Mr. Joseph G Nance
19614 Scenic Harbour Dr
Northville, MI 48167

D1567994

The Edge *of* Terror

Also by Scott Walker

This book is dedicated to the beauty, graciousness, hospitality, and love of the Filipino people. The greatest gift of my childhood is to have lived in their midst.

I also pause to remember my friend, Kathy Fertig, who encouraged me to research and write this story. As she was a healthy influence in my teenage years, so was she an inspiration in death. She taught me that life is to be lived to the fullest and that death is a friend to embrace.

Faith faints to understand.

—Emily Dickinson, "Too Much"

Contents

Contents

Acknowledgments

To write narrative history is to know both the living and the dead. This is the privilege and honor of authorship.

Over the last six years while I was researching and writing this book, many have shared with me the gift of their personal story. Their story is told through letters, diaries, poetry, and books. It is heard in the voices of their children and grandchildren. Through such conversations my life is enriched by discovering Milton Meyer, Carol Park, Bob Chambers, David Covell, Dylan Rounds, Dodie Borroughs, Elmo Familiaran, Kathy Fertig, Susan Fertig-Dykes, and Mark and Jason Phelps—people whose parents and grandparents live their lives on the pages of this wartime saga. For their friendship and contributions I am profoundly grateful.

I am most fortunate to have Claudia Cross as my literary agent. For two decades she has given me expert guidance, professional expertise, and continuous encouragement. Most of all, she has shared with me friendship. Claudia, you are the very best!

In 2004, Sean Desmond read a book proposal that I submitted to St. Martin's Press about one of the most intense and gripping stories to emerge from World War II. Sean offered me a chance to write this book. And I am thankful.

Peter Joseph, my editor at St. Martin's Press, is not only gifted but also a pleasure to work with. He has the ability to see what a book might become and guide the author toward the best expression of his or her gifts. Blessed with the ability to balance patience with firmness, he ranks with the best of coaches, knowing how to shape each unique writer.

Twenty-five years and ten books ago, I sat down with a pad and pencil and wrote the first page of my first manuscript. I could not know then what joy and what demands the life of writing brings. Thankfully, my wife, Beth, was also equally and blissfully unaware. Since then she has enabled me to be an author, giving me permission to spend long hours in research and writing. She has encouraged me, loved me, and taken delight in a journey traveled together. Without Beth, the writer's muse would not have spoken. She is God's most precious gift to me.

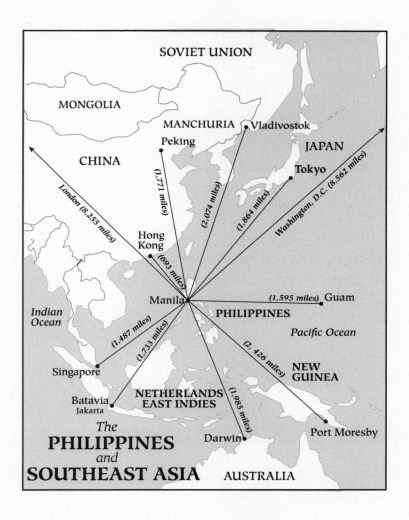

SOVIET UNION

MONGOLIA

MANCHURIA • Vladivostok

Peking

JAPAN

CHINA

Tokyo

(1,771 miles)

(2,074 miles)

(1,864 miles)

Washington, D.C. (8,562 miles)

London (8,255 miles)

Hong
Kong

(693 miles)

Manila

(1,595 miles) Guam

PHILIPPINES

Indian
Ocean

Pacific Ocean

(1,487 miles)

(1,733 miles)

(2,426 miles)

NEW
GUINEA

Singapore

Batavia
Jakarta

NETHERLANDS
EAST INDIES

(1,985 miles)

Port Moresby

The

PHILIPPINES

Darwin

and

SOUTHEAST ASIA AUSTRALIA

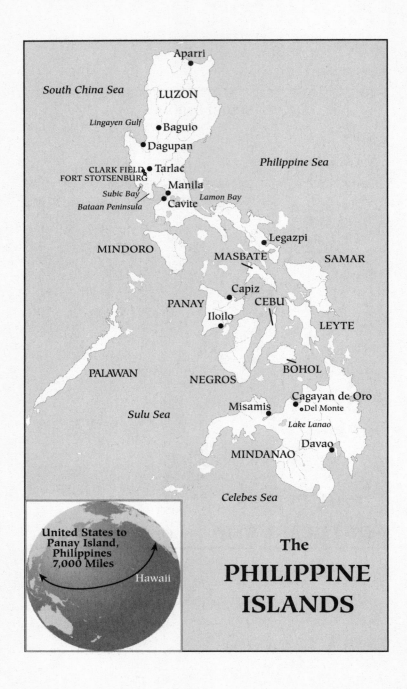

Aparri

South China Sea

LUZON

Lingayen Gulf • Baguio

• Dagupan

CLARK FIELD • Tarlac
FORT STOTSENBURG
Subic Bay   • Manila
Bataan Peninsula • Cavite   Lamon Bay

Philippine Sea

MINDORO   Legazpi •

MASBATE   SAMAR

Capiz
PANAY   • CEBU
Iloilo •
LEYTE

BOHOL

NEGROS

Cagayan de Oro
Misamis •   • Del Monte
Lake Lanao
Davao •
MINDANAO

Sulu Sea

Celebes Sea

United States to
Panay Island,
Philippines
7,000 Miles
Hawaii

PALAWAN

The
PHILIPPINE
ISLANDS

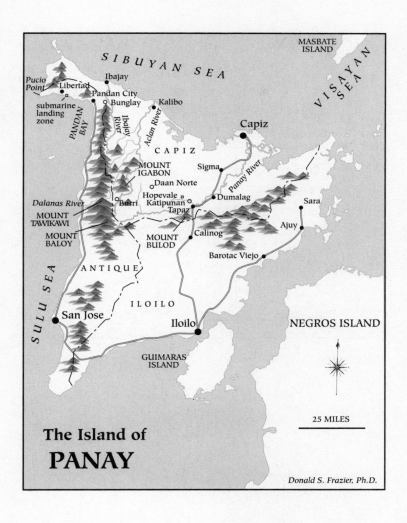

The Island of

PANAY

Donald S. Frazier, Ph.D.

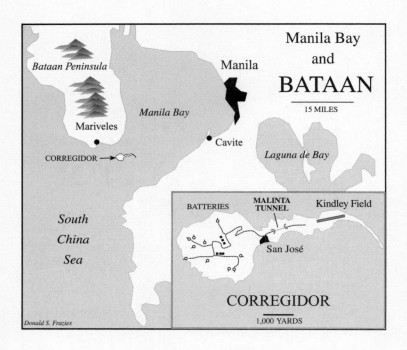

Manila Bay
and
BATAAN

15 MILES

Bataan Peninsula

Manila

Manila Bay

Mariveles

Cavite

CORREGIDOR ➜

Laguna de Bay

South
China
Sea

Donald S. Frazier.

BATTERIES   MALINTA TUNNEL   Kindley Field

San José

CORREGIDOR

1,000 YARDS

The **Edge** *of* **Terror**

Prologue

Antique Province,
The Island of Panay,
Philippine Archipelago

Sound precedes light in the tropical predawn of the Philippine Islands. Small, colorful birds rustle in dense trees. Roosters crow and swayback pigs root in pungent mud. Dogs bark as dim forms move down narrow footpaths and monkeys chatter in the darkness. Awakened by this primeval chorus, the Filipinos in rural barrios glimpse the first ripples of red, orange, and purple hues tinting the horizon. In rainy season the air is hot and humid, a steamy sauna before sunrise.

On this October day there is a new sound in the darkness. It is the plodding of boots and rubber sandals mixed with the grunts and curses of soldiers. As Filipinos wake, a Japanese punishment or terror force marches down the Antique-Capiz national road. These hardened veterans, recently transferred from the Japanese war with China, are crossing the northwestern corner of the island of Panay, bearing down on the unsuspecting village of Ibajay.

Nearing the outskirts of Ibajay, the Japanese abduct a few

hapless Filipino men found wandering in the early morning. The khaki-clad soldiers forming the special task force over one hundred strong are tired and hungry. Most of all, they are angry.

They are angry because their control in this new war has been slipping away. For nearly two years Japanese armed forces have occupied the Philippine islands. They have crushed the defending military forces of the United States and the Philippines. Yet, with every month that has passed, stubborn Filipino and American guerrilla resistance has grown stronger and more effective. On the small island of Panay, there are no more than 3,200 Japanese soldiers to subjugate a population of nearly a million and a half Filipinos. The defiance of the Filipinos is escalating.

To quash this revolt, punishment squads have been sent out to bludgeon and unnerve the Filipino people. Any Americans still resisting capture and imprisonment were special prey. The Japanese believed that only through the use of harsh brutality and intimidation could they retain authority.

Upon entering Ibajay, the Japanese quickly took control of the second-largest town in the northern coastal region of Aklan. By midmorning, the Japanese commander had ordered that the town's citizens gather in the plaza. At noon, over one hundred people milled around the central monument, to Dr. José Rizal, the national hero of the Philippines, who was executed by a Spanish firing squad forty-seven years earlier. In the shadow of this martyr, Filipino families now waited in fear.

Staring at the frightened crowd, the Japanese commander cleared his throat and addressed the assembly, smiling amiably. He introduced several nervous Filipino men who were not from Ibajay. On cue, they gave short, awkward speeches urging Filipinos and Japanese to unite in the building of a new and unified Asia, free from the control of America and Western imperialism. Then, his Filipino interpreter standing by him, the Japanese officer's mood grew sinister, and he launched into a clipped tirade demanding the citizens of Ibajay obey the Japanese and defy the guerrilla movement. As his voice rose in intensity, he moved toward his dramatic conclusion, beckoning a barefooted teenage boy to come and stand before him. Placing his hands gently on the boy's shoulders, the commander spoke rapid words that the boy did not understand. The interpreter motioned the boy to kneel. Smiling shyly, the boy obeyed. In a flashing instant, the Japanese officer drew his long *katana* sword and severed the boy's head from his shoulders. As the head thumped in the dust and blood arced from the neck, the officer screamed out in English that this was a "sample" of what would happen to any Filipino who did not accept Japanese control.

Panicked, the stunned crowd spun around to find that they were surrounded by the rest of the squad, bayonets gleaming. Quickly, a dozen young Filipino men were seized and thrown to the ground, and their hands tied roughly behind their backs. Arrested as suspected "guerrilla bandits," they were lashed together and led to the opposite side of the plaza. Then, wiping the blood from his sword on a handkerchief, the commander ordered the citizens of Ibajay to cook lunch for his troops.

After gorging on dried fish, rice, and other hastily prepared dishes, the Japanese returned to the tethered men, forcing them to their feet and prodding them with bayonets and rifle butts toward a bridge a half kilometer away from the town. Crossing the bridge, the soldiers whirled on the hog-tied men, slashing them with swords and using their bodies for bayonet practice. The mangled and gutted corpses were thrown into the shallow stream.

Paralyzed with fear, the rest of the villagers looked on in horror. Though temporarily subdued, they hated the Japanese more than ever. Never would the searing brutality of this day be forgotten or forgiven in Ibajay.[1]

Continuing fourteen kilometers east, the Japanese entered the town of Makato late in the afternoon. An elderly woman, hoping to placate the soldiers, invited several into her home and offered refreshments. The young men were polite in the presence of an elder until one noticed a framed photograph of an American warship hanging on her wall. The panicked woman explained that her brother had been in the United States Navy many years before but had long since returned to farming. Instantly, politeness disappeared and hatred flared. The woman was seized and dragged into the street. Stripped of her clothes, she was beaten savagely and, once unconscious, bayoneted to death. Leaving her ravaged body as warning against American allegiance, the Japanese marched into the gathering dusk, intent on occupying the town of Kalibo by nightfall. A full day of breaking the spirits of Filipinos had exhausted them. But tomorrow the terror would begin again.[2]

Far in the mountainous interior of Panay, American and Filipino guerrillas endured such brutal physical and psychological warfare. In truth, these terror tactics only made Filipinos more determined to resist the Japanese. But for Americans still alive and hiding in the remote mountains, the message was clear. They would receive no mercy if captured. And the length of time a fugitive could survive on an isolated island was limited.

Months before, when the Japanese first invaded the Philippines, an odd assortment of twenty-two American and Canadian missionaries and gold miners, along with their four young children, had bound their fates together and vowed to elude the Japanese. Preferring the risk of death to life in a Japanese prison camp, they had so far escaped capture, huddled within a secluded river gorge in the foothills of central Panay. But another year of freedom seemed improbable. Now, as Japanese control drew tighter, they teetered on the edge of terror.

Their story is a saga of sacrifice and survival, of faith and despair, of triumph and defeat. It is a far-reaching epic of Filipinos, Americans, Canadians, Australians—indeed, an international cast of characters—all embroiled in the world's greatest armed conflict, yet isolated and trapped on one small island. Ultimately their experience is one of the great adventures to emerge from World War II, yet its memory is now fading into obscurity. Their heroic story is an account that must be told again and not forgotten.

What was it that brought missionaries and gold miners from the United States to the shores of the Philippine islands? What was the passion that transported them thousands of miles and gave them a purpose to live and a reason to die? Who are these Filipino guerrillas and rural villagers who fought the Japanese occupation so tenaciously and risked—indeed, sacrificed—their lives for their American friends? It is the answers to these questions that provide understanding of the characters who star in this incredible story.

Chapter One

The Philippine Islands, 1898–1935

Until the end of the nineteenth century few Americans had heard of the Philippine islands. Those who had would be hard-pressed to locate the archipelago on a map, much less know how to spell it. Caught up in their own affairs, sheltered by an isolationist mind-set, and still recovering thirty-three years later from the trauma of the American Civil War, most Americans did not pay attention to affairs "on the other side of the world."

That distance would disappear at midnight on February 15, 1898, when the USS *Maine* exploded in Havana's harbor, killing 266 American sailors. The venerable old battleship had been sent to Cuba to monitor the partisan revolution against Spain and to protect American interests. It was immediately assumed—though never proven—that the Spanish had blown up the *Maine*. On April 25, 1898, the United States declared war on Spain. Two days later, the U.S. Asiatic Squadron of five cruisers and two gunboats steamed from Hong Kong for Manila, under the command of Commodore George Dewey. The Philippines, a Spanish colony since 1565, provided anchorage in Manila Bay for Spain's Pacific fleet. It was Admiral Dewey's mission to prevent this fleet from sailing to reinforce Spanish military forces in Cuba.

Cloaked in darkness, Dewey's squadron crept into Manila Bay on April 30 at three o'clock in the morning, slipped past the harbor defenses on Corregidor Island, and opened fire on the slumbering Spanish fleet. Nine hours later the Spaniards raised a white flag of surrender. Only one of the twelve Spanish vessels engaged in battle was still afloat.

Upon receiving the news of this stunning American victory, an elated President William McKinley asked for a map in order to locate the Philippines. Later, he admitted to a confidant that he "could not have told where those darned islands were within two thousand miles." But now the Philippine islands were front-page news. Nearly four hundred years after Magellan had claimed the Philippines for Spain, a maturing American giant had blundered into this same Pacific archipelago and was feeling an adolescent surge of imperialism.[1]

The Spanish-American War was short-lived. Six months after Dewey's victory commissioners from the United States and Spain met in Paris on October 1, 1898, to discuss the cessation of hostilities. On December 10, 1898, the Treaty of Paris was signed. The Spanish colonies of Puerto Rico and Guam were placed under American control, the United States paid Spain $20 million for possession of the Philippines, and Cuba was soon granted independence. Earlier that same year the United States had annexed Hawaii, making the islands a territory in 1900. The result of the year's sudden gains in territory was the rise of the United States as a Pacific and Asiatic power and a major new player in international affairs.

Yet, what would the United States now do with the Philippines? What would be the advantage of obtaining this new protectorate and incurring heavy and costly responsibility? Why not grant the Filipinos their independence in the same liberating spirit as Cuba? The American answer was both muddled and multifaceted.

The United States was keenly aware of the competition among multiple nations vying for influence and profit in Asia. Soon after Dewey defeated the Spanish Pacific fleet, Japanese, German, French, and British warships appeared along the coastline of the Philippines and entered the harbor of Manila. American strategists assumed that without a strong American presence for protection, the Philippines islands would soon become the domain of Japan or another European power.[2]

There was also a rising thirst for expansion within the United States. This tone was set by both the media and key political figures, such as Theodore Roosevelt. This new American imperialism was not projected as a naked grab for power or profit. Rather, it was often cloaked in more benign and compassionate terms as "manifest destiny" and a desire to help the oppressed. According to such thinking, America, if she were to be a great and benevolent power, must seize her God-given destiny of worldwide influence and become a Christian and humanitarian presence in needy and struggling parts of the world.[3]

Finally, the United States had clear economic and strategic interests in assuming the role of "protector" of the Philippines. For decades America had seen increased business ventures and profits in Asia, particularly in China. In order to secure future commerce, and to build a foundation for an American economic presence in Asia, the United States needed a base of operations for both business and military installations. The Philippines was a ripe choice. Manila harbor would provide one of the best naval bases and commercial shipping ports in the world. The location of the Philippines would position an American presence directly astride the major ocean trade routes of Asia. And the islands were rich in minerals, timber, iron ore, and gold. The Philippines was an economic plum to be picked.

There was one major problem, however. At the same time that Cubans had been fighting for their independence from Spain, revolutionary embers were igniting in the Philippines. The breath that most fanned the fire came from a young man named José Rizal. Rizal was an unlikely figure to spark a revolution. Born in 1861 into a well-educated and distinguished farming family from Laguna province, south of Manila, Rizal was quickly recognized as a brilliant and precocious child. Far from exuding military bearing or a revolutionary disposition, Rizal was a refined intellectual with creative and artistic sensitivities. As a teenager he decided to become a doctor and entered the University of Santo Tomas, the most elite Roman Catholic university in the Philippines. Soon, however, Rizal perceived that Filipino students were being discriminated against by their Dominican professors and tutors. Disgusted, he then applied to attend medical school in Madrid, Spain, and left the Philippines as a twenty-year-old to discover Europe.

In 1884, at the age of twenty-three, Rizal received his licentiate in medicine with a specialization in ophthalmology. He then continued his education at the University of Paris and the University of Heidelberg, where he earned a graduate degree in philosophy and letters. While in Europe he wrote and published two novels, *Noli Me Tangere* and *El Filibusterismo*, which developed themes of Spanish oppression and despotism in the Philippines. Rizal particularly criticized Spanish priests, and he implicated the Catholic Church in the persecution of the Filipino people. He continued to tour Europe, Asia, and the United States after his graduation and returned to the Philippines on June 26, 1892, one of the most talented, educated, and charismatic young men of his emerging generation.

Within hours of returning to Manila, Rizal learned that he was under surveillance by Spanish authorities because of his critical books. He had in effect become an enemy of the state. One week after stepping on Philippine soil, he formed a civic movement, La Liga Filipina, which sought to make social reforms through legislative efforts and legal stratagems. However, the constituency of La Liga Filipina soon split into two camps: those who supported Rizal's desire for change through peaceful means and those who advocated open and armed rebellion against Spain.

On July 6, 1892, Rizal was arrested by Spanish authorities and banished from the major island of Luzon to the more remote southern island of Mindanao, where he resided under virtual house arrest in the community of Dapitan in Zamboanga province. On the day that Rizal was exiled, the more radical branch of La Liga Filipina—under the primary leadership of twenty-eight-year-old Andrés Bonifacio—formed a secret revolutionary organization in Manila and named it Katipunan, translated variously as "the Society" or "the Gathered." Without his knowledge or permission, José Rizal was initially named the honorary president, an action for which Rizal would later pay with his life.

Over the next four years, the Katipunan worked covertly, quietly expanding their organization, gathering weapons, training revolutionaries, and preparing for armed revolt. In May 1896, Andrés Bonifacio secretly sent Katipunan representatives to Mindanao to seek José Rizal's formal support for armed revolution. Rizal, opposed to violence, rejected their appeal, stating that armed rebellion was premature.

Disappointed at Rizal's decision, Katipunan leaders decided to concentrate their forces and attack Manila on August 29, 1896. However, Spanish intelligence discovered their plot, and a series of preemptive skirmishes broke out that weakened the strength of the Katipunan, disrupted their organization, and robbed them of the element of surprise. As the Katipunan offensive waned, the Spanish government achieved critical time to reinforce their army and regain stability. Katipunan forces had no choice but to retreat to mountainous enclaves throughout Luzon and engage in guerrilla warfare.

As the Spanish army licked their wounds and fought to keep Katipunan forces at bay, the Spanish increasingly focused blame for the Katipunan revolt on the exiled José Rizal. He was arrested, tried, and convicted of rebellion, sedition, and conspiracy. On December 30, 1896, Rizal was executed in Manila by firing squad. The young and gentle doctor became an instant national hero, and his death only intensified the resolve of Filipinos to gain independence.

In the midst of the Katipunan revolt, a serious schism erupted among the Katipunan leadership. The bickering parties met in Cavite province, twenty miles southwest of Manila, to mend fences and try to form a more viable revolutionary government. Andrés Bonifacio was challenged for leadership by twenty-eight-year-old Emilio Aguinaldo, an ambitious young man with strong political connections in Cavite province. Bonifacio lost the vote for president, and the cordial relationship between the two men quickly disappeared. Exploding in anger, Bonifacio pulled a pistol, threatened the gathered leadership, and declared that the new election was void. Summoning his newly appointed powers, Aguinaldo soon ordered Bonifacio arrested. Under conditions that still remain murky, Bonifacio was then murdered on May 10, 1897, while being led to a place of exile by Aguinaldo's soldiers. Bonifacio's death effectively ended the existence of the Katipunan, and a new revolutionary government was created under Aguinaldo's leadership.

Emilio Aguinaldo, a Chinese-Filipino mestizo, was now faced with stabilizing the Filipino revolutionary movement while defending his forces from an aroused Spanish military presence. At best, the situation seemed to point toward a prolonged and bloody stalemate. On November 1, 1897, Aguinaldo did complete the writing of a Philippine revolutionary constitution and formed the Biak-na-Bato Republic. The constitution provided for a republican government, and was modeled on the Cuban constitution of Jimaguayu of 1895.

One month later, the Spanish government took the initiative to propose peace negotiations with the Biak-na-Bato Republic. Both sides had reasons to seek a truce and saw benefit in doing so. For the sake of a tenuous peace, the Spanish government agreed to pay the Biak-na-Bato Republic an immediate indemnity of four hundred thousand pesos and to allow Emilio Aguinaldo and thirty-four other key Filipino revolutionaries free and safe passage into exile in Hong Kong. On December 14, 1897, the Pact of Biak-na-Bato was signed and concluded. Aguinaldo departed to Hong Kong with four hundred thousand pesos in his suitcase, money that soon purchased arms for the smoldering revolution. The exiled Filipino leadership bided their time and waited for a better day.[4]

Aguinaldo's better day arrived four months later, when the United States declared war on Spain on April 25, 1898. Following the defeat of the Spanish Pacific fleet by Commodore Dewey, Aguinaldo returned to the Philippines at the invitation of Dewey. Transported from Hong Kong on an American vessel, Aguinaldo arrived in Manila on May 19, 1898. Dewey hoped that Aguinaldo would now help American forces defeat the Spanish in the Philippines. Instead, Aguinaldo soon left American ranks and returned to his home in the town of Cavite el Viejo.[5]

There was reason for Aguinaldo to go his own way. A leading scholar on Philippine-American relations, Stanley Karnow, notes:

> In the spring of 1898, [President] McKinley still lacked a plan for dealing with the Spanish in the Philippines; and he was paying even less attention to the Filipino insurgents.

The evidence suggests, indeed, that he was oblivious to their existence. The absence of guidance from Washington licensed Dewey, Merritt and other American officials to improvise. Their only preoccupation at that juncture was to defeat the Spanish. To achieve that goal, they sought the help of the Filipinos, indulging them with pledges that had no foundation in reality. The Filipinos naively believed the promises until they discovered, to their dismay, that they had been manipulated. Within less than a year, tensions were to spark a tragic war between the Americans and Filipinos that almost surely could have been averted had McKinley, at the outset, proceeded into the Philippines with a policy.[6]

Realizing that Dewey's promises and allegiance could not be trusted, Aguinaldo set as his primary objective the goal of keeping Philippine independence publicly visible and alive. More as symbol than fact, Aguinaldo commissioned the creation of a national anthem, a flag, and a declaration of independence. On June 12, 1898, Aguinaldo publicly read his declaration of independence from the balcony of his home before a small crowd of one hundred people. He then began the task of preparing his guerrilla forces for possible combat against the Americans. When the Treaty of Paris was signed on December 10, 1898, and Cuba was given independence but the Philippines was ceded to the United States, Filipino patriots were infuriated. Faced with the prospects of being ruled by yet another foreign country, the revolutionaries now turned their attention and anger toward the American occupation.

On January 1, 1899, following a constitutional convention, Aguinaldo was declared the president of the Philippine Republic. The United States refused to recognize his authority or government, and President McKinley instructed the American occupying army to use force, if necessary, to impose American sovereignty.

The Edge of Terror

Open hostility soon escalated into warfare. After three Filipino solders were killed by American forces in Manila, Aguinaldo and his newly formed government declared war on February 4, 1899.

Reacting swiftly and forcefully, a determined United States committed a cumulative total of 126,000 troops to crush the "Philippine insurrection." The fighting was savage, reflecting some of the worst events in the history of Western imperialism. There could be no dissimulation: America was openly fighting for territory. Her military methods often made the bloody Spanish look benevolent.

In describing how the Filipinos were treated by American troops, a Filipino historian, Professor Roland G. Simbulan, writes, "The most barbaric forms of torture and interrogation, such as 'water cure' as well as scorched earth military tactics and the brutal 'reconcentration' of civilians, were applied against the Filipino people. The most inhuman and brutal tactics experimented earlier against American Indian tribes in the American frontier were again applied and practiced by the U.S. military veterans of the Indian campaigns."[7]

General Jacob Hurd Smith, a lackluster Civil War veteran, gained perhaps the worst reputation for atrocities during his command of American troops on the island of Samar. Filipinos on Samar were well-known for their intense patriotic ardor and staunch resistance. Smith freely applied the rule of the noose or firing squad upon guerrillas, or *insurrectos.* He made public threats that he would reduce Samar "to a howling wilderness," and encouraged his troops to "kill everyone over the age of ten."

On September 28, 1901, Filipinos in the Samar village of Balangiga revolted against the oppression of some of General Smith's troops. Balangiga was garrisoned and patrolled by seventy-four American soldiers of Company C, Ninth U.S. Infantry, under the command of Captain Thomas W. Connell. Connell was an arrogant and foolish officer who flagrantly antagonized the citizens

of Balangiga. In a display of his unbridled authority, he forced
nearly one hundred men into forced labor to "clean up" the town,
refusing to pay or reward them for their work. He quartered the
laborers under guard in two small tents designed to hold sixteen
men each and made them live in squalid conditions. While these
men worked against their will, Connell's soldiers preyed on the
citizens of Balangiga, stealing from them, beating them, and even
raping at least one woman. The villagers finally were pushed
beyond their endurance and united with guerrillas, who then
secretly infiltrated Balangiga. Early on a sleepy Sunday morning
they attacked the American garrison as the soldiers gathered in
their mess tent for breakfast. Concealed in nearby dense jungle as well as in an adjacent church building, dozens of Filipinos
wielding long knives, or *bolos*, charged the tent, hacking and stab-
bing forty-eight officers and men to death.

The American army on Samar immediately retaliated. General Smith's superior, Major General Adna R. Chaffee, ordered
Smith to seek vengeance for the Balangiga massacre, telling Smith
in a letter that he must "give [your troops] a fair opportunity to
kill off the bands of utter savages who have hibernated in the
brush in that vicinity." Smith needed no further encouragement.
American military records state that between October 10 and
December 31, 1901, Smith's troops killed or captured 759 *insurrectos*, slaughtered 587 *carabao* (water buffalo), and razed acres
of rice, 1,662 houses, and 226 boats.[8] Such examples of American brutality and destruction were not rare. It was a savage war.

By the end of 1901, the American army had worn down and
splintered the guerrilla resistance, intimidated the civilian population, and captured Emilio Aguinaldo, hiding in the high mountains of northern Luzon in Palanan, Isabela. Aguinaldo accepted
an offer: He would not be executed if he swore allegiance to the
United States. With Aguinaldo's capitulation, armed rebellion
in the Philippines gradually dwindled, and the Philippine insur-

rection was declared officially over on July 4, 1902. The cost was high. The butcher bill was forty-two hundred American soldiers and sixteen thousand Filipino guerrillas killed. A minimum of two hundred thousand Filipino citizens, perhaps many more, died from combat conditions, internment camps, disease, and starvation.[9]

With the war over, America was now faced with the responsibility of deciding what its role would be in the future of the Philippines. After allowing the military free rein in carrying out a ruthless war for civil control, President McKinley now moved in a more democratic spirit to quickly replace military governance with civilian rule. With the passage of the Philippine Organic Act in July 1902, two important political principles were established. First, that a Philippine government be instituted, modeled on the American republican form of government. Second, that the protections of the American Bill of Rights would be extended to all Filipino citizens.

William Howard Taft, then a federal court judge in Cincinnati, was appointed by the McKinley administration to be the first American governor-general of the Philippines, from 1901 to 1903. Taft was a large man—indeed, a huge man—who was also wise, warm, good-natured and yet firm. He was an excellent selection and proved popular with both Americans and Filipinos.

Taft's primary job was to establish the civilian government in the Philippines. He also worked to improve health care, education, and infrastructure to aid the Filipino people. He negotiated with Pope Leo XIII to purchase vast lands owned by the Catholic Church in the Philippines, so that they might be sold at affordable prices to Filipino farmers and civilians. Later, upon his departure from the Philippines, Taft would serve as the secretary of war in the Roosevelt administration (1904–8), be elected president of the United States (1909–13), and serve as chief justice of the Supreme Court (1921–30). Taft's intimate

love and understanding of the Philippines greatly strengthened trust and relationships between the two countries as Taft
rose to the pinnacle of power in the United States and interna-
tionally.

In 1907 a Filipino assembly was elected, and the first Filipino
president, Manuel Quezon, was inaugurated. Over the years an
increasingly large measure of self-rule was given to the Filipino
government. On March 24, 1934, the U.S. Tydings-McDuffie Act
established the Philippine Commonwealth under the protection
of the United States. It was agreed that this commonwealth would
be granted independence eventually. The date set for independence was July 4, 1946. At the time, few could have anticipated
the approaching horrors of World War II that would come before that date.

In his Pulitzer Prize–winning history of American and Filipino
relations, *In Our Image*, Stanley Karnow writes:

> [American] policy was enlightened compared to the repres-
> sive practices of the European powers in their colonies at
> the time. But the effort of the United States to transplant
> its values and institutions in the Philippines eventually be-
> came what the historian Glenn Anthony May has termed
> an *"experiment in self-duplication,"* spurred by a belief still
> ingrained in Americans; *that they can remold other lands
> in their own image.* A noble dream, it proved in later years
> to be largely an exercise in self-deception.[10] (Emphasis
> added.)

Karnow is correct in his assessment that the United States
was basically well-intentioned in attempting to bring the
Philippines—over a period of time—to independence and self-
government based on a democratic system. The bestowal of the

liberties found in the U.S. Bill of Rights was, indeed, a gift unique among imperial powers. And within a few short months, an emerging generation of young and bright-eyed Americans would symbolize this benevolent spirit by flooding into the Philippines to be teachers, instructors, and public servants in the remotest parts—the Peace Corps of an earlier era. But within it all was an imperial spirit that also said "We want to make you just like us and create you in our image. We want you to be as good, and healthy and hopeful as America."

Perhaps there is a beautiful, admirable, and authentic American generosity found in this response. But there is also an inherent and naïve arrogance that says "We know the truth. We've got it right. Join our family of democratic nations and all will be well." This tapestry of American imperialism was—and is—woven and colored by both of these threads of thought, inseparable and intertwined. Such American international relations are sparked by a parental passion to experiment in self-duplication.

In reality, America would discover—and today is still in the painful process of discovering—that each country to which we relate is culturally unique and must find its own indigenous answers and forms of government. But to find its own way, it must have the freedom to succeed and the freedom to fail; the freedom to relate to America and the freedom to drift apart. And that when an alien country such as the United States takes up residence for an extended time within the borders of a host country—no matter how good American intentions might be—it is not long before the United States becomes the enemy.

Into this ferment of Philippine and American relations came many types of Americans. Some would be soldiers and sailors, the "peacekeepers" of the world. Some would be teachers and doctors and humanitarians. Some would be missionaries with a zeal to save souls and bring the virtues of the kingdom of God to earth. And some would be industrialists and gold miners eager to develop a burgeoning industry that would enrich the young Philippine economy and provide personal wealth and profit. And, in due time, some would be Japanese soldiers, intent on creating a new Asia for Asians, and in so doing making the Philippines a vassal subject to a sprawling Japanese empire.

Chapter Two

The Missionaries, 1892–1919

Frederick Meyer was born in 1892, six years before the Spanish-American and the Philippine-American wars became national and international news, and grew up in Milwaukee, Wisconsin. Frederick spoke both English and German, taught by his father, Reverend William Carl Meyer, who had emigrated from Germany to the United States shortly after the American Civil War. After attending Yale Divinity School, Reverend Meyer became a minister in the German Baptist church. Later he served as a professor at Rochester Theological Seminary, a school known for academic rigor combined with concern for practical social ministry.

While growing up in an evangelical Protestant family, young Frederick Meyer excelled in academics and music, and he chose a classical studies curriculum in the North Division High School in Milwaukee. Influenced by his father, he enrolled at Yale University in 1910, though with dreams of studying medicine. Money was always tight, so he soon found a job as a waiter in the university dining hall, "slinging hash." In between long hours of study and scrambling for spending money, he became involved in the Student Volunteer Missionary Movement.[1]

Unlike some preacher's kids, Frederick did not shed his faith once he left home and gained independence. His religious beliefs seemed comfortable and consistent with who he was as a young man. He had inherited a Germanic no-nonsense attitude about life, and was quite intense and serious.[2] He soon found the Student Volunteer Missionary Movement fit his idealistic and driven personality. Frederick wanted to make a difference in the world, and this missionary organization was a vehicle for doing so.

Begun in 1886, the Student Volunteer Missionary Movement spread like wildfire among American college campuses for the next forty years. The movement's motto was: "Evangelization of the world in this generation." Interested students were encouraged to sign a succinct but life-shaping pledge that stated, "It is my purpose, if God permits, to become a foreign missionary." By the end of World War II, over twenty thousand American college students who had signed these commitments had actually become "foreign missionaries."[3]

One of them, Dr. Wilfred Grenfell, was well-known among these students. He was an English physician who had received his medical education at Oxford University. When he was twenty years old, a rather secular Grenfell was converted to Christianity by the American evangelist Dwight L. Moody. A year later, in 1886, Grenfell became concerned about the plight of North Seas' fishermen and their isolated families. He decided to become a medical missionary among the cod fishermen in Newfoundland, whose families had little access to medical care. Grenfell established schools, hospitals, nursing stations, and an orphanage for these struggling communities. A talented and charismatic speaker, Grenfell often talked at student gatherings in America, where he urged the "brightest and best" to become "laborers for God."[4]

It is not known if young Frederick Meyer ever signed a commitment card to become a foreign missionary, but he did hear Grenfell lecture at Yale. Grenfell and others stirred within Frederick a spiritual and vocational passion. Sometime during his junior year, Frederick firmly decided that he, too, would become a doctor. He wrote to his mother, "My present plans compel me to stay here for the medical course. As you probably know that means four years of medical studies, with at least fifteen months of hospital work. It seems like such a long time to me, but I'll go ahead and work my way through." As World War I exploded and enveloped Europe, Meyer entered Yale Medical School, in 1915.[5]

During the years of the war, Frederick enlisted as a private in the Medical Enlisted Reserve Corps on inactive duty, which allowed him to stay at Yale and complete his medical training. For this young American, who still had cousins and extended family in Germany, the absurdity of war now grew real. The horrors of this conflict—of cousins fighting cousins—only emphasized for many of Frederick's generation the need to devote their lives to the pursuit of world peace, and Frederick's desire to make a contribution increased his missionary zeal. Like the famous Dr. Albert Schweitzer, who had built a medical hospital in remote equatorial Africa a decade before World War I, Frederick also dreamed of finding his own small corner of the world to bring health, nutrition, and Bible teachings to those who were in need.

Amid the demands of medical school, Frederick took a few weeks of vacation in 1918 to return home to Wisconsin. While there, he attended a German Baptist youth conference and met Ruth Schacht. Her father, August Ludwig Schacht, had also emigrated, with his three brothers, from Germany, in 1878 to escape the military draft of Chancellor Bismarck. Mr. Schacht settled in the factory town of Racine, Wisconsin, which was nestled on the banks of Lake Michigan at the mouth of the Root River. Now, a generation later, his talented daughter, Ruth, was studying in Chicago to be a professional singer.[6]

Frederick Meyer and Ruth Schacht at the time of their engagement, 1919.   *Milton Meyer*

Frederick was captivated by this young lady with the beautiful soprano voice. He was also delighted to discover that they both shared a wish to be involved in Christian missions in distant parts of the world. Fueled by infatuation, their dreams of the future blended together and they soon became engaged. In the whirlwind year of 1919, Ruth and Frederick traveled together to Denver, Colorado, where in May they were commissioned as medical missionaries to the Philippines by the Baptist Missionary Union of the American Baptist Convention. In June, Frederick returned to New Haven, Connecticut, to graduate from Yale Medical School. Then, on August 22, 1919, Frederick and Ruth were married by Frederick's father in Ruth's Baptist Church in Racine.[7]

In October 1919, eleven months after the signing of the armistice that ended the war, Frederick and Ruth departed for San Francisco, where they would set sail on the first part of their missionary career. As they said good-bye to parents and friends, they fully expected that they would spend their entire lives in the Philippines. A missionary appointment was seen as a lifelong commitment, and not to honor this commitment would be tinged with failure. Though they would return to the United States for year-long furloughs every four to five years, the Philippines would now become their permanent home. As they stepped on the deck of the Pacific Mail Steamship Company liner SS *Venezuela* to begin a month-long cruise to the Philippines, they were ripping up roots and transplanting their lives into the soil of another world. They were anxious, eager, and blessedly naïve; their eyes were alight with the idealism and hope that only youth can engender.

The *Venezuela* steamed out of San Francisco on October 22, 1919, and under the Golden Gate Bridge carrying eighteen Baptist missionaries bound for various Asian countries. Ruth wrote to her mother, "There is quite a strange feeling that comes over one as [we are] leaving the States. . . . We all just stood there rather deep in thought and watched the coast line disappear in the distance."[8]

Reverie changed to gladness as the ship made port periodically, in Honolulu, Yokohama, and then Shanghai. Frederick and Ruth were particularly interested in Japan, and spent several days touring the cities of Kyoto, Tokyo, and Kobe. Reflecting on what he observed in Japan, Frederick wrote to his father a foreboding message: "Everybody distrusts and hates the Japanese in the Orient. Japan is strong in finance and militarism, able to conduct war, if it wishes. . . . Japan is the most troublesome nation of the present and the future due to her domineering military attitude. . . . It is too bad that thousands and thousands of Japanese, yes the majority, must suffer from the military party. TROUBLE is coming."[9]

On Sunday, November 23, 1919, the Meyers sailed into Manila Bay to meet their new homeland. Looking around, they were charmed by an edenic beauty mixed with exotic aromas, tropical colors, and oppressive heat. Manila was an exotic city adorned with an Old World allure. This "Pearl of the Orient" brought together the cultures of the Philippines, China, Malaya, India, Indonesia, Spain, and America. Soon the Meyers also noticed the financial affluence of Americans, Europeans, and wealthy

Filipinos set side by side with the poverty and physical need of
the vast majority of Filipinos. Yale and the heartland of America
were another world away.

The Philippine Islands make up the second-largest archipelago
in the world, after Indonesia. They comprise over 7,000 islands
and a population speaking over eighty different dialects. Only
466 of the islands are larger than one square mile, and no more
than 700 islands were populated in 1919. The 11 largest islands
compose 95 percent of the landmass, and even today contain
the vast majority of the population. Listed in order of size, the
primary islands are Luzon, Mindanao, Samar, Negros, Palawan,
Panay, Mindoro, Leyte, Cebu, Bohol, and Masbate. Though the
combined coastline of the islands is twelve thousand miles—the
same as the continental United States—the combined landmass
is only slightly larger than Arizona. If the ocean mass that sur-
rounds the islands were overlaid on the United States, the archipelago would stretch from the Great Lakes into Florida, and from
West Virginia into Arkansas. As the Meyers would discover, a
sprawling archipelago of 7,000 scattered islands is primarily
water, not land.[10]

The Meyers were assigned to the island of Panay, in the
central portion of the archipelago. The Philippines is divided
into three regions: Luzon, the largest island, is in the north; Mindanao, the second-largest island, is in the south; and an assortment of smaller islands in the center collectively are called the
Visayas. Panay is on the western side of the Visayas.

Catching a small interisland steamer from Manila going
south to Panay, the Meyers were greeted by six of their fellow
Baptist missionaries on the docks of Iloilo, the largest city on
Panay, with a population then not exceeding ninety thousand
people. On December 4, the twenty-seven-year-olds boarded an
ancient and colonial-looking train in Iloilo for a five-hour—

seventy-four-mile-long—trip due north to their new home in the small coastal city of Capiz (modern-day Roxas City).[11]

The Meyers' train slowly creaked and clattered down the narrow-gauge tracks, leaving the southern coast and heading north across the central plain of Panay toward Capiz, the major city on the northern coast. Frederick and Ruth gazed with honeymoon glee at the varied and beautiful topography of their new home. Panay extends approximately 105 miles from north to south and 70 miles from east to west. Far to the west rise the silhouetted peaks of the rugged western Cordillera mountain range running north to south along the gorgeous coastline of the Sulu Sea and rising to a height of 6,722 feet at Mount Nangtud. Closer to the railroad, the foothills of the Cordilleras merge onto a 20-mile-wide central plain called the central lowlands. To the east of the railroad tracks a shorter range of mountains again ascends to a height of 2,736 feet at Mount Agudo, and then descends to the eastern coast, flanking the Guimaras Strait and the Visayan Sea.

As the train chugged up the central lowlands plain, flanked by distant mountain ranges on both sides, the Meyers studied the rich tropical vegetation and the densely cultivated fields of corn and sugarcane. Rice paddies glistened everywhere. Crossing networks of frequent streams and rivers, they marveled at the thick green clumps of bamboo drinking moisture from the streambeds. Looking toward the horizon where the central plain stretched toward the foothills, they saw verdant agricultural land give way to steep slopes of native Cogan grasslands, rising to mountainous jungle and even to weathered moss forests at the highest elevations. Panay was a beautiful island with immensely varied topography crowded into a small confined space. Soon the Meyers would also discover the wonder of their new coastal home of Capiz on the northeastern shore of Panay, laced with coconut trees, mangrove and nipa swamps, and pristine beaches. Frederick

and Ruth realized that they were a long way from Wisconsin in a
tropical land of lush and vibrant beauty.[12]

As Frederick and Ruth stepped down on the station platform at
Capiz, they gazed at a small colonial town of fewer than twenty
thousand citizens. It had been founded on the banks of the
Capiz River in 1693, several miles upstream from where the
river met the Visayan Sea. Perched on high ground at a bend of
the river, the city was built over the ancient seat of a kingdom
that had existed during the Indo-Malay era of the Philippines
(after 3,000 B.C.).

The Meyers soon noticed that the most prominent structure
in Capiz was a new concrete bridge that crossed the river at the
center of the town. Near the bridge a quaint central plaza had
been laid out adjacent to the widest curvature of the river, beau-
tifully framing the Catholic church, the municipal building, and
a statue of José Rizal. The plaza and river were flanked by several
streets lined with the attractive houses of the affluent business
class. These houses usually consisted of a first floor constructed
of stone and stucco and a second story made of wood. Nearby
were their shops and businesses. Poorer dwellings, constructed
primarily of nipa palm and thatch, were scattered on the outskirts of the city, extending into the farmland and rural barrios.

The crown of the Capiz region, however, is her beautiful
beaches. Baybay Beach is sixteen miles long, often a mile wide
at low tide, and forms the fifteenth-largest natural bay in the
world. The white beach sand is pristine and thickly lined with
lush and majestic coconut palms. Capiz is often called the "sea-
food capital of the Philippines." The balmy salt air and the lap-
ping surf suffuse the region with quiet tranquility.

Inland from the beaches is rich agricultural land, with the
primary crop being coconuts. Copra is the dried meat, or kernel,
of the coconut. When the coconuts are harvested and the meat

is extracted and dried, the copra is boiled and the coconut oil separated and processed. In addition to copra, the rich land also produced sugarcane, fruit, rice, hemp, and tobacco.

As Frederick and Ruth took in their exotic surroundings and unpacked their few belongings, they joined a sixteen-year effort by Baptists to secure a three-pronged approach to ministry in Capiz that focused on medicine, education, and evangelism. In 1903, Dr. Peter Lerrigo had begun this ministry when he visited Capiz and decided to begin a medical mission there. In the initial days a small Bible study and worship service was begun in a private home. A children's Bible study class soon took form, which included a local boy named Manuel Roxas, who would later become the first president of the Philippine republic in 1946.[13] A medical clinic was finally started in the basement of Dr. Lerrigo's rented home. But tragedy struck with the death of Dr. and Mrs. Lerrigo's infant son and the subsequent failing health of Mrs. Lerrigo. After only four months, the Lerrigos returned to the United States for her medical treatment.

Over the next fifteen years, the mission work in Capiz limped along sporadically, with missionaries, doctors, and nurses coming to reside for only short tenures. Yet, there was much encouragement as well. Faraway in New York City, Mrs. Laura "Cettie" Rockefeller, wife of John D. Rockefeller Sr.—a devout Baptist and noted philanthropist—heard a missionary on furlough speak of the struggling ministry in Capiz. She was moved by the story and donated funds to purchase land in Capiz to build a compound to house educational facilities, a hospital, and mission residences.[14] Her gift was used to buy seven acres of undulating land covered with bamboo one mile south of the city. When the Meyers arrived in Capiz in 1919, the land had been cleared and landscaped; on the property was a modest "Home School" for children, a simple two-story, wooden hospital building named "Emmanuel," a small nurses' training school, and two missionary residences.

Though the availability of missionaries had not been constant—
there had not been a doctor at the hospital in two years—the
medical practice had grown slowly. Now Frederick and Ruth
would attempt to stabilize the ministry and expand it. In future
decades they would be consistently present in overseeing "healing, teaching, and preaching" in Capiz.[15]

Chapter Three

The Gold Miners, 1901–1937

Energetic, mischievous, fearless, and full of themselves, the young Fertig brothers were tough as boots before they ever wore shoes. Wendell and Claude were reared on the high plains of southeast Colorado in the small town of La Junta, a Wild West community on the Santa Fe Trail, where both Bat Masterson and Kit Carson had played starring roles in its earliest days.

Wendell and Claude were born Colorado cowboys for only one reason—the grit and determination of their father, Welby Lee Fertig. Welby was born in 1864 during the final months of the American Civil War in Kaiser, West Virginia. Orphaned at an early age, he lived with his older brother, John, before striking out on his own at the age of twelve and heading west. This strong and independent boy supported himself by working on railroad construction gangs as an emerging rail system spread its iron web west of the Mississippi River and on toward the Pacific. Welby finally settled down in La Junta, Colorado, and married Olive Florence Baxter from Old Granada, Colorado.[1]

Wendell Fertig was born to Welby and Olive in 1901. Four
years later his kid brother, Claude, was born. The boys' relationship was tight-knit, and they hung together in this frontier community. Wendell was the bigger, bolder, and louder of the two.
But Claude could hold his own against his brother. After each
boy graduated from La Junta High School four years apart, they
each attended the Colorado School of Mines to become mining
engineers. Claude stood just five feet seven inches tall and weighed
all of 145 pounds when he tried out for the Colorado School of
Mines football team. Quickly given the nickname "the runt," he
gained respect as a fast, agile, and durable running back.

Wendell and Claude each enrolled in the Army Reserve Officers Corps while in college and spent their summers training
to be army engineers. A photograph shows Claude at Fort Sam
Houston in San Antonio, Texas, during the summer of 1926, striking a pose in his officer's uniform by a sign that states, "Company
27, 2nd Engineers." Both young men received their commissions
and entered the army reserves.

As Claude graduated from the Colorado School of Mines
in the late 1920s and entered the first years of young adulthood,
the Dust Bowl was beginning to choke the Colorado high plains:
Crops were poor, cattle were being sold for less than cost, and
America was careering toward the Great Depression. Mines cut
back production and young mining engineers found it difficult to
secure employment. After surviving on odd jobs, Claude finally
joined the Civilian Conservation Corps, a financial salvation for
thousands offered by the Roosevelt administration in 1933.[2] The
CCC created federally funded jobs for unemployed men in construction, forestry, and flood prevention. With his degree in engineering and his military background, Claude was soon placed
in a position of leadership responsibility on construction sites.
Through the remaining years of his twenties and early thirties, he
worked on the construction of two of the greatest engineering

feats of this era—the Hoover Dam on the Nevada-Arizona border, and the Moffat Tunnel near Winter Park, Colorado.

The Moffat Tunnel was of particular interest to Claude. Soon to be one of the most famous railroad tunnels in America, this passageway was blasted through six miles of Colorado Rocky Mountain slab at an elevation of 9,239 feet. By penetrating James Peak and the continental divide the tunnel eliminated the necessity of operating tracks over the highest parts of Rollins Pass. Claude always looked back on this feat with a sense of pride for his contribution to his home state.

While working with the CCC, whenever Claude returned home to La Junta, he noticed a slender, vivacious, blue-eyed blonde, Laverne Shockley. Laverne had been just a freshman when Claude graduated from high school, too young to take seriously, but he had always kept his eye on her. Now in his late twenties, Claude was mesmerized by the mature Laverne. He suddenly felt ready to settle down.

Like many people in the region, Laverne's family had gone through hard times. Her mother, Nora, had been raised as an orphan in Colorado. When she was a teenager she was introduced by a friend to a man twice her age, Joseph Shockley, and they struck up a pen-pal relationship. While he was living in the small town of Stoutland in central Missouri, Joseph Shockley, age thirty-one, wrote to Nora, age sixteen, and proposed marriage. Reflecting the poverty of the times, he suggested, "If you can pay for your ticket to Stoutland, I'll pay you back when you arrive." Nora bought the ticket and they were married in 1896.[3]

During her first twelve years of marriage Nora gave birth to five daughters, the last being Laverne, born in 1908. Weakened by repeated pregnancies and poor nutrition, Nora developed tuberculosis. The Shockleys traveled to arid Colorado in search of a drier climate conducive to healing lung disease. When Laverne was three, her family settled on a farm outside of La Junta, in 1911. Ten years later Nora and Joseph divorced and Joseph traveled on to California, leaving Nora alone to raise the five daughters.

Despite being dirt poor, Nora managed to pay her bills, and her daughters became a tight and supportive sorority that helped their mother. When Laverne graduated from high school, it was obvious that she was bright, talented, and wanted to go to college. Her older sister Bee, who had dropped out of school in the eighth grade to work, sat her down and said, "You're going to college, and I'll help you pay for it." With Bee's help Laverne enrolled at Colorado State Teachers College in Greeley, Colorado, to study education and develop her natural gifts in drama and singing.[4] Bee's friendship and support bonded the two sisters in an intimate and sustained friendship that would later help Laverne cope with the trauma she endured during World War II.

Claude Fertig walked back onto the stage of Laverne's life after her college years were complete. Short, with a gymnast's taut physique, Claude had a broad, devilish grin and twinkling blue eyes that were accentuated by a thick mane of auburn-tinted brown hair. Though reserved, Claude was full of energy. He liked to dance and laugh, and loved the outdoors. He was dashing in a quiet way, romantic and adventuresome. He was a man's man but never macho. He loved people and parties, but at heart he was a solitary person.

Claude adored Laverne. That was clear to everyone. Petite, weighing ninety-eight pounds and five feet four inches tall, Laverne was lively and energetic. A natural blonde with engaging light-blue eyes, she exuded beauty and an alluring softness that covered her strong-willed determination and no-nonsense attitude. She was a realist with no false pretense about life. Though in contrast to Claude she seemed an extrovert. She, too, liked time alone to think,

Claude and Laverne quickly fell in love. Not wanting the frills and costs of a wedding, they eloped on June 14, 1935, and were married in Denver in the home of a Congregational minister. Claude was twenty-nine years old and Laverne was twenty-six. Both had enjoyed their years of independence and now embraced commitment. From 1935 through 1937, they lived in

Claude and Laverne Fertig on their wedding day, 1935.   *Kathy Fertig*

Grand Junction, Colorado, while Claude continued his engineering work with the CCC.[5]

As the United States sank further into the Great Depression, positive economic conditions emerged in the Philippines that would affect Wendell and Claude Fertig for life. The Philippines had some of the largest copper, gold, and chromite deposits in the world.[6] Primitive gold mines date back to at least 1000 B.C. in the Philippines.[7] As early as 1524, Spanish explorers had reported the existence of gold mining throughout the scattered archipelago. However, extensive exploration and processing of gold did not begin until the United States invested in the natural resources of the Philippines in the early twentieth century.[8]

In 1933, President Franklin D. Roosevelt sought to stabilize the flagging United States economy by passing legislation that prohibited the exportation of gold from the continental United States. This created what amounted to a gold rush in the Philippines as American gold miners saw the undeveloped Philippine gold deposits as an excellent opportunity to fill the new vacuum in the international gold market. Soon American mining companies were infiltrating the islands, and gold mines multiplied.[9] This mining boom did not escape the notice of Wendell and Claude Fertig in Colorado.

As the Depression years wore on in the United States, Claude's older brother, Wendell, was also struggling to support his wife and two young daughters. Ever adventurous, Wendell seized upon the prospect of living the good life in the Philippines and making a fortune, soon swinging into action and using his small savings to buy four tickets on an ocean liner bound for Manila. He packed up his wife, Mary, and his young daughters, Pat and Jeanne, and sailed to the Philippines to secure work in the gold-mining industry.

Arriving in the Philippines in the middle years of the 1930s, Wendell and Mary initially settled on the northern island of Luzon in the province of Batangas, south of Manila. Wendell spent several years working as a mining engineer, supervising the on-site operations of start-up mining projects, and then moved his family from Batangas to the exotic capital of Manila and a more urban lifestyle. His work as an executive for a mining firm soon enabled Wendell and Mary to live the Manila country club life. Within the Philippine economy a dollar went a long way. Their standard of living soared. Comfortable housing with servants became standard fare. Their daughters attended a private international school. Membership at the Polo Club or the Yacht Club was expected and affordable. Within a short time their lives had changed radically.[10]

Soon Wendell wrote to his brother, Claude, urging him to come to the Philippines as well. Just as work on the Moffat Tunnel was nearing completion, Claude and Laverne decided to join Wendell and Mary. Selling their few possessions, they purchased passenger ship tickets to Manila and set out on the adventure of their lives. Married for two years and without children, they now enjoyed a long-awaited honeymoon. Claude, age thirty-two, and Laverne, age twenty-nine, sailed into the unknown filled with youthful excitement.[11]

Chapter Four

Capiz City, Panay,
1919–1941

When Frederick and Ruth Meyer stepped off the wheezing narrow-gauge train in the provincial capital of Capiz in 1919, the twenty-seven-year-olds could not have imagined that this coastal city would be their home for the rest of their professional lives. With the exception of one-year furloughs in the United States, the Meyers would remain in Capiz, developing deep roots and relationships with their Filipino neighbors. What the Baptist mission in Capiz now needed was a long-term commitment by and consistency from a missionary couple. And in the Meyers, this need was fulfilled.

Upon arrival, Frederick and Ruth were confronted with Emmanuel Hospital—a small and delapidated twenty-bed facility that had been closed for three years. Emmanuel—a Hebrew word meaning "God with us"—was made of wood, which deteriorated quickly in the tropical climate if not continually painted, repaired, and treated for termite infestation. Due to the annual rainy season, most buildings were also saturated with mold and mildew. In his first letter to his parents Frederick wrote, "The hospital needs thorough cleaning in every department, which will require very much time, as I cannot secure enough men. People do not understand this situation, but come for treatment, even from a distance of 50 kilometers. The doctor has come and so the patients come. I believe a new floor of reinforced concrete must be laid in the operating room. The hospital unoccupied for many months demands an overhauling."[1]

Dr. Meyer did far more than an *overhauling*. Slowly he increased the technological capability of the hospital through the development of a laboratory and the acquisition of an X-ray machine and new surgical apparatuses. Much later, with the completion of a new annex in 1940, the hospital expanded to a maximum capacity of ninety beds. After his first full year of medical practice, in 1920, Frederick reported that he had treated a total of 130 inpatients at Emmanuel Hospital. Twenty years later, in 1940, the annual total of inpatients had mushroomed to 2,368.[2] Such rapid growth and success was created by the Filipinos' acute need for medical care combined with Dr. Meyer's intense work ethic and devoted care.

Within the first year of Dr. Meyer's arrival he led the reinstitution of a lapsed nursing school program. Desperate for competent nursing staff, the hospital needed to train its own nurses. He soon mailed flyers throughout the Visayan Islands announcing the beginning of the nursing program and stating the requirements for acceptance into the program: applicants over eighteen years old who had completed the seventh grade in a public school. The advertisement explained that the nursing curriculum would consist of "practical nursing, anatomy, physiology, *materia medica*, medicine, surgery, obstetrics, care of children, hygiene, massage, house-keeping, dietetics, English, and all other subjects included in the curriculum required by the Government."[3]

The biggest problem was, who would train the nurses? One of the American elementary schoolteachers in Capiz was Cora

Sydney. Cora was also a professional nurse and had passed her examinations in Manila. In June 1920, she became the sole instructor and director of the nursing program. Three years later, the first nursing class graduated, and seven nurses received their diplomas and caps.

After the first graduation, Cora Sydney resigned due to deteriorating health, and returned to the United States. She was soon replaced by a new, twenty-seven-year-old missionary appointee, Jennie C. Adams. Upon meeting her, Frederick enthusiastically wrote, "She is a very nice young lady from Chambers, Nebraska, and will fit into the work most admirably. The girls love her. She had her training at Lincoln [Nebraska], and at Cook County Hospital, Chicago. She has a very nice disposition."

Jennie Adams began a long and healthy partnership with the Meyers at Emmanuel Hospital. Under her capable leadership, the nursing school would graduate 142 nurses prior to the outbreak of World War II. The graduates made a significant contribution to the health care of Panay and the central Philippines.[4]

One of Frederick's ardent beliefs was that he must "work himself out of a job" by training and encouraging a new generation of Filipino doctors. Over his years of medical practice, he sought to recruit and enlist young Filipino medical associates and interns. He played a teaching and mentoring role in their lives, setting an example of exacting professionalism and selfless commitment to his patients.

In addition to their roles at Emmanuel Hospital, Frederick and Ruth often ran temporary health clinics in the remote areas of Capiz province. As they worked throughout the rural barrios, more Filipinos became aware of the medical mission in Capiz and later would travel long distances to the hospital for surgery and treatment of chronic illnesses. Frederick's reputation as a superb doctor spread by the "bamboo telegraph" to the

most remote regions of Panay. As the only board-certified surgeon in the sole hospital in a province of some three hundred
thousand people, Frederick soon had more patients than he
could handle.

He also had to adjust to treating exotic medical cases he
had rarely observed at Yale Medical School. Some of the diseases
he most frequently treated were advanced amoebic dysentery,
intestinal parasites, complications of childbirth, and heart disease; he also had to perform emergency surgeries that had been
delayed until the patient was at the point of death. One such delayed surgery Frederick discussed in a letter to his parents: "The
other week, I had a dreadful neglected mistreated transverse presentation obstetrics case—details too horrible to relate—she died
under the operation; couldn't save her, she was too far gone, in
a dreadful condition for a day and night, before brought to the
hospital."[5]

In other letters to his relatives, Frederick took muted delight
in describing gross tropical maladies and surgical procedures:
"But listen, here's a case, a young boy with five large eight inch
worms coming out of the umbilicus. How's that for an oddity. I
am going to write up my oddities in worm complications. . . .
And yesterday I took out my heaviest tumor, twenty-six pounds,
a multilobar ovarian cyst, which had pushed up the diaphragm
and displaced the heart, it filled the whole abdominal cavity,
poor twenty year old girl, suffering thus for three years. Today I
had a dynamite case, in which the forearm was blown off to
parts unknown, and so an amputation was necessary. . . ."

Frederick's initial months in Capiz were spent in wonder
as he observed medical cases he had never seen before and
was forced to perform surgeries rarely done in the United States.
His medical experience was growing, and he loved his work.

In addition to being a skilled surgeon, Frederick was also
a talented musician and an able preacher. Ruth, trained as a

concert soloist, sang on many occasions throughout the Philippines. Frederick often accompanied her on either a piano or an
organ. He also had gifts as a choral conductor, and in 1941 directed a choir from the provinces of Capiz, Iloilo, and the island
of Negros in the presentation of the oratorio *The Holy City*. Like
the famed Dr. Albert Schweitzer, missionary to Africa, medicine
was Frederick's heart but music revived his soul. Ruth and Frederick shared their love of music, and it strengthened their friendship and marriage.

On many weekends Frederick also could be found preaching in church services in small rural barrios as well as in provincial cities throughout Panay. He was a natural teacher and liked
to use stories from his medical practice in his sermons. He did
not see himself simply as a physician. Rather, he was a man who
loved and helped people through every skill and talent that he
possessed.

Such a varied and active life in the tropics often exhausted
Frederick. In 1932, he wrote, "I am just over loaded with work,
and lack sleep. I really do the work of three men up here. It is
getting just a little bit too much. . . . I have to run the finances,
and keep the records, cases, all hospital secretarial work, etc.
It is too much. My nerves react peculiarly a wee bit. I am longin'
for sleep." Later, in 1941, he wrote, "I have been overladen with
talks this month . . . on top of all my hospital duties, local
church work, and the direction of *The Holy City* for the Baptist
Convention. People must think my days consist of 72 hours
each. And no vacation this year. I do not know what will happen."[6]

In addition to their demanding medical work, Frederick and
Ruth also learned to be parents. Arriving in Capiz as newlyweds,
they did not waste time starting a family. Seventeen months af-
ter their wedding and thirteen months after arriving in Capiz,
Frederick Willer Meyer (Buddy) was born, on January 3, 1921.
Milton Walter Meyer (Milt) joined the family two and a half

years later, on August 7, 1923, and the family was completed with the birth of Richard Allen Meyer (Dick) on August 13, 1927. Eight short years after their marriage vows, Frederick and Ruth's lives had changed radically.

Frederick and Ruth Meyer, with their sons (from left) Richard, Frederick (Buddy), and Milton, 1933.

Milton Meyer

Growing up in Capiz was delightful and idyllic in many ways for the Meyer boys. The Baptist mission had built a comfortable house for the doctor-in-residence, which was wired for electricity upon the Meyers' arrival. The house was in the midst of a scenic mission compound. In her first letter to her family in Wisconsin, Ruth wrote, "How should I begin to tell you of our compound! It's one of the most beautiful mission compounds in the Islands and we are both very much in love with it and the people. It is located on a high hill overlooking the city and [you can see] out on the ocean with beautiful flowers, palms, and shrubs."[7] Later, their first house, in need of much renovation, was razed, and a new one built.

In addition to their Western-style home in the mission

compound, the Meyers had access to a nearby beach house constructed in a simple native style. Throughout the Philippines small
thatched huts—called "nipa huts"—are made from the long feath-
ery leaves of the nipa palm found growing in soft mud along
coastal riverbanks and mangrove swamps. The nipa leaves are
harvested and processed into a thatch material that can be woven
to make walls and partitions. The nipa hut is then constructed
on top of stilts made of stout bamboo poles or tree trunks. The
stilts lift the hut four to eight feet above the ground and protect
it from incoming tides and flooding from torrential rains. On
top of these stilts a bamboo framework is constructed on which
to attach the exterior nipa palm walls and the thick cogan-grass
roof. The bamboo framework is laced and tied together with split
strands of the banban plant. The interior floor is made of thin
strips of split bamboo, which allows cool air to flow through the
raised flooring. Within such native housing Ruth and the boys
vacationed for weeks on the northern coast, whiling away the
long summer months. Dr. Meyer would break away from the hospital to drop in on the family whenever he could. Some of their
fondest family memories took place in this seaside setting.[8]

However, all was not perfect in Eden. Milton would later reflect that his father's total dedication to his medical practice did,
in Ruth's words, sometimes "make him a stranger at home."[9] He
recalled that he grew to dread Christmas Eves, because it seemed
that his father was always called away from the family to stitch
up some drunken reveler who had been carved up in a knife fight.
Dr. Meyer's devotion to his work resulted in the boys relying on
their mother for affection, closeness, and intimacy. Though they
never doubted their father's love and commitment, they often
felt in competition with his profession for his attention and time.
There was a certain "Germanic distance" to the doctor that could
make him seem aloof and formal, both to family and friends.[10]

The most difficult family challenge, however, was schooling

for the children. The Meyer boys' playmates were Filipino, Spanish, Chinese, and mestizo. Thus, these young "Americanos" became bilingual as small children. Upon reaching school age, they attended Home School in Capiz, a small school extending from first grade through high school, with approximately one hundred students in 1925. The teachers were both Filipino and American, though the Meyer brothers often were the only American students. Their education was supplemented by Calvert correspondence courses, a popular form of homeschooling for Americans living abroad. Ruth became their tutor as well as their mother.

When the high school years arrived, Frederick and Ruth reluctantly chose to send their three boys to Bordner School in Manila, a 250-mile voyage north to the island of Luzon by inter-island steamer, requiring two days of travel. At Bordner School their classmates were primarily American students. They studied a curriculum that prepared them to attend universities in the United States. During the nine-month school year they lived with another missionary family in Manila, and then returned to Capiz for summer vacation. Buddy was the first to leave home for Manila, in 1933, followed by Milton in 1937, and finally, Dick in 1941.

The separation from their parents during high school was a necessary but painful change for both the children and their parents. Young teenagers were forced to "grow up quickly," and younger siblings were prematurely separated from their older brothers and sisters. Parents typically felt guilty about sending their children away from home for months at a time. They also struggled to pay the additional cost of private school education. Yet Bordner was one of only three American schools in the Philippines that could prepare the Meyer boys to attend their father's alma mater, Yale University. The feeling of acute separation—from America, from parents, from home, from siblings, from security and safety—was an inherent part of being the children of missionaries. The pang of such separation anxiety plagued many missionary children for the rest of their lives.

During the period Buddy and Milton left home for high school in Manila, the growth of Japanese militarism was spreading fear and uncertainty across southeast Asia. Overcrowded on its home islands, lacking essential natural resources and depending on other nations for vital petroleum and oil, Japan had an intense desire to conquer and expand her territory. Japan had ruled Korea and Formosa since 1895. But it now desired above all to invade China. As the decade of the 1930s evolved, China was becoming a vulnerable nation weakened by a massive civil war between the nationalist government troops of Chiang Kai-shek and communist rebels led by a young Mao Tse-tung. Taking advantage of this instability, Japan successfully invaded the northeastern province of Manchuria in 1931, virtually unopposed.

After consolidating its gains within Manchuria, Japan struck again in 1937, crossing into China across the Great Wall at the ancient Marco Polo Bridge near Peking. Within six months the Chinese forces collapsed, and Japan occupied Peking, Shanghai, the nationalist capital at Nanking, and the essential ports of Amoy and Canton. By 1939, Japan had seized military control of eastern China and was making obvious plans to invade the rest of southeast Asia.

As Japanese troops spread across China, so did Hitler's efficient military machine conquer vast areas of Europe. When Hitler invaded Poland on September 1, 1939, England and France were bound by treaty to declare war on Germany. They did so on September 3, 1939, and within the next nine months Hitler invaded and crushed Poland, Belgium, Denmark, Norway, the Netherlands, and France. Only Great Britain was left on her secluded islands, barely resisting the might of Germany. British

prime minister Winston Churchill openly (and covertly) begged
President Franklin Roosevelt and the American people for aid
and assistance. Roosevelt sensed that American intervention in
World War II was inevitable, but he faced an American public
that was largely opposed to U.S. involvement in foreign wars. It
was a perilous and anxious time.

During the uncertain year of 1939, Dr. Meyer reflected on
his college days at Yale during the nightmare of World War I,
and wrote to his family in America, "Europe is again engulfed in
war. . . . I try to get the latest news via radio and pray that we of
the U.S.A. conserve neutrality through thick and thin; no more
participation in any European fracas."[11]

Yet despite Dr. Meyer's isolationist wishes, American neutrality seemed to grow more unlikely. A year later, in November
1940, he reflected on the deteriorating situation in Asia and
strained to be optimistic: "The tenseness of the Japan situation
is quieting down, evidently Japan sees we mean business, and
so does not want war with America. But still evacuation is going
on from Japan, and Shanghai, and parts of China. America is
increasing her air and navy forces out here [in the Philippines]
and in regard to land troops will use 50,000 Filipino soldiers."[12]

By June 1941, Dr. Meyer—along with most Americans in the
Philippines—knew that war was all but inevitable. Only months
before the U.S. Pacific Fleet had been permanently moved from
its traditional home base in San Diego to Pearl Harbor in Hawaii, to place the fleet nearer to potential combat in Asia. Many
American civilians in the Philippines also noticed that the wives
and children of American military personnel were quietly returning to the United States. With such thoughts whirring in his
mind, Dr. Meyer wrote of contingency plans being made for the
use of Emmanuel Hospital in the event of a Japanese invasion of
Panay: "We had several [hospital] staff meetings, to aid along in

the Volunteer movement of the civilian evacuation of wounded, with the hospital as a center, plans are being drafted as to what to do in bombing. The tense situation between Japan and the U.S.A. has not abated, although the Japanese are hesitant to involve themselves in war with us. Hitler is doing his best to involve the Orient, there is pressure upon Japan, but Japan will not risk too much, as she is heavily involved with China. But we must prepare for emergency so are committeeing and planning and looking for safe spots."[13]

A month later Frederick recorded the appearance of a new wartime symbol at the hospital: "Our hospital on orders from Manila has four red crosses painted on the different roofs of the hospital, as if that would insure safety from air attack by the enemy." A week later he wrote, "Japanese tension is terrific last week, I thought things would ease up, but this week it is a different story. The fleet has left Honolulu for destination unknown, that means, to us [the Philippines]. Japanese steamers hesitate to make American ports, and we have frozen all credits, and in addition, MacArthur becomes commander-in-chief out here of the federalized Filipino troops as well as American soldiers. It seems we are ready. Japan must go slow, and we hope the hotheads of Japan realize the situation. We are far from prepared for an attack on us. Those four red crosses on our hospital roofs will not protect us in these totalitarian wars."[14]

In the last six months of 1941, preceding the war between the United States and Japan, Emmanuel Hospital and the Capiz Baptist Mission became increasingly identified with the United States military, a decision that would later affect the decisions and the welfare of the Meyer family. Two small military bases on Panay, at Banga and Panitan, were reinforced and made ready for war. Emmanuel Hospital soon became a major medical center for treating and supporting American and Filipino troops at these bases. On September 8, 1941, Frederick wrote, "The American

camp commanders have been in to pay their respect. I have op-
erated upon the first army case; two colonels, a major and three
captains have inspected us, as our hospital will be a base hospital in case of war, we shall be ranking officers, and so we must
be prepared." Frederick clearly expected to be actively involved
in the military effort should war be declared.

In addition to dealing with the military in an official capacity, Frederick and Ruth developed friendly relationships with
the officers. Frederick wrote, "Last Sunday we entertained for
dinner also at tea the American camp commanders of the two
camps, one at Panitan and the other at Banga, with their aides.
They certainly enjoyed the full meal of capon, green jello salad,
Ruth's special, and all the other trimmings." Ruth and Frederick
were becoming personally and emotionally involved in the welfare of the officers and soldiers.

A month later, Frederick wrote a note in his journal that reflected his waning hope that war might be avoided: "We shall
be drawn soon into warfare. Coming Wednesday night we have
scheduled a national blackout for two hours, and so are busy preparing for proper methods of maintenance in a hospital, so that
we can take care of our patients properly, operate without being
seen on the outside. We can evacuate fairly nicely now without
too much confusion, to three places if need be, fire precautions,
emergency squads; yes, we must be prepared."[15]

As the final days before the outbreak of war between the United
States and Japan flew by, Dr. Meyer was prepared for Emmanuel
Hospital to become a vital part of an American-Filipino defense
of Panay. His youthful days in the Medical Enlisted Reserve
Corps during World War I were coming back to him again. He
felt it was his duty to give medical services to American and
Filipino troops, as well as civilians, and to help in the defense of
the Philippines.

The Gold Miners
1937–41

When Claude and Laverne Fertig first arrived in the Philippines, they were reunited with Wendell and Mary, a long way from Colorado. By now Wendell had a firm grasp of the gold-mining business in the Philippines, and he helped Claude find employment as an engineer and mining supervisor. In their first months in the Philippines, Claude and Laverne moved sixty-eight miles southwest of Manila to the scenic province of Batangas to work in a developing gold mine. Soon, however, they moved farther south to the remote island of Masbate at the northern end of the

Claude Fertig's mining house in Batangas, 1937.   *Kathy Fertig*

Visayan chain of islands, exactly in the center of the Philippine archipelago. Claude was employed at the Capsay Mine on Masbate. The island is only forty miles northwest of the port city of Capiz on the island of Panay.[16]

    Mining in the Philippines in the late 1930s was difficult work. Much of the labor was physically demanding, mechanized mining equipment was not obtained easily and the tropical heat and dampness was oppressive. But there were benefits as well. While the salary of a mining engineer was not unusually high, costs for most essential goods were also inexpensive. Claude and Laverne lived in a comfortable wooden house provided by the mining company. The pace of life was slow and leisurely, like the rest of rural Filipino culture, and there was time to savor life. Evenings were quiet. Wives were not expected to work outside the home. There was time to enjoy a young marriage and to socialize with other mining families.

One of the customs in the Philippines that both the missionaries and the gold miners benefited from was the employment of household servants. Upperclass Filipinos and Americans frequently hired at least one servant to cook, wash clothes, and clean the house. This was an important form of income for poor Filipinos who lacked an education or profession. This household help was a luxury that the Americans had not experienced in the United States, and it freed up much time to enjoy a less frenetic lifestyle than they were used to. Claude arranged for Federico Condino to assist Laverne with housekeeping and cooking. Federico, along with his wife, Catalina, and daughter, Bienvenida, soon became almost a part of the Fertig family.[17]

Laverne Fertig, about 1941.
Kathy Fertig

Both Laverne and Claude relished their solitude. They enjoyed long walks and quiet reflection. They read and they listened to music. But they also liked the chances for friendship and parties that the mining community provided. Laverne developed friendships with two other American miners' wives, Louise Spencer and Laura Schuring, who lived in neighboring mining towns within an hour's drive of one an-other.[18] Each Saturday these young women met in one of their homes for a day of playing bridge and catching up.

The Americans working in the scattered gold mines on Masbate would also get together frequently for volleyball games, beach parties, and dances. For many of these Americans—young and old—their social lives in the Philippines were more intense, enjoyable, and festive than they had ever been in the United States. Their frequent interactions with one another reduced their homesickness.

The Fertigs soon met Cyril (always called Spence) and Louise Spencer. Both couples were relative newlyweds and close to the same age. Spence, an American, had been involved in gold-mining operations in South America and Canada, and was a seasoned traveler. He met Louise Reid, who was from Montreal, Canada, and could not forget her. He sailed alone to the Philippines, but wrote back proposing marriage, and asking her to sail to Manila for their wedding. Louise accepted Spence's proposal through the mail, and in 1937 bravely boarded a passenger liner bound for Manila. She was met at the dock by an eager and wide-eyed Spence, nervously holding a dozen red roses. They spent their honeymoon in Manila, and then moved several times, to remote gold-mining towns. For the last year they had been developing a mine on Masbate."[19]

Spence was six feet tall and slender, and had reddish blond hair and blue eyes. He was a chain-smoker and fiercely independent. Louise was also tall and attractive, and had soft brown hair and a quiet disposition. She was twenty-six when she sailed for Manila and thirty as the war approached.[20]

As the end of 1941 drew near, all American civilians living in the Philippines felt the tension of the impending war with Japan. As early as the summer of 1941, passenger-ship travel to the Philippines was restricted, and the wives and children of American military personnel were continuing to quietly and unofficially return to the United States. Wendell Fertig took no chances and sent his wife, Mary, and their two children back to Colorado. Yet the United States government refused to evacuate all American civilian families officially for fear of spreading panic and appearing weak to the Japanese.[21] This government decision sealed the fate of many American wives and children, and would cause incalculable suffering.

On July 1, 1941, the Meyers' second son, Milton, was able to sail to the United States on the SS *President Pierce*, the last regularly scheduled passenger ship to depart from Manila. He joined his older brother, Buddy, at Yale.[22] One year later the SS *President Pierce* became a U.S. Army troop transport, was renamed the USS *Hugh L. Scott*, and was sunk by a German submarine off the coast of North Africa in 1942.

As the final months of 1941 flew by, the fear of a Japanese attack on the Philippines was palpable. Yet no one knew when that moment would come. General MacArthur had been forewarned by Washington as early as November 27, 1941, of the possibility,[23] but he felt confident that there was still adequate time to prepare to repel a Japanese invasion successfully. He had somehow come to the conclusion that if the Japanese attacked at all, it would not be before April 1942.

He was badly mistaken.[24]

Chapter Five

December 4, 1941,
Chicago, Illinois

By Thursday, December 4, the presses were rolling in Chicago, printing the final copies of the newest weekly edition of *Life* magazine, perhaps the most popular magazine in America at the time with sales of over one million copies each week. The cover date was Monday, December 8, 1941. And the cover was a photograph of General Douglas MacArthur wearing a richly gold-embroidered dress cap and looking supremely confident

The feature editorial for the week took aim at the lackadaisical attitude its editors found among most Americans toward the likelihood of war in Asia:

> For a nation poised on the precipice of two-ocean war, the U.S. was extraordinarily complacent last week. Washington cocked tense ears for the first sounds of shooting on the wide Pacific. . . . There was no question that the country was thoroughly aware of the situation. Newspaper headlines loomed heavy with portents. Yet no one

worried. . . . All of this indicated just one thing; that Americans were not frightened by the Japanese. . . .

What few pondered, in the enthusiastic nationwide
endorsement of the administration's tough Pacific policy,
were the immense strategical problems involved in fighting a war west of the Philippines. For the time being the
classic American naval principle of an undivided fleet,
acting as a unit, has been scrapped in the interest of aid-
to-Britain. For the time being the classic naval theory that
a Pacific conflict must involve three years of slow west-
ward progress from fortified base to fortified base has been
conveniently forgotten. The American people felt secure
in the belief that America's superb Navy could cope with
all difficulties. Americans felt confident, rightly or wrongly,
the Japs were pushovers.[1]

This edition of *Life* magazine arrived in American homes and
was on the shelves of drugstores and magazine shops the day
after Japan's catastrophic attack on Pearl Harbor. For those who
took time to look at the self-assured face of General MacArthur
and read the prophetic editorial page, the magazine struck a dis-
sonant chord of taunting horror and shame. The Japanese were
no pushovers.

December 7–10, 1941,
Luzon Island

The Philippines and Hawaii are located on the opposite sides of
the international dateline that bisects the Pacific Ocean. Because
of this, the Philippines is "one day ahead" of Hawaii, by eighteen hours. When Pearl Harbor was attacked on Sunday morning, December 7, it was already early Monday morning, December
8, in the Philippines. At three o'clock on that dark Monday

morning an urgent message reached Manila from Hawaii addressed to Rear Admiral Thomas C. Hart, commander of the U.S. Asiatic Fleet and ranking naval officer in the Philippines. The words were terse: *AIR RAID AT PEARL HARBOR—THIS IS NO DRILL*. With this shock, military plans and efficiency unraveled in the Philippines with unbelievable speed and ineptness.[2]

Admiral Hart and General MacArthur had always had a strained personal and professional relationship. Professionally, there was a lack of a clearly defined chain of command and "coordination of mission" between MacArthur and Hart. Much of this was due to the traditional vying between the army and the navy as to "who ruled the roost and who called the shots." As a result, in the opening hours of World War II in the Philippines there was obvious discord between the responses of the navy and the army. To complicate matters further, Hart personally could not abide MacArthur's ego and theatrics and MacArthur refused to share center stage with anyone. As a result, each man kept his guarded distance. Unbelievably, Hart did not notify MacArthur immediately of the Japanese attack on Pearl Harbor, and the general would slumber for nearly an hour before being awakened by his chief of staff, Major General Richard Sutherland, who heard the news via an enlisted army signalman who was listening on a shortwave radio to a California radio station.[3]

Slowly the enormity of the Japanese attack on Hawaii would filter through radio transmissions and became clear to both MacArthur and Hart. Secretly transported by aircraft carriers to less than two hundred miles north of Oahu, Japanese naval aircraft had sunk or badly damaged twenty American warships at Pearl Harbor, destroyed most U.S. aircraft on the ground, and killed 2,403 American servicemen and left 1,178 wounded. The only good news was that the American aircraft carriers were safely at sea and untouched.

What was not known was that the Japanese naval air offensive on December 7 (8) would be a two-pronged attack. At the same time that Japanese planes were returning from Pearl Harbor to their carriers, Japanese fighters and bombers of the Eleventh Imperial Air Fleet, based on the island of Formosa (as Taiwan was known at the time)—100 miles east of the southern China coast—were being fueled and armed for a multitarget raid on the island of Luzon in the Philippines, 450 miles due south. Their principal objectives were to take out the American bombers at Clark Field northwest of Manila and to destroy American fighter planes at nearby Iba Field.

Two hundred Zero fighters and Mitsubishi bombers were supposed to be in the first wave, and their crews were restless as the planes sat on Formosan runways, socked in by thick fog. As minutes ticked by, they knew that news of the Pearl Harbor attack was circling the globe. They now feared that a preemptive strike by an angry United States bomber fleet based in the Philippines would catch them on the ground. Finally able to take off as the fog lifted, the Japanese pilots assumed that they had lost the element of surprise. The United States army and navy would be on full alert in the Philippines. The Japanese pilots anticipated the worst.[4]

MacArthur was officially contacted by Washington at 3:40 A.M. by Brigadier General Leonard T. Gerow, head of Army planning. Gerow confirmed the attack on Pearl Harbor and warned MacArthur to prepare for an imminent Japanese attack. MacArthur was well aware that the initial strike would likely come from aircraft based on Formosa. Yet for nine hours MacArthur did little to aggressively prevent such an attack.[5]

As early as 5:00 A.M. on December 8, Major General Lewis Brereton, commander of the Far East Air Force in the Philippine Islands, had rushed to General MacArthur's headquarters and asked for an immediate meeting with him. He had come in person to request permission to send his B-17 bombers from Clark Field on a preemptive strike to destroy Japanese air bases in Formosa. Though he knew he lacked adequate reconnaissance and would have to fly without a fighter escort due to the long distance, he felt that a poorly planned attack was better than no attack at all. Champing at the bit, Brereton was curtly informed by Mac-Arthur's protective chief of staff, Major General Sutherland, that MacArthur was in conference and unable to see him. Sutherland then told Brereton to proceed with preparations for a bombing strike on Formosa but to await MacArthur's direct permission, which Sutherland would obtain personally.

While waiting for MacArthur's response, his staff stewed in Brereton's office at Nielson Field on the southern outskirts of Manila. When Lieutenant Colonel Eugene Eubank was asked if the B-17 force at Clark Field was prepared for attack, he snapped, "Sure they're ready. They've been ready since before daylight. What're we going to do with 'em? That's what I want to know." The frustration over delayed orders from MacArthur was growing by the minute.

Two hours later, at 7:15 A.M., Brereton returned to Mac-Arthur's headquarters and was again stopped from direct conversation with him by Sutherland. Though MacArthur was alone, Sutherland informed Brereton that MacArthur still could not be disturbed, and that he had not yet responded to Brereton's request to bomb Formosa. Losing patience, a livid Brereton again demanded a face-to-face meeting with MacArthur. Sutherland refused, but grudgingly said, "I'll ask the General." Sutherland disappeared into MacArthur's inner sanctum and returned with a terse order, "The General says no. Don't make the first overt act."[6]

Brereton stormed out of MacArthur's office and ordered his staff car to return to his headquarters. His options were now limited to defensive operations until further word from an isolated and vacillating MacArthur. He immediately ordered all B-17 and B-18 bombers at Clark Field into the air to avoid destruc-

tion on the ground. The bombers were to stay within control-
tower range of Clark Field until ordered to land.

At 8:25 A.M., as American bombers were lifting off at Clark, the
first seventeen Ki-21-IIAs Japanese bombers appeared over the
mountainous "summer capital" city of Baguio, ninety miles north
of Clark Field. The Japanese bombed a small military base, Camp
John Hay, a favorite rest and relaxation center for American servicemen. Japanese intelligence suspected that MacArthur was
vacationing at Camp John Hay and intended their first bombs to
fall on him.[7] Though they missed MacArthur, it was now obvious that Japanese bombers were taking offensive actions against
the Philippines. However, MacArthur still withheld permission
from Brereton to unleash his bombers and attack Formosa.[8]

As the sun grew higher in the sky on the morning of December 8, Brereton's bombers continued to circle idly above Luzon
and the South China Sea, slowly expending their fuel supply.
Finally, at 10:14 A.M., MacArthur personally telephoned Brereton. Brereton told MacArthur that even though he lacked proper
photoreconnaissance, he wanted to mount an attack on Formosa
as soon as possible. MacArthur finally gave Brereton permission
to attack at his own discretion. Elated, Brereton immediately ordered his circling bombers to return to Clark for refueling and
the loading of armaments.[9]

As the scattered American bombers landed, they lined up
with peacetime precision into neat rows and were attached to fuel
trucks and loaded with one-hundred- and three-hundred-pound
bombs. The tense and jittery bomber crews gulped down lunch
in the mess hall, and some forty senior officers gathered for a
briefing on the bombing mission to Formosa, slated for the afternoon. At this most vulnerable of moments the delayed Japanese attack on Clark Field and nearby Iba Field finally struck at
12:35 P.M. It was a repeat of Pearl Harbor. The first wave of fifty-
four bombers crossed the field at 18,000 feet and dropped their

bomb loads. The bombers were followed by Japanese fighters that strafed the field at ground-top level. In a matter of minutes, twelve B-17s were destroyed, along with thirty-four P-40 fighters and thirty other aircraft. It is also estimated that 77 airmen and ground crewmen were killed and another 148 wounded. MacArthur had lost over half of his air force.[10]

Two days later, on December 10, sixty Japanese bombers and fifty fighters attacked Cavite Naval Base, eight miles southwest of Manila, as well as Clark, Nichols, and Iba airfields. The Cavite Naval Base—the major port and equipping station for the American Asiatic Fleet—was gutted and left in flames. Further naval operations by the U.S. Navy in the Philippines were now impossible. More precious aircraft had also been destroyed, and by December 12 only a few B-17s were left on the southern island of Mindanao, and thirty-five outclassed fighters were dispersed throughout the islands. Admiral Hart soon directed the primary elements of the Asiatic Fleet to safer ports in Asia. MacArthur was now left with an army without air support and a naval fleet consisting mostly of PT boats.

On December 10, two small Japanese infantry forces from Formosa, each consisting of about two thousand men, made the first amphibious landings on the northern coast of Luzon near the cities of Aparri and Vigan. The first Japanese soldiers had set foot on Philippine soil. Thousands more would soon follow. To combat these invaders, MacArthur had a combined American and Filipino army of between twenty-five thousand and thirty thousand trained and reliable regular infantry troops—troops who could be expected to perform well in battle. To augment these professional forces, MacArthur could also turn to one hundred thousand Filipino reservists, but they were poorly trained, inadequately equipped, and not ready for combat. MacArthur's troops were concentrated primarily on the island of Luzon, divided into the North Luzon Force commanded by General Jonathan Wainwright and the South Luzon Force commanded by General George Parker. Much smaller infantry units were assigned to the Visayan-Mindanao Force commanded by General William F. Sharp, and scattered ineffectively throughout numerous islands of the archipelago.[11]

Within three days after Pearl Harbor, disaster had struck the Philippines, and MacArthur was left reeling. Without an air force or a navy—and with inadequate infantry and supplies—MacArthur had little hope of reinforcement and no prospect for victory.

December 8–22, 1941,
Masbate Island

As Louise Spencer awoke on Monday morning on the secluded island of Masbate, she could smell coffee brewing and hear her house servant gathering up clothes for washing. The lure of sleep swept her back toward slumber, but the lure of hot coffee won out. Slowly swinging her long girlish legs over the bedside, she felt the coolness of the waxed mahogany floor and fumbled for her slippers. Throwing on a robe, she slowly moved through the den, or *sala*, squinting in the bright sunlight filtering through the kapok trees and refracting through the windows. Absently, she reached out and turned on their radio—their only connection with the larger world—and heard the strains of big-band music ebbing toward conclusion.

Nearing the kitchen door she could smell Spence's cigarette smoke and suddenly yearned for one herself. In that fleeting moment of craving cigarettes and coffee, her world changed forever, when the distant voice of a Filipino radio announcer broke into the comfort of the morning excitedly announcing that the Japanese had bombed Pearl Harbor and savaged the American fleet.

As she whirled to face the radio, static broke in and the distant voice was lost. Unable to believe what she thought she had heard, she rushed into the kitchen to find Spence polishing off breakfast and luxuriating in the morning stillness. When she blurted out what she'd just heard, Spence looked at her as if she had awoken from a nightmare. He calmly assured her that what she thought she'd heard could not possibly be true. She must have heard a sentence out of context. Certainly the Japanese had not sailed all the way to Hawaii and caught the American navy with her britches down. That was impossible.

Reassured by Spence, Louise poured her coffee while Spence sauntered out the door to face another day's work at the mine.[12] Within a few short minutes he burst back through the front door and he was not laughing. Other miners had confirmed hearing the same news broadcast. The rumors were real. Japan had attacked the United States. And with this news, the Spencers' quiet and simple world fell apart. They were cut off from home, from safety, and soon, from basic supplies that were usually shipped from Manila to their small island.[13]

Four days later, on Thursday, December 11 the Spencers and other Americans waited anxiously at the Masbate docks for the arrival of their supply boat from Manila. The day before the Japanese had bombed Manila harbor and American naval installations heavily. Interisland shipping was now in disarray. The Americans on Masbate were totally dependent on this weekly shipment for canned and processed foods, mail, household supplies, and payroll money.

As night fell and no boat arrived, a grim reality set in. They now knew they were on their own. Soon, pantries would be bare of canned goods, and niceties such as toilet paper and toothpaste would be scarce. Contact with family and friends in the United States was severed, available cash depleted, and the payroll for Filipino miners could not be met. Some Americans took refuge in a false hope that the war would be short and they could simply ride it out. Others faced reality and scrambled to make long-term survival plans.

Most alarming, though, was the fact that the Japanese army was making new invasion landings almost daily. Radio broadcasts from Manila confirmed that on December 12, the Japanese landed twenty-five hundred troops from the Sixteenth Infantry Regiment near the city of Legaspi in southern Luzon, only fifty miles across a narrow ocean channel from Masbate. Though these troops were headed north to occupy Manila, it was clear to Americans on Masbate that soon there would be troop landings there.

By December 13, most of the U.S. Army and Navy planes in the Philippines had been destroyed. If a plane was seen in the sky, it could now be assumed to be Japanese. Any remaining heavy bombers on Luzon were withdrawn to the Del Monte airfield on Mindanao. On December 15, the surviving B-17s at Del Monte were ordered to fly to Darwin, Australia. With their flight came one of the first intimations that the Philippines were being written off and abandoned by the military strategists in Washington.

The high point of the crisis came on December 22, when forty thousand troops from Lieutenant General Masahara Homma's Fourteenth Army arrived off the western coast of Luzon from Formosa and the nearby Pescadores Islands, south of Formosa, and landed at Lingayen Gulf. MacArthur's Northern Luzon Force, under the command of Major General Jonathan Wainright, attempted to oppose the invasion at the beach. However, the outnumbered American and Filipino troops were routed quickly, and by nightfall, Japanese infantry columns led by tanks were heading south toward Manila. By Christmas, Homma had enough troops on Luzon to eventually defeat American and Filipino ground forces. With complete control of the air and with full access to supplies and reinforcement, the Japanese knew the American lion was lodged in the trap. All they needed now was to let the cat starve to death.

Claude Fertig, still on Masbate, was surely worried about his brother, Wendell. As a reserve army officer, Wendell had opted to go on active duty some months before. Now he was part of MacArthur's defense force being mauled on Luzon. As the first days of the war flew by, Claude did not know if Wendell was dead or alive. The isolated Americans on Masbate were confined in solitude.

December 8–29, 1941,
Capiz City, Panay Island

As the news reached Capiz of the Japanese attack on Pearl Harbor and the bombing of American bases on Luzon, Frederick and Ruth Meyer were stunned and shaken. They turned for support to their new neighbors in the mission compound, Erle and Louise Rounds.

The Roundses were among the youngest of the thirty or more American Baptist missionaries on Panay. Erle and Louise arrived in the Philippines in 1930, while still in their twenties, and they were both from Wisconsin. Erle was tall, lean, and athletic, with a high forehead, deep-set eyes, and a strong, masculine jaw. He struck many as a "man's man."[14] He was neither a doctor nor a professor as were most of his missionary peers on Panay; he was a preacher and an evangelist. For the previous twelve years he had wandered far into the mountainous interior of Panay, hiking trails and camping out for days, preaching in the most remote places. He had started many small barrio churches. Erle was a strong and rugged individual with a compassionate heart. Everyone liked him.[15]

Louise Rounds was perhaps the most beautiful of the missionary women. At age thirty-eight, she was a tall, shapely blonde with high cheekbones and a pretty, engaging smile. As a child, she had been mentored by an elderly aunt, Emma Louise Cummings, for whom she was named. Mrs. Cummings had been a missionary to Japan in the nineteenth century, and Louise had always wanted to follow her example. Louise now embraced her missionary life in the Philippines, often living in far more remote areas than other missionary women. Each year she homeschooled her two sons, Donal and Erle Douglas, teaching them their Calvert correspondence lessons and doting on them. Once Donal reached his teenage years and Erle Douglas entered elementary school, the Roundses moved from the isolated interior of Panay to settle in the Emmanuel Hospital compound in Capiz, where a school was available. The Meyers and Roundses were an ideal pair of next-door neighbors.[16]

Erle, Louise, Donal and Erle Douglas Rounds, about 1940. *Courtesy American Baptist Historical Society, Atlanta*

In the dawn light of December 8, these two American families huddled together to share what war news they had heard. Their fears focused on the fates of their two fourteen-year-old sons, Richard Meyer and Donal Rounds, both in their first year of boarding school in Manila and separated from their parents by hundreds of miles of ocean. Now inter-island transportation by boat would be limited and extremely dangerous.

Dazed with shock and anxiety, the Meyers and Roundses calmed their nerves by immersing themselves in their work, and in frantic preparation for war. Dr. Meyer and his medical staff at Emmanuel Hospital worked alongside U.S. military forces stationed on Panay, the USAFFE (United States Armed Forces, Far East). On December 10, labor parties assembled to dig air-raid shelters around the hospital and throughout the mission compound. The Home School building was transformed into an emergency medical center. Young Filipino men who joined the military ranks of the USAFFE were given physicals by Dr. Meyer and his staff at the compound.

Louise Rounds described in her diary the confusion in Capiz during the first hours of war.

> Orders from Manila were to close all schools. The road out of Capiz passes our house. On it all day has been a steady stream of cars and trucks taking people away [to the safety of the interior]. Davao, Baguio, Tarlac and Camp Clark have been bombed. . . . Of course we are worried about Donal. . . . [President] Quezon has advised all Manila residents who live in the provinces to get there but as far as we know there are no definite arrangements for evacuation. The ocean certainly wouldn't be a very safe place. The Japanese [civilians] in the town [of Capiz] have all been interned at the constabulary. There was quite a crowd gathered around to see them taken away. Even two Germans were brought in from one of the big haciendas but were later released. Someplace on Luzon the Japanese dropped leaflets saying they have come to liberate the Filipinos! Such rot! We are in total blackout tonight which means that all street lights are out and the light by which I am writing just about reveals this tablet and not much more.[17]

The next day, the homes of the Roundses and Meyers were converted into emergency evacuation stations in the event that the hospital was bombed. As the missionaries scrambled to stock provisions, they realized that they had waited too long. Louise Rounds writes:

The Edge of Terror

67

The Chinese food stores have been busy. Even yesterday they were sold out of milk and today word went around there was no more gasoline. That is a false rumor, I hope. We have our car tank filled up and that is all. We will try to keep it so in case we need to leave in a hurry. No word yet from Donal. We sent a wire to him this morning. We have the utmost confidence that they are as well cared for as possible.[18]

On December 16 the Meyers and Roundses received a much-delayed telegram sent on December 9 from a missionary in Manila, Reverend W. H. Fonger, informing them that Richard and Donal would be sent to Panay on the first available boat transport. The very next day, December 17, tragedy struck. Louise writes:

We were sitting listening to the radio at 5 o'clock [a.m.] and heard the news that the [passenger ship] *Corregidor* had left Manila for the Visayan Islands with officers and civilians. It struck a mine and sank in 10 minutes. All we could think of was the telegram from Mr. Fonger saying they would send the boys on the next available transportation. No civilian can send a wire now so Doc [Meyer] rushed to the Post Office and got Governor Hernandez to sign one to Mr. Fonger. Erle left on the morning train for Iloilo. The waiting for the answer is long and cruel. Jane [Adams], Ruth [Meyer] and I (with Doug on my lap) prayed and were comforted. Jane will stay with me all night. After Doug was in bed we talked about anything that would keep our mind off the boys. . . . Such a night! Why is it that in the dark of the night a mind which during the day is well-behaved can go completely hay-wire? Ruth kept seeing two boys' heads bobbing up and down in the water. I saw sharks.[19]

The next morning, around 9:30, Ruth Meyer ran across her yard toward the Roundses house. Louise remembered that "Ruth was crying and I got weak all over." Rushing into the house, Ruth blurted out between sobs that the boys were safe. Word had arrived that Richard and Donal were not on the *Corregidor.* Louise later scribbled in her diary, "I came as near to fainting as I ever have in my life. . . . My body and my soul breathed again."[20]

On December 18, Iloilo was bombed for the first time, and on the 19th the Roundses evacuated from Capiz to Bagong Barrio, where Erle had been working on an experimental agricultural education center for several years. On December 20, the air-raid shelters at Emmanuel Hospital in Capiz were used for the first time as a flight of Japanese planes approached. It proved to be a reconnaissance mission, but a vivid warning of things to come.[21]

As Christmas arrived, the Meyers spent an anxious Christmas Eve without their three sons—Buddy, Milton, and Richard— at home. It was comforting to know that the older boys would be with family in the United States, but they still did not know Richard's whereabouts. The thought of a fourteen-year-old alone and frightened in Manila at Christmas tore at their hearts. Two days before Christmas General MacArthur had given orders for USAFFE troops to evacuate Manila, and to withdraw to the peninsula of Bataan to make a final defensive stand. Now Manila was left undefended as Japanese forces approached from both the north and south. The Meyers knew that Richard was trapped in a combat zone and might not come home for the duration of the war.

Amid the gloom of this Christmas, Frederick and Ruth invited four American officers to have dinner with them. If they could not have their own children home for Christmas dinner, they could be parents for lonely soldiers. It was a Christmas when everyone was severed from family and friends, and people sought comfort in the presence of colleagues, and even strangers.

On the day after Christmas, orders were received that would alter forever the Meyers' twenty-six years of work at Emmanuel Hospital. Major Dwight M. Deter, USAFFE medical officer, knowing that Emmanuel Hospital was vulnerable to attack, issued a directive for the hospital to be abandoned and all medical staff to evacuate to the interior of the province to the town of Dumalag.[22]

Chapter Six

January–February 1942,
Masbate and Panay Islands

The week following Christmas at Emmanuel Hospital was filled with the frantic packing and crating of medical supplies to be sent to the new temporary army hospital in rural Dumalag. This decision caused great unrest and anger among the citizens of Capiz. They felt abandoned in the face of imminent invasion by the Japanese.

On December 31, Erle and Louise Rounds returned to Capiz to pick up supplies at their house and felt the tension. Louise remarked in her diary, "[Capiz] is quite deserted—especially with the hospital gone. Such a furor as that move caused! The governor had a terrific quarrel with Doc Meyer and the people of the town felt the mission was deserting them."[1]

In order to appease Governor Hernandez and the residents of Capiz, a temporary emergency medical station was kept operative at Emmanuel Hospital under the direction of the head nurse, Jennie Adams. Jennie was forty-five years old, a veteran missionary and professionally competent. Never married, she had spent nineteen years at Emmanuel Hospital and was the heart of the nursing program. She was short, thin, with heavy jet-black hair and alluring large brown eyes framed by glasses. The nurses idolized Jennie, and she could handle any situation that came her way.[2]

A train was commandeered by the military to take most of the nurses and one hundred Filipino bed patients to San Jose, the closest rail station to Dumalag. On December 27 to 28, the patients were transferred inland to Dumalag during a heavy rainstorm. Drenched and exhausted, they finally bedded down in a makeshift infirmary inside a damp, cinder-block elementary school.

On January 2, 1942, the Japanese army entered Manila, which had been declared an "open city" by MacArthur. With American and Filipino troops barricaded in the jungle fortress of Bataan, forty miles northwest of Manila, the Japanese marched through the streets of Manila without opposition, watched intently by a tense and frightened populace, including Richard Meyer and Donal Rounds.

On the same day that Manila capitulated, Japanese planes flew over Dumalag on a reconnaissance mission, probably sighting the building of the new hospital. The Meyers felt exposed and vulnerable even in the interior of Panay. The island was too small to hide from Japanese observation.[3]

As the new year began, the military assumed full command of all medical operations on Panay. A warehouse was built in Dumalag to store the remaining milk, flour, rice, canned goods, and medical supplies. A simple but symbolic directive was given that all nurses and doctors were to wear khaki uniforms. As Dr. Meyer received his uniform, he drew one step closer to being publicly seen as an officer in the United States Army. Whether he ever wore the uniform is unknown.

At the same time that the Meyers and Emmanuel Hospital moved to Dumalag, the Baptist hospital in Iloilo—Iloilo Mission

Hospital—on the southern Panay coast also withdrew into the interior of Panay, and relocated at Calinog, an hour's drive south of Dumalag. Dr. Henry Waters and Dr. Dorothy Chambers, American Baptist missionaries, were the physicians of this hospital. Both hospitals were now away from the seacoast and closely associated with the USAFFE. Each medical staff would make their own independent decisions concerning the operations of their hospital, the extent of their cooperation with the USAFFE, and how they would relate to the Japanese should Panay be invaded and conquered.

On the island of Masbate, Louise Spencer sat alone at her kitchen table, monitoring the radio as the sun rose higher in the sky on the last day of 1941. She nervously tapped her fingers to the beat of distant music that was interrupted by static and interludes of silence. What she yearned to hear was news—any tiny bit of encouraging news that she could cling to, any news that would help her remain hopeful. But there was nothing.

Refusing to succumb to fear, she grabbed her pen and reached for her calendar. If she could plan and organize even the next week, the world would seem a safer place. But then she remembered that the 1942 calendars had not yet been shipped from Manila, and now would never arrive. Grimacing with anger and raw determination, she snatched up a yellow pad, ruler, and pencil and began to construct her own calendar.

Louise designed a yellow page for each month, divided into rows and columns, and strained to remember which months had thirty days and which had thirty-one. She scribbled in holidays, birthdays, and anniversaries. Several hours later, when Spence returned home from the mine, she had completed her project, and she showed him her creation. Smiling at her beaming face, Spence flipped through the homespun calendar and quipped, "That's fine. But you're sort of pessimistic, making it for the whole year. The war will be over long before that."[4]

Spence was not alone in this assumption. Many Americans in the Philippines believed that help was coming just over the horizon.

Despite Spence's brave prediction, things did not look good. New Year's Day brought the feel of ominous calm that precedes the worst of storms. It broke sooner than expected. On January 2, the Spencers huddled together by their radio as the noon broadcast from Manila crackled across the miles. A Filipino voice breaking with emotion announced that Manila had fallen to the Japanese. His weeping could be heard as the Philippine National Anthem played defiantly across the airwaves. Slowly Spence and Louise stood at respectful attention and determined that they would never surrender, never give in. They were still standing at attention with fists clenched when the radio went deathly silent.[5]

On January 3, a small Japanese military unit landed on Masbate. Not large enough to forge inland, this Japanese presence only warned that a beachhead was established and that more troops would arrive in the near future. The Spencers and many other miners immediately evacuated farther inland. A week later, when they realized that the Japanese intended to remain along the shoreline, the Spencers returned to their home, only to find that it had been ransacked and most of their possessions stolen by looters. In the midst of anger and grief, their material losses freed them to think of moving to a safer place. Now they were not tied to clothes, wedding gifts, and furniture.

Soon after, Claude and Laverne Fertig visited the Spencers. Claude, an officer in the U.S. Army Reserve, announced that he had been notified by the USAFFE to report for active duty with the sixty-first Philippine Army Division on Panay. In the immediate future Major Fertig would inspect the mines on Masbate and decide what materials, such as dynamite and earth-moving equipment, might be transported to Panay to help build airfields and defensive positions. Just the thought of doing something to thwart the Japanese brought the Fertigs and Spencers encouragement.[6]

Yet, what was increasingly clear to all Americans on Masbate was that someday soon they would be forced to decide

Claude Fertig.   *Kathy Fertig Family*

between surrendering to the Japanese or seeking to evade them under threat of death if captured. There was dire risk involved with either option. Most American civilians would ultimately decide to gamble on being prisoners of war. But one night, as the Spencers discussed their options, Spence could not erase from his mind the horrors of the rape, pillage, and atrocities committed when Japanese troops captured Nanking, the ancient capital of China. Balling up his fists, he angrily exclaimed, "Louise, I'll never see you put in a concentration camp! I'll never give the Japs a chance to get close enough to you so you would be at their mercy."[7] In that moment their decision to evade the invaders was firmly made.

The Fertigs concurred with the Spencers' decision, and both couples worked out plans to escape from the small, confined island of Masbate and sail to the larger one of Panay, where they would be closer to an American military presence. At that time the American and Filipino forces on Panay were commanded by Brigadier General Bradford Chynoweth and had a total troop strength in excess of eight thousand officers and men, primarily Filipinos.[8]

Escaping separately, the Fertigs and Spencers arranged for local fishermen to ferry them under cover of darkness, in twenty-foot outrigger *bancas,* or sailboats, across sixty miles of open sea to the northern coast of Panay. On February 3, the Fertigs

left Masbate, followed by the Spencers on February 7. It was a
narrow escape. On February 8, all remaining Americans at Spencer's mine were arrested by the Japanese and taken into custody.[9] Most of the Americans on Masbate would eventually be
transferred to prisoner-of war-camps in Manila.

As the Spencers and Fertigs reached Panay, they were not aware
that the first American attempt to counterattack the Japanese
and slowly advance across the Pacific back toward the Philippines was taking place. On February 1, U.S. Navy and Marine
planes from aircraft carriers, under the command of Admiral
William "Bull" Halsey, attacked Japanese air and naval installations in the Marshall and Gilbert islands, inflicting serious damage. This was the first step in a long journey that would last three
and a half years.

As February continued, Dr. Meyer helped design and construct the temporary two hundred-bed hospital building in
Dumalag. Jennie Adams and the nurses who had remained at
Emmanuel Hospital in Capiz were finally evacuated on January 22
and joined the Meyers. They now helped Dr. Meyer serve the
medical needs of an increasing military-civilian complex.

On the northern Panay coast, the Spencers and Fertigs ren-
dezvoused in Capiz and temporarily checked into the Riverside
Inn, close to the deserted Emmanuel Hospital. Within a few days
Louise and Laverne moved farther inland in case the Japanese
invaded the northern coast. The women found comfortable quarters in a rented bungalow at a sugar *central*, or plantation, near
Sara-Ajuy, twenty-five miles southeast of Capiz.

Both Claude and Spence immediately went to work on military projects. As an army engineer, Claude was assigned to the
construction of an airstrip on the outskirts of Sara, and he remained close to Laverne and Louise. As a civilian, Spence was
involved in airfield construction, at Pilar, a coastal town fifteen
miles north of Sara. For the next two months their lives would

settle into an uneasy lull as Japanese troops focused their attack against American and Filipino troops isolated on Bataan and Corregidor on the northern island of Luzon.[10]

January–February 1942, Luzon Island

On the island of Luzon, 250 miles north of Panay, the American military situation had grown desperate. General Douglas Mac-Arthur was no stranger to combat or to the Philippine islands. But even his extensive experience could not reverse a rapidly deteriorating state of affairs.

MacArthur had spent a major part of his life in the Philippines. He was the son of Major General Arthur MacArthur, a hero in the American Civil War. Arthur MacArthur had later served as the U.S. military governor of the Philippines in 1900 and 1901 while Douglas was a cadet at West Point. Upon graduating from the military academy, Douglas MacArthur served from 1903 to 1906 with the military survey department in the Philippines, gaining detailed knowledge of the geography of the islands, particularly Luzon.

Following his distinguished combat service in Europe during World War I, Douglas MacArthur returned to the Philippines as commander of the Manila District, and was promoted to major general. From 1928 to 1930 MacArthur served as commander of the entire Philippine Department, and was promoted to general in 1930. Though he left the Philippines from 1930 to 1935 to serve as U.S. Army Chief of Staff, he returned again to the islands in 1935 as director of national defense. In 1937 he retired from the U.S. Army after an illustrious career, and accepted a private contract to serve independently as a field marshal in the Philippine army.

As the threat of war with Japan grew, MacArthur was recalled to duty as a general in the U.S. Army on July 26, 1941, and appointed commander of the United States Armed Forces, Far East (USAFFE), headquartered in Manila. No American general had more experience in the Philippines than MacArthur, and few could match his combat record and career excellence.[11]

When the United States declared war on Japan, military conditions were dangerously askew in the Philippines due to decisions that MacArthur had recently made. As soon as the United States obtained the Philippines at the conclusion of the Spanish-American War, military contingency plans were developed to protect the islands in case of attack. A plan emerged, and was often revised over the ensuing years, titled War Plan Orange. In essence the plan stated that if the Philippines was invaded by an overwhelming enemy force, American and Filipino troops would withdraw into the mountainous jungle of the Bataan peninsula facing Manila Bay. Once there they would establish successive defensive lines, prohibiting entrance into Bataan by the enemy. They would then secure the fortified island of Corregidor guarding Manila Bay, and defend Manila and its harbor until naval reinforcements arrived from the United States or Pearl Harbor.

War Plan Orange was a strategy that many felt was unrealistic. It was designed for an American-Filipino force to endure on Bataan for a maximum of six months without reinforcement. However, most navy planners anticipated that in a total war against Japan, it would take at least two years before the navy could slowly fight its way across the vast Pacific, conquering key Japanese strongholds as it progressed, and finally bring reinforcements to the Philippines. As time would show, even this pessimistic estimate was nearly a year too short.[12]

MacArthur had always been critical of War Plan Orange. When he became field marshal in the Philippine army in the late 1930s, he grew even more so. He particularly did not like the plan's defensive nature. MacArthur preferred to take the offensive and defeat a military foe on the invasion beaches rather than hunker down behind a siege wall, waiting for the navy to rescue the army. He had presented his case for increased financial support and supply from the United States. Once he had enough resources, MacArthur planned to build an army—composed of both Filipino and American forces—that could successfully defend the Philippines. This was a strategy that he believed would become particularly important after the islands were granted independence, as promised, in 1946. Slowly MacArthur convinced United States military leadership to accept his strategy—to unofficially shelve the latest version of War Plan Orange (Orange Number 3, or WPO-3)—and to send more military personnel, weapons, supplies, and air support to the Philippines.[13]

MacArthur's position was based on two assumptions that were soon obliterated: First, Japan would not attack the United States prior to mid-1942 or 1943, and second, that the U.S. Navy based in Pearl Harbor would be able to resupply his army in the Philippines. With this strategy in mind, MacArthur had begun to enlarge his Filipino and American troop strength, and to construct supply bases not only on Bataan, but throughout Luzon.[14]

All of this changed on December 8, 1941, when Japan attacked the Philippines before MacArthur was fully prepared and organized. He had not been able to build up adequate supply and troop strength. His critical air support was effectively wiped out during the first hours of combat, and the great American fleet in Pearl Harbor, which might have supplied him additional forces, was crippled. MacArthur was caught "spraggle-legged" between two strategic plans—War Plan Orange Number 3 and "MacArthur's Dream"—inadequately prepared to use either one.[15]

When General Homma's primary infantry force invaded Luzon on December 22, 1941, through Lingayen Gulf in northwestern Luzon, and also through Legaspi and Lamon Bay in southern Luzon, MacArthur's Filipino and American troops were not able to stop them on the beaches or slow their progress inland.

Soon MacArthur was forced to order a well-orchestrated retreat of all American and Filipino forces on Luzon—from north and south—into the Bataan peninsula. MacArthur had no option but to revert to War Plan Orange Number 3.[16]

However, there was one huge problem. Instead of ammunition, medicine, and food supplies being well stocked in "fortress Bataan," these supplies had been scattered to strategic points all over Luzon. There was no time to transfer these irreplaceable supplies back to Bataan. Instead, supply warehouses and ammunition dumps were abandoned or burned as American and Filipino units retreated. It is estimated that six million gallons of gasoline and a half million artillery shells were left behind or burned. Fifty million bushels of rice were abandoned at a supply depot in Cabanatuan, enough to feed military personnel and civilians on Bataan for nearly four years. Instead, troops there faced a scarcity of food that required them to go on half rations as soon as they entered the Bataan lines.[17] Americans and Filipinos could put up a stubborn and heroic defense, but they could not do so for long on empty stomachs.

By January 6, 1942, MacArthur had completed his retreat to Bataan, only twenty-nine days after the first Japanese bombs fell on Luzon. By January 9, the last straggling American troops had either filtered into Bataan or melted away into the Luzon mountains to become guerrillas. Ensconced within his defensive perimeter, MacArthur had fifteen thousand American and sixty-five thousand Filipino troops—along with twenty-six thousand frightened civilians—to fight against Japan. General Homma was now free to commence a concentrated infantry attack on Bataan with total freedom in the skies and unrestricted naval reinforcements.

Bataan is a compact peninsula twenty-five miles long and twenty miles wide, and its rugged topography makes this natural bastion a defender's dream. The peninsula is formed by the steep southern ridge of the Zambales Mountains descending into Manila Bay. Covered in thick steamy jungles, Bataan had only two roads that could be used for motor transport. The offensive use of armor was restricted, aircraft had limited visibility, and the Americans could establish concentric defensive lines that would be difficult to breach.[18]

For the next six weeks MacArthur's troops fought tenaciously and successfully in these sweltering environs, wiping out large bodies of Japanese assault troops and blunting several Japanese attempts at amphibious landings. By February 8, Homma's forces had bled so badly—and tropical diseases were so virulent—that he ordered a general withdrawal to the outer lines of Bataan to reorganize, rest, and await troop reinforcements. In a matter of six weeks Homma lost seven thousand troops in combat and another ten thousand to malaria, beriberi, scurvy, dengue fever, and dysentery. He was reduced to three infantry battalions within the Bataan peninsula.[19] Despite Japan's avowed intentions to conquer Luzon in fifty days, and the whole archipelago in seven weeks, Homma had failed to secure victory. Risking disgrace, he momentarily disengaged his Bataan offensive, rested the bulk of his depleted troops, and waited on reinforcements.[20]

Yet the same diseases also attacked Americans and Filipinos, and their lack of food and medical supplies was taking a horrendous toll. Soon they would be reduced to one-third rations— less than 1,000 calories a day—virtually a starvation diet. While the Japanese waited for fresh troops and supplies, the Americans could only hope that admirals and generals in Washington were making an all-out effort to resupply them. However, it became increasingly clear that that hope was futile. Because of the destruction at Pearl Harbor, naval reinforcement was all but impossible. One estimate by the War Department projected that it would require no less than seven battleships, five carriers, fifty destroyers, sixty submarines, and fifteen hundred aircraft to bring prompt and adequate aid to MacArthur, an impossible feat.[21] And even if it had been feasible, the top priority of the Joint Chiefs of Staff was the war in Europe. For the rest of 1942, the majority of American supplies would be crossing the Atlantic, not the Pacific.[22]

Over the next eight weeks MacArthur's troops were not pressed by Japanese infantry assaults. However, they were constantly pounded by artillery and aerial bombardment. More than anything they suffered from depression, disease, and malnutrition. They were exhausted.

One of the officers trapped in the hell of Bataan was Wendell Fertig. Having gone on active duty with the USAFFE after sending his family back to the United States on the last passenger ship to leave Manila, Fertig had been in the thick of battle on Luzon. Now totally cut off from his brother, Claude, on Panay, Wendell was serving as the director of construction engineering on Bataan.[23] However, he knew that the end of American resistance on Bataan could not be far away. Already he was contemplating how he might escape. Combat with the Japanese had taught him one sure thing—he would rather risk death than surrender.[24]

Chapter Seven

March–April 1942,
Bataan, Luzon

While Japanese troops temporarily disengaged their infantry assault and awaited reinforcements, top-secret plans were transmitted directly by radio from President Roosevelt to General MacArthur on February 22, ordering the general and his family to attempt evacuation to Australia. Roosevelt could not afford the international embarrassment and political repercussions of a famous American general being captured by Japan. And the general's skill and experience were needed to defend Australia and to forge a counteroffensive against the Japanese in the Pacific. MacArthur was directed to proceed from his headquarters on the island fortress of Corregidor to Australia, where he would become supreme commander of the South West Pacific Area (SWPA). Admiral Chester Nimitz was selected to be commander-in-chief, Pacific Ocean Area (CINCPOA), and to serve as MacArthur's naval counterpart.[1]

MacArthur was stunned when the coded presidential order came over the radio at 11:23 A.M., February 23, Manila time.

On the one hand, he was relieved that his son and wife would be spared capture. But he recoiled at the thought of leaving his troops, of inevitably being seen as a deserter. Yet, if he disobeyed Roosevelt, he could be court-martialed. Initially he considered resigning his commission. He talked dramatically of turning in his general's stars and crossing from his bunker in the Malinta Tunnel on Corregidor to Bataan to fight as a "simple volunteer." But finally he buckled under, feeling that he had no option but to obey a direct order. He began to prepare for departure.[2]

Prior to leaving, MacArthur divided the defense of the Philippines into three sectors: the Luzon Force, under Major General Jonathan Wainwright; the Mindanao Force, under Brigadier General William Sharp; and the Visayan Force, under Brigadier General Bradford Chynoweth (including Panay). MacArthur intended to retain direct command of overall operations in the Philippines from his distant new headquarters in Australia. However, the army chief of staff, General George C. Marshall, wisely overruled MacArthur and made Wainwright commander of all forces in the Philippine islands. Major General Edward King replaced Wainwright as commander of the Luzon Force.[3]

Jonathan Wainwright and Douglas MacArthur were a fascinating study of similarities and contrasts. Both men were the sons of successful and decorated U.S. Army officers. MacArthur's father, General Arthur MacArthur, received the Medal of Honor at Missionary Ridge during the American Civil War. Wainwright's father, Robert Powell Page Wainwright, fought with the First Cavalry in the American Indian wars following the Civil War. Later, in the Spanish-American War, Robert Wainwright was a captain commanding a cavalry squadron in Cuba at the Battle of Las Guasimas and at San Juan Hill. Returning from Cuba, Robert Wainwright, now a lieutenant colonel, was transferred to the Philippines during the insurrection, and he served there as assistant to the adjutant general under the command of General Arthur MacArthur. In 1902 Robert Wainwright died in the Philippines, not from combat, but from tropical disease. Now, forty years later, the sons of these deceased officers found themselves together, and repeating history in the same exotic islands.[4]

Both MacArthur (1903) and Wainwright (1906) were graduates of West Point. Both men attained a cadet's highest honor when each was appointed first captain of cadets. As young officers, MacArthur and Wainwright were both baptized by combat in World War I, and each received the Distinguished Service Medal.

However, in personality and temperament, the men were vastly different. MacArthur had emerged from World War I as one of the youngest brigadier generals, and as a commander of a regiment. He quickly rose to the top of his profession—achieving celebrity status—and became superintendent of West Point at age thirty-nine, a major general at forty-five, and chief of staff before he was fifty. MacArthur was a man of privilege, refinement, competency, brilliance, courage, and unbridled ambition, and he possessed a world-class ego bordering on outright narcissism. On Bataan he had remained aloof from his troops, and did not engender their fondness or respect.

Wainwright, on the other hand, returned from World War I as a major, and continued his father's career path as a cavalry officer in the United States. Slowly making his way through the arduous peacetime promotion process, he was promoted to brigadier general in command of the U.S. First Cavlary Regiment when he was forty-seven years old. Wainwright was then transferred to the Philippines shortly before the outbreak of World War II.

"Skinny" Wainwright was known as a colorful, hard-fighting, hard-drinking general who endured privations and dangers in the front lines with his men. His troops loved him. Heavy drinking was as much a mark of cavalrymen as tattoos were for sailors. There were times when MacArthur wondered if Skinny had the sobriety, moderation, and judgment necessary for high command. But, as he surveyed his officer corps in the Philippines and assessed the needs of his demoralized troops, MacArthur knew that Wainwright was his best and obvious choice. The men loved him and would die for him.[5]

A day before evacuating from the Philippines and leaving Wainwright to seemingly certain doom. MacArthur—known for melodrama—met with Wainwright. He presented the general with a box of Philippine president Quezon's best cigars and two jars of scarce shaving cream, and then gave him final instructions: "Jonathan, I want you to understand my position very plainly. I'm leaving for Australia pursuant to repeated orders of the President. Things have reached such a point that I must comply with these orders or get out of the Army. I want you to make it known throughout all elements of your command that I'm leaving over my repeated protests."[6]

After asking Wainwright to uphold his reputation, MacArthur continued, "If I get through to Australia, you know I'll come back as soon as I can with as much as I can. In the meantime you've got to hold." He shook Wainwright's hand and then made a solemn promise that must have smacked of insult in the midst of such gravity: "Good-bye Jonathan. When I get back, if you're still on Bataan, I'll make you a Lieutenant General."[7]

Wainwright's least concern was another promotion. As a good soldier, he had only one ambition: to wage an effective war and preserve the lives of as many of his soldiers as possible. He would earn the moniker given to him by the Battling Bastards of Bataan—"The Last of the Fighting Generals."

Turning to MacArthur, Wainwright grimly responded, "I'll be on Bataan if I'm alive."[8]

On the night of March 11, MacArthur, his wife, Jean, his three-year-old son, Arthur MacArthur IV, and their Chinese amah, Au Cheu, slipped down to the loading docks on Corregidor. Joining twenty-one personally selected staff members whom

MacArthur would need in Australia, this small band of evacuees was secretly loaded aboard four surviving seventy-seven-foot-long PT boats commanded by thirty-year-old Lieutenant Commander John Bulkeley. Slowly these well-worn, mahogany-hulled torpedo boats threaded their way through the mined harbor protecting Corregidor, raced fifty miles out to sea, and then veered south toward Mindanao.[9]

The Japanese had expected such a move, and their navy was on alert. In recent days Tokyo Rose, the Japanese radio propagandist, had announced that if captured, MacArthur would be publicly hanged in Tokyo's Imperial Plaza.[10] MacArthur later gave a curt but tense account of his escape in his wartime reports.

> Departed from Corregidor at dark on the 12th making the trip with four U.S. Navy motor torpedo boats. Air reconnaissance revealed one hostile cruiser and one destroyer off the west coast of Mindoro but we slipped by them in the darkness. The following day was passed in the shelter of an uninhabited island but we risked discovery by air and started several hours before dark in order to approach Mindanao at dawn. Sighted an enemy destroyer at 15,000 yards but escaped unseen, making the scheduled run despite heavy seas and severe buffeting.[11]

Thirty-seven hours later, on March 14, MacArthur safely reached Mindanao, over eight hundred miles due south of Corregidor. Veteran sailors on Corregidor had given him one-in-five odds of making it. His luck held out. On March 17, MacArthur and his staff flew from Del Monte airfield in two crowded B-17 bombers and landed at Batchelor Field, forty miles south of Darwin, Australia. MacArthur's covert escape from Corregidor shattered any remaining hope among American and Filipino defenders that U.S. military leaders would rescue them.[12] Their despair gave birth to the popular wartime phrase of writer William L. White: "They Were Expendable."[13]

When MacArthur escaped, he left on Bataan an emaciated army in which four out of five troops suffered from malaria, three-quarters had dysentery, and more than a third had beri-beri.[14] On April 1, rations on Bataan were again reduced to one fourth of normal daily consumption, barely enough to keep a soldier alive.

Already MacArthur had acquired the sobriquet of Dugout Dug for staying concealed in his bomb-proof headquarters on Corregidor. He had crossed from the island to Bataan only once to visit his troops, on January 10. But now his exit seemed like a captain stealing a lifeboat and being the first to leave a sinking ship. Anger turned to bitterness among the abandoned men and women.[15]

On Good Friday, April 3—twenty-three days after MacArthur left Corregidor—the Japanese army resumed their all-out offensive against the Bataan line. General Homma's army was reinforced by 21,000 new troops, 150 artillery pieces, and 60 bombers.[16] It was indeed the day of crucifixion for American troops. Though the American and Filipino troops resisted valiantly, their lines were brutally overrun. Six days later, Major General King surrendered his 76,000 troops on Bataan to General Homma, leaving only General Wainwright and his remaining garrison on the tiny island of Corregidor to continue the fight on Luzon.

For most American and Filipino troops hunger and sickness had ravaged their bodies and crushed their spirits. There was no energy left to resist or escape. And an order was an order— *surrender!* But for a few Americans and Filipinos, a primal urge to fight or flee remained. Two young American officers, Russell Volckmann and Donald Blackburn, were assigned to the Eleventh Philippine Infantry Regiment. Late in the afternoon of April 9, 1942, the Eleventh Regiment, deep in the jungles of Bataan, received orders from headquarters to surrender. With night descending, the Eleventh Regiment raised white flags and lit torches to illuminate their emblems of surrender. Volckmann recalls,

> The flags could be clearly seen in the dark. [Yet], the Japs ignored the flags and rushed in firing madly. I nudged Don [Blackburn] and said, 'This is when!,' and we slumped down and rolled over a bank into a dry streambed. Once there we slowly crawled away from the command post and in a few seconds we were completely blanketed by the darkness and the thick undergrowth of the jungle. Quietly and steadily we crawled along the streambed. I knew we were heading north. . . . How long and how far we crawled that night I will never venture to guess.[17]

Volckmann and Blackburn continued to head north for days and weeks. Settling into the wild northern mountains of Luzon in the midst of headhunter tribes, they slowly put together a guerrilla resistance organization. By the closing months of the war, Volckmann commanded a guerrilla force made up of over twenty thousand Filipinos and escaped Americans. They would play an indispensable role in the liberation of the Philippines.

Such "no surrender" roles were played by many American soldiers. But for the vast majority of American and Filipino troops, there was no option but to obey orders and capitulate. The extent of the cruelty that followed their surrender could never have been expected.

Within hours of the surrender, surviving American and Filipino troops on Bataan were corralled and herded north along the infamous sixty-five-mile "death march" to hastily prepared prisoner-of-war camps in central Luzon. Japanese troops supervising this exodus had not been trained or prepared for the task. Nor had essential elements like food and medicine been supplied and distributed. The march was pandemonium.

Some Japanese soldiers demonstrated acts of kindness, such as letting the men stop to drink from streams and rest. But most Japanese troops—men who had been taught by the ancient Bushido military code to prefer suicide to surrender—treated the captive Filipinos and Americans brutally. Stanley Falk writes of this experience:

> Time after time prisoners who straggled or fell out of line would be shot, bayoneted, or beaten to death. . . . Some exhausted stragglers were even buried alive, often by other prisoners who were forced at bayonet point to carry out this grisly task. One dying Filipino, rolled into an open ditch for burial, was revived by the water standing at the bottom and tried to stand up. A Japanese soldier kicked him back into his grave and motioned for the horrified American who was burying him to hurry up.
>
> When rest periods were allowed the marching men, there were always a few prisoners who were slow in getting to their feet. Then the guards rushed in and hurried them along with kicks or blows with their rifle butts. To Captain George W. Kane, it seemed as if the Japanese got "some animal pleasure" out of beating the men.[18]

The worst abuse of prisoners was reserved for Filipinos. The 350 to 400 survivors of the Ninety-first Philippine Army Division were slaughtered en masse by the Japanese on April 11. Separated from their American officers and forced off the path of march into an open field, each soldier had his arms tied behind his back with telephone wire and his wrists linked to three other prisoners. The bound men were again lined up along the trail. At a given signal, Japanese officers unsheathed their swords and walked slowly down the long line of bound soldiers, beheading each Filipino soldier. From the opposite end of the line, Japanese enlisted men methodically advanced, plunging their bayonets

into the backs of the prisoners. The gruesome slaughter lasted
for two hours, until all appeared dead and the Japanese were
exhausted from their grisly work. Only a few hideously wounded
Filipinos, hidden under the bloody pile of bodies on top of them,
lived to tell of the massacre.[19]

Approximately 10,000 Americans and 62,000 Filipinos began
the forced Bataan death march. An estimated 2,300 Americans
and 8,000 Filipinos succumbed to exhaustion, hunger, or disease, or were executed before they reached their prison destination.[20] Another 2,000 Americans managed to avoid the death
march by escaping into the jungle or across the three-mile ocean
channel to Corregidor Island, most by boat, and a few by swim-
ming.[21] One of those to reach Corregidor was a defiant Wendell
Fertig.[22]

March–April 1942,
Panay Island

In the final weeks prior to the fall of Bataan, Dr. and Mrs. Meyer
continued their work assisting the army in building a medical
support structure and a new field hospital in Dumalag in anticipation of the invasion of Panay. Amid their hectic schedule, time
was found for the final commencement of the nursing school. Eighteen nurses graduated, the largest prewar class, and then they
returned to their homes and families. As these proud young Filipinas began the war years with competent medical skills, Dr.
Meyer could see that his life's work was proving worthwhile.

With increasing frequency, Japanese planes flew over Panay.
On March 22, the Meyers were in their temporary makeshift
quarters in the economics building of a school when Japanese
fighter planes dove out of a cloud bank, bombing and strafing
the nearby Dumarao airfield then under construction. Scrambling for cover, the Meyers huddled in their kitchen until the air

raid was over. Jumping to his feet, Dr. Meyer rushed to the partially constructed field hospital to receive four badly wounded soldiers. Dr. Meyer was soon facing an increasing number of war casualties.[23]

As the Meyers worked to complete the hospital, the Spencers and Fertigs settled in on Panay. Claude and Spence continued to work on the construction of various airfields scattered across the island in the hope that reinforcements would soon come from Australia. A rumor was circulating that the first American planes had landed in Cebu, and would soon be sent to reinforce the defense of Panay.[24]

While the men worked, Louise and Laverne remained at the sugar *central* in Sara. Secure in a bungalow decorated with beautiful Chinese furniture, their comfortable surroundings were a temporary escape from a dire reality. Both women gathered supplies in preparation for an expected evacuation farther into the rustic interior of Panay. A Russian friend, who as a child had escaped the ravages of the Russian Revolution suggested that if they bought nothing else, they must stock up on shoes and soap. However, money was scarce, shoes even scarcer, and canned food rose to the top of their list. Louise and Laverne would soon regret that they did not take her advice.[25]

To help the women secure groceries and cook, Claude Fertig sent money back to Masbate and requested that their former servant, Federico Condino, and his wife and daughter leave Masbate and join them on Panay. They did so, bringing with them Laverne's Airedale terrier, Debbie.[26] A sense of normalcy took shallow root in the final days of March.

Easter came on April 5, in 1942. On this special Sunday most of the American Baptist missionaries on Panay—twenty-four men and women—gathered in the afternoon at Barong Barrio, where the Roundses had started a small church and were living temporarily. They planned to enjoy one another's company, share an early "covered dish" supper at the Roundses' home, and then join in an outdoor worship service at sunset.

As they gathered for the meal, every conversation seemed focused on what they would do when—not if—the Japanese invaded Panay. Soon the dinner turned into an open discussion concerning whether they should make a decision together as to what they would do and how they should respond. It was clear to everyone that there were only two options: surrender and be placed in an internment camp, or attempt to evade and hide from the Japanese in the interior of the island. Within a short time it also became obvious that the twenty-four missionaries differed in their opinions. Ultimately it was decided that each family or individual would choose their own best option and have total freedom to do so. As Dr. Fred Chambers, president of the Central Philippine College in Iloilo, later wrote in his memoir, "It was an understanding group, for it was agreed at the beginning that whatever each decided to do, no one would stand in judgement."[27]

After they left the supper tables and turned their attention to the beauty of the late afternoon, Ruth Meyer led her mission family in singing hymns and then sang a solo. Fred Chambers gave a short devotional thought and led the group in prayer. As the sun dipped lower, the missionaries shared emotional good-byes and drove back to Dumalag and Calinog.[28]

As they traveled to their evacuation locations and temporary homes, it seemed that all of their lives were in absolute turmoil. Approaching Calinog and topping a scenic hill, Fred Chambers pulled his 1941 Chevrolet slowly over to the side of the road and coasted to a stop. The sun was exploding in its final flare of color and twinkling lantern lights could be seen in Calinog, in the valley below them. It seemed a natural time for Fred and Dorothy to talk, reflect, and make decisions.

As Dorothy gazed across the Panay countryside, she was still amazed that she was in the Philippines. It seemed like a dream from which she would soon awake. Fifteen years ago she had boarded a ship in California, in 1927, and sailed to India to spend the rest of her life. An attractive twenty-seven-year-old single woman, she had recently graduated second in her class from the University of Colorado School of Medicine with a specialization in obstetrics. Now she was embarking on the dream of her life, to be a medical missionary.

For the next nine years Dorothy was the only physician at a small, forty-five-bed hospital in Gauhauti, India. The hospital was in the poorest of conditions. Dorothy performed surgery by the dim light of kerosene lanterns, hauled buckets of water from a well to the hospital, delivered hundreds of babies, and even

Fred and Dorothy Chambers, Carol, Bob, and playmates.

Carol Chambers Park

taught herself to perform delicate cataract surgery. She was an impressive, brilliant, committed, and independent young lady.

At the same time, Dr. Fred Chambers was also a Baptist missionary in Jorhat, India. A theology professor and education specialist, he was in charge of the Christian schools in Jorhat. Shortly after his young wife, Irene, tragically died from complications during her first pregnancy, he met and began to court Dorothy Chambers. In 1936 they were married, and Dorothy moved to Jorhat to be the surgeon at Jorhat Hospital for women and children. The next year their first child, Carol Joy Chambers, was born, and in 1939 they returned to the United States on furlough.

During their furlough they were reassigned to the Philippines, where Fred was to serve as dean of the Department of Theology at Central Philippine College and Dorothy was to be a physician at Iloilo Mission Hospital. When they arrived in Iloilo, Fred discovered that he was also to serve as president of the college. Soon their second child, Robert Bruce, was born, and then the war suddenly descended upon them.

Now, as they reflected on their lives, it seemed that in the years since they had first sailed for India their experiences had been incredibly intense, fast-paced, dramatic, exhausting, exhilarating, and fulfilling. Yet as the sky before them turned totally dark, it seemed that their future was shrouded in impenetrable darkness as well. What should they now do with their two small children in the midst of violent chaos? Would it be best to retreat to the mountains with part of their mission family or to stay at the hospital in Calinog and take their chances? Remembering that Easter night sitting by Fred on the hillside, Dorothy later wrote, "We did a lot of talking and a lot of praying. We felt that we should stand by the hospital. I had a sense of assurance that we would come out O.K."

In the profound silence of that night they had made their decision. It was a decision that brought little comfort. But some peace had been found in making a resolution.[29]

Four days later on April 9, 1942, American forces on Bataan surrendered. Now the Japanese military was free to occupy the rest of the major islands in the Philippines. On April 10 a Japanese invasion force of twelve thousand troops came ashore on neigh-boring Cebu Island, engaging American and Filipino troops and quickly shattering Brigadier General Chynoweth's defense struc-ture there.[30] Knowing that time was running out for Panay, on April 13 the Meyers were somehow able to smuggle out a mes-sage to their parents in the United States, one of two letters re-ceived from them during World War II. Ruth wrote that they were currently safe "as are all the other missionaries and have enough food so far." Frederick added a scribbled note, "These have been the busiest months of my career; some day may release the news to you."[31]

Things grew even busier at dawn on Friday, April 17, when 4,160 Japanese troops transported from Luzon landed on Panay in three locations: Capiz, in the north; Oton, in the south; and San Jose, on the west coast. Having learned from MacArthur's failed attempts on Luzon to fight an offensive battle against the Japanese at the shoreline, Brigadier General Albert F. Christie's Panay force of nearly 7,000 American and Filipino troops suc-cessfully withdrew into the mountains to take stronger defen-sive positions and begin a campaign of guerrilla warfare.[32] After the invasion the Meyers could no longer return to Emmanuel Hospital in Capiz for supplies or possessions.

The next day, April 17, Dr. Meyer noticed smoke and flames billowing from the hospital under construction at Dumalag and from other support buildings and warehouses. Without his knowl-edge or input, the army had secretly ordered the razing of all fa-cilities and supplies that might be of help to the Japanese. In doing so, they burned the only remaining medical supplies and surgi-cal equipment available to Frederick. He was enraged. The same army that he had tried so hard to support had now tied his hands. He no longer had a hospital or medical supplies to work with. He felt helpless, and angry.[33]

But the Meyers' first priority was to make an immediate retreat from the path of the invading Japanese. Some of the

American Baptist missionaries on Panay—both in Capiz and
Iloilo—had made a contingency escape plan.[34] Near the center
of Panay is the small barrio of Katipunan, where a Baptist pastor, Reverend Delfin Dianala, resided. Dianala had agreed to
offer the missionaries refuge.

Reverend Dianala was a most unusual man. He had grown
up an orphan, with no siblings. As a young teenager he had wandered onto the Central Philippine College campus in Iloilo and
been befriended by some of the earliest American Baptist missionaries teaching at the college. They had recently started an
orphanage, and they gave young Delfin his first real home. While
living in the orphanage, he was educated by the missionaries.
Later, he attended their college and became one of the first graduates of its College of Theology. He then left Iloilo and went into
the countryside, an earnest and fervent evangelist. As part of his
ministry he organized the fledgling barrio of Katipunan, a name
that means "a place of gathering."

Dianala centered the life of the young barrio around the
founding of a new church, the Katipunan Evangelical Church.
Most of the indigenous people with whom he lived, and to whom
he ministered, were animists who had very little knowledge of
Christianity. Dianala personally brought most of them into the
Christian faith, and was seen as the father of the barrio.

Because of his background, Reverend Dianala was a close
friend of many of the missionaries, and welcomed them to come
and find safety at Katipunan. As they had adopted him years
before, now he adopted them and brought them to "the place of
gathering."[35]

Katipunan is a two-and-a-half mile hike from the nearest
highway, national Highway 2, and is nestled in the midst of rolling foothills at the base of the rugged Western Cordillera mountains.[36] The Cordillera mountains run north to south parallel to
the western coast of Panay. This steep range is densely forested

and sparsely populated, and it reaches an altitude of 6,722 feet at Mount Nangtud. From remote Katipunan, the safety of these isolated mountains could be reached quickly. Katipunan is also near the Panay River and its tributaries, an important source of water. The escape plan called for a retreat to rural Katipunan until the extent and nature of the Japanese invasion of Panay could be assessed.

Late in the afternoon of April 17, the Meyers, Jennie Adams, and the remaining nursing students hurriedly packed and crammed a total of ninety-seven people into Dr. Meyer's old Ford automobile and two large trucks marked with red crosses. As they sped south from Dumalag down Highway 2 toward Katipunan, eight miles away, a Japanese fighter plane spotted their convoy and peeled off to strafe them. At the last minute the fighter pulled up, perhaps honoring the red crosses. In the rush to escape, one truck slid into a ditch, and all the vehicles were quickly abandoned. As night came to the foothills, Dr. Meyer led his hospital entourage off the highway and onto the narrow footpath leading to Katipunan. They stumbled through the tropical darkness, following the beam of a single flashlight.[37]

Eight miles south of Katipunan is the town of Calinog, where the Iloilo Mission Hospital staff had relocated, including most of the professors from Central Philippine College. Following the Japanese landings on Panay, Louise Spencer and Laverne Fertig had also fled farther inland to Calinog to join American miners they had known in Masbate. Claude and Spence could not join them immediately because of their work with the army. In Calinog a fateful meeting took place between Louise, Laverne, and an older Baptist missionary couple, Francis and Gertrude Rose.[38]

Dr. and Mrs. Rose had served on Panay since 1912. For

thirty years they had taught at Central Philippine University in
Iloilo. Both Francis and Gertrude were seminary graduates and
had completed further graduate degrees at Columbia University
and the University of Chicago, respectively.[39] Francis was from

Francis Rose   Gertrude Rose
Courtesy American Baptist Historical Society, Atlanta

Connecticut and Gertrude from Vermont, and though they spoke
indigenous Filipino dialects such as Hiligaynon and Ilonggo, the
echo of their New England accent was still prominent.

When Louise and Laverne encountered the Roses in Calinog,
they immediately sensed they were kind and caring people. Francis was of medium height, and though he was healthy and vigor-
ous, he had put on extra pounds as he approached his retirement
years. He had a full head of regal white hair that framed intense
and intelligent blue eyes. He was gregarious, energetic, indus-
trious, unusually creative, and a delight to be around. Francis
seemed the perfect grandfather.

Gertrude was short and plump, and she exuded a sense of prudent New England reserve that often melted away when her keen humor broke through. An attractive woman, she kept her hair short and in a permanent wave. Though she was gentle and caring, she also was strong willed and independent. She was a woman who had seen the world and could take care of herself.[40]

The Roses had had two children, a son, Weston, who had died at age six in 1926, and a twenty-two-year-old daughter, Elinor, who was in college in the United States. Elinor later characterized her parents:

Daddy was an artist at heart, though a scientist by education. He not only loved music, he wrote it. He also painted and wrote poetry. . . . Daddy was an exception to the rule that a man can handle only one job and do it well. I remember that one year he taught twenty-four classes a week [at Philippine Central College], was acting Vice-President of the College, Manager of the school printing-press, Advertising Manager for the College, architect, and solicitor of funds, and still he found time to keep the organ tuned, and had his fingers on the steering wheel of the school carpentry and automotive shops. . . .

I don't believe Mother was too fond of the tropics. She suffered terribly from arthritis. However, she believed that a man's work is where his heart is, and that his wife's place is at his side. Though she may not have had the unbounded enthusiasm which my father possessed, she must have absorbed some of his, for she taught three or four classes a day, proof-read the products of the school press, and helped in the treasurer's office, in addition to being a good hostess and home-maker. We were seldom without guests, either personal friends or those of the College, and during the last year I was there, mother's guest

book showed that we had entertained at meals 765 guests,
and over 400 of these had spent one or more nights in our
home.[41]

It was this energetic and hospitable couple who met Louise and
Laverne at Calinog and took the two young women under their
protective wings. The Roses invited them to live at their mission's
temporary hideaway at Katipunan, where they could be close to
other Americans as well as a doctor, Frederick Meyer. Louise and
Laverne accepted the offer, as did two other gold-mining families from Masbate, the Schurings and the Clardys.

From April 16 to 18, the missionaries and gold miners filtered into the temporary safety of Katipunan. With a population
of less than one hundred Filipinos, the arrival of at least twenty-
three Americans was no secret. The word traveled far and wide
via the so-called bamboo telegraph.

South of Katipunan, in Calinog, Fred and Dorothy Chambers,
along with Henry and Anna Waters, remained at the temporary
hospital. By chance this hospital had not been burned by the
USAFFE, and was still operational. In addition to local patients,
they were caring for at least fifty convalescing soldiers who had
been evacuated from Bataan and Corregidor during the early
weeks of the war. Dr. Chambers and Dr. Waters had decided to
stay with their patients until the Japanese arrived.

The Chambers had two small children and the Waterses had
three. The welfare of these children was their greatest concern.
Rather than wait for the Japanese to approach them in their homes,
they decided that both families would move into the hospital. In
this way they would be clearly associated with the humanitarian
facility and might be afforded neutrality and mercy.

Late on Friday, April 17, retreating American and Filipino
soldiers informed the town that the Japanese would be arriving
no later than midnight. Instantly, stores were looted for provi-

sions as the populace of Calinog panicked and rushed to retreat to the hill country. Running past the hospital, they warned the Americans that they must evacuate, too. Having made the decision to stay, Fred Chambers remembers that "there was an inde-

Henry and Anna Waters, Billy, George, Mary Alice.

Courtesy American Baptist Historical Society, Atlanta

scribable peace that took possession of my mind, with the deep conviction that whatever came, we would fare all right."[42]

As expected, around midnight automatic rifle fire cut loose outside the city. The sentries on the bridge near the hospital had been mowed down. By sunrise the town was filled with Japanese soldiers with machine guns set up on each corner of the town square facing the hospital. Later, tanks clanked through the town. The missionaries were surprised and relieved that none of the Japanese troops had entered the hospital grounds. Finally a Japanese officer approached the hospital and told the Americans that if they stayed inside the hospital they would not be harmed. A little later other officers quietly entered the hospital and ate their breakfast in the dining room.

As the day wore on and more troops came into town, some soldiers came to the rear entrance of the hospital and asked for medications. Many had been transferred from Panang and Singapore, and they were suffering from malaria and wanted quinine.

In the afternoon Dr. Chambers asked one of the Japanese officers if she could return to their temporary home and get some supplies for their small children. A Japanese guard was sent to accompany her. When they entered their house, they found that it had been ransacked by soldiers, who had broken in and pilfered. Looking at the mess they had left, the Japanese guard shook his head sadly and said, "Bad soldiers in every army." He allowed Dr. Chambers to gather whatever she wanted from their home and walked with her back to the hospital.

The next day two Ford trucks rambled up to the hospital, and the Chamberses and the Waterses were ordered to climb up into the back of the trucks, taking only what possessions they could carry in their hands. The Chamberses brought only a few toys for Carol and Bob and waited in the truck as the Waterses gathered up their three little children—Billy and George, and the infant, Mary Alice. This young cargo was so precious and delicate. What awaited them at the end of this journey was unknown.[43]

The truck headed south down the national highway toward Iloilo. Bob Chambers sat on top of a suitcase holding his teddy bear while his sister, Carol, played mother with her doll. When some of the Japanese soldiers sitting by the tailgate motioned with their hands, indicating that they wanted to examine this American toy, she became protective and started crying. Her pure emotions expressed clearly the feeling her parents were repressing.

Arriving in Iloilo, they were not taken to the hospital as hoped but rather to the provincial jail. For the next month this would be the home for many Americans and Europeans rounded up in Iloilo. Because American and Filipino soldiers had successfully sabotaged the city's electricity and water supplies as they retreated, all drinking water was carried in by buckets. Food was brought into the jail through arrangements made between the internees and Filipino civilians. Though the internees could walk freely inside the walled prison yard during the day, they were locked into cells at night. It was a claustrophobic experience for most.

After four weeks, the male internees were put on a work detail to build a fence of corrugated roofing tin around three elementary school buildings. When this was completed, the three buildings were fashioned into a new internment camp. One building was used as a dining hall and crude kitchen. The second building was made into a dormitory for mothers and children, and the third building housed all other adults. This would be the Chamberses' and Waterses' home for the next thirteen months. During the summer of 1943 the entire camp would be loaded on an interisland steamer and shuttled to Manila to be interned in the massive Santo Tomas prison camp. There the Waterses and Chamberses would find Donal Rounds and Dick Meyers waiting to greet them.[44]

At the very moment these American civilians were fleeing to Katipunan or being interned in Iloilo, the United States aircraft carrier *Hornet* was secretly plying her way toward Japan. On April 18, as Katipunan welcomed her American refugees, sixteen B-25 army bombers under the command of Lieutenant Colonel Jimmy Doolittle lumbered off the *Hornet*'s short flight deck and flew seven-hundred miles toward Tokyo. Arriving successfully over their unsuspecting target, Doolittle's Raiders dropped their bombs and then fled toward China, crash landing or bailing out amid fog and darkness. This daring raid caused only minor physical damage to Tokyo but resulted in a major morale jolt for Japanese military personnel and civilians. As one Japanese witness of the bombing expressed, "We started to doubt that we were invincible."[45]

In Katipunan and Iloilo, Americans were desperately trying to convince themselves that the Japanese were, indeed, not invincible. Though all steadfastly expected an eventual American victory, they couldn't help wondering how long it would take for American forces to return to the Philippines. Some believed that it would be only a matter of months. But others who knew more about world affairs and the sober realities reflected in War Plan Orange had to acknowledge that it would be a wait measured in years; they prayed it would not be decades.

It soon became clear that Katipunan would not be safe. Though the barrio was over two miles from Highway 2 and secluded, the surrounding countryside was rolling grassland without dense tree cover. Japanese planes frequently flew over at low altitude, surveying the terrain and looking for guerrilla troop movement. A decision was made to move farther into the foothills, where the foliage was denser.

On April 18, Reverend Dianala led a scout party to a location he judged to be a suitable hideout, two and a half miles from Katipunan. It was readily apparent that this friendly and caring pastor walking in the midst of seemingly lost and bewildered refugees was dedicated to the welfare of the American missionaries who had shaped his Christian faith and supported his ministry in Katipunan. He was quite aware that his continued aid to the Americans might endanger his own family. But he—and many of his church members—were committed to these American friends and colleagues.

As they clambered higher up into the foothills, Reverend Dianala stopped and pointed out a narrow footpath leading down a steep embankment, which dropped nearly vertically for two hundred feet into a rocky ravine through which a small stream flowed. The stream soon disappeared out of sight around a sharp bend and entered a dense, forested canyon. It was within this nearly inaccessible and hidden spot that the miners and missionaries decided to build their hideaway. The missionaries optimistically named the locale Hopevale.[46]

As the first day progressed, the American refugees erected an odd assortment of canvas tents under the dense tree cover along the rocky streambed. The tents would have to do until grass nipa huts could be built. Reverend Dianala and his confidant, Mr. Rio, agreed to be paid a monthly salary to provide both food and security for Hopevale. Mr. Rio would travel to local markets and covertly purchase and transport fresh food for the community. Reverend Dianala would enlist trusted citizens in Katipunan to serve as sentries to warn the Americans of any nearby Japanese troop movements. As the Americans settled in, a system for providing basic needs began to evolve.[47] Food was cooked over open fires, and stream water was purified by boiling. Hopevale would be the home of these miners and missionaries for months to come

Trail to Hopevale from Katipunan. *Milton Meyer*

May 1942,
Luzon and Panay

As Bataan fell and the community of Hopevale took quiet shape in the interior of Panay, a fierce battle still continued for the fortress island of Corregidor, which now became the symbol for a new American Alamo in the Pacific. The island already had a storied history. At the conclusion of the Spanish-American

War, when the Philippines became an American territory, American military strategists did not forget how easily Admiral Dewey had sneaked into Manila Bay by night and destroyed the Spanish fleet. Not wanting to see this repeated by another military power, the United States immediately moved to fortify Manila's harbor to protect American and Filipino interests.

In 1902 a survey was made of five small islands within Manila Bay that had already been fortified lightly by the Spanish. The Americans selected these same islands and decided to greatly strengthen their ability to repel invading naval fleets. The largest island was Corregidor, and it was transformed between 1904 and 1910 into Fort Mills. Over the next twenty years, smaller defensive installations were constructed on the remaining four islands: Fort Frank, on Carabao Island; Fort Drum, on El Fraile Island; Fort Hughes, on Caballo Island; and Fort Wint, on El Grande Island. This network of mutually supportive harbor forts, studded with artillery emplacements, could provide interlocking coverage against an invading naval force. However, many of the emplacements for the seacoast artillery weapons were pointed out to sea and not designed to fire on an infantry force advancing at their rear, by land across Bataan.[48]

When Bataan fell, the only refuge for escaping American and Filipino forces who did not surrender was on Corregidor, which was separated from that mainland province by a 3.5-mile-wide, shark-infested ocean channel. This compact island is 4 miles long and 1.5 miles wide at its broadest point, and its total area comprises approximately three square miles. Crowded onto this "rock" were 9,377 Filipino and American military personnel and 2,302 frightened civilians.

From the air Corregidor appears to be shaped like a tadpole, with its elevated bulbous head pointing west toward the South China Sea and the entrance of Manila Bay. Its tapering tail points east across the harbor toward Manila. Protecting this island were twenty-three batteries with a total of fifty-six coastal guns and mortars, as well as antiaircraft installations. Though some of the batteries—particularly the mortars—could be turned to fire effectively toward Bataan, some of the larger coastal artillery guns were ineffective, due to their permanent reinforced emplacements and flat trajectories.[49]

The troops that manned the batteries were quartered near their artillery guns. However, the majority of the military personnel were protected inside a massive underground tunnel complex underneath Malinta Hill, near the Middle of the island. This cavernous tunnel, constructed between 1931 and 1938, was 1,400 feet long and 30 feet wide. From this major tunnel extended multiple lateral tunnels, providing quartermaster storage, barracks, a large hospital, and MacArthur's former headquarters. Built primarily for protection from air bombardment, the Malinta Tunnel was fortified with thick concrete floors and walls and strong overhead arches, and it had ventilation equipment to supply fresh air. During peacetime the main supply of water was brought by launch from Bataan.[50] There were also water wells on Corregidor whose electric pumps required dwindling supplies of fuel and electricity.

The ability of the American and Filipino force to survive on Corregidor was limited by their food and water supply. At half rations there was food to last for only six to eight weeks. Water was rationed to one canteen per person each day. Yet among the troops there was the determination to last until resistance became impossible. The siege would extend for twenty-seven days.

By April 12 the Japanese had increased their artillery capability to 18 batteries consisting of 116 guns that could fire, on Corregidor from multiple directions; artillery fire, supported by aerial bombing, grew in intensity and effectiveness over the next month. Lieutenant Juanita Redmond was an army nurse who had been evacuated from the field hospitals on Bataan to Corregidor during the final hours before Bataan surrendered. She recorded the

intensity of her claustrophobic life in Malinta Tunnel during the
bombardment of Corregidor:

> The roar of shells and bombs was not so muffled as I had
> thought at first, but echoed and reverberated through the
> laterals; and the lack of real ventilation was hard on ev-
> eryone, for even the elaborate system of fans did not keep
> the air from getting very stuffy and hot. And as the shell-
> ing of Corregidor became heavier and the bombings more
> frequent, our luxuries disappeared one by one. Double-
> decked and triple-decked beds in the hospital; civilian
> refugees sleeping in packed rows on the Tunnel floors; two
> meals a day, again, and scanty rations.[51]

On one night two weeks after arriving on Corregidor, Lieutenant Redmond endured an artillery barrage she would never
forget. During a long lull in the firing, a group of soldiers and
civilians took a chance and wandered outside the mouth of Malinta Tunnel to enjoy the cool evening and breathe the wonderful fresh air. Suddenly a shell landed and the concussion blew
the front gate to the tunnel shut. Unable to reenter the tunnel,
the small group could not hide from the incoming shells. They
were trapped in the open and their bodies were shattered by
the explosions and torn by shrapnel. Redmond recalled that
moment.

> Inside, we had heard the screaming of the shells. All the
> doctors and nurses hurried to duty, as the gates were opened
> and the corpsmen ran out with stretchers to bring in the
> wounded. The shells had done their work well.
>   We worked all that night, and I wish I could forget
> those endless, harrowing hours. Hours of giving injections,
> anesthetizing, ripping off clothes, stitching gaping wounds,
> of amputations, sterilizing instruments, bandaging, settling

the treated patients in their beds, covering the wounded that we could not save. . . .

The litter bearers kept bringing in more and more. Once, as I stooped to give an injection to one that they had just put down on the floor, I saw that it was a headless body. Shock and horror made me turn furiously on the corpsman.

"*Must* you do this?" I cried.

The boys looked at what they had carried with consternation almost equaling mine.

"It's so dark out there," one of them stammered. "We can't use lights. We feel for the bodies and just roll them onto the stretchers."

The doctors were so busy with the more severe cases that they turned minor injuries over to the nurses. . . . I was ordered to take care of a patient whose great toe was badly cut by shrapnel. I asked the doctor:

"What shall I do?"

"Remove it. It's practically off now; you won't have to do much to finish the job."

When I dropped the toe from my instrument into the container in which we disposed of the amputated parts, it fell into the open hand of an arm that had just been removed.[52]

Every day and night on Corregidor such ghastly scenes were recreated. The only fear that seemed worse than dying was the fear of surrender.

As the end of the siege drew near, General Wainwright contacted MacArthur in Australia with the urgent request that seaplanes be dispatched secretly to evacuate 150 nurses, the few remaining civilian women, and older American officers who could not withstand captivity. On April 29, Wainwright received word that two seaplanes, Navy PBYs able to land on water, were en route and would land under cover of darkness. Only fifty personnel could be evacuated, and Wainwright must make the difficult choices as to who would be chosen.

MacArthur sent Wainwright a list of essential personnel he needed on his staff to continue to wage war and fight his way back to the Philippines. These individuals would receive first priority. With the remaining space, Wainwright had room for American civilian women, 6 ailing officers, 1 pilot, and only 30 of the 150 nurses. He asked Captain Maud Davison, chief of nurses, to select them.[53]

Near midnight on April 29, the two PBYs glided through the darkness and splashed down undetected. Hurriedly, the fifty passengers boarded small boats to be ferried out to the planes. As they stepped aboard the boats, Wainwright shook hands with each man and hugged each nurse. One of the nurses suddenly turned her face and kissed the general on the cheek. It was Juanita Redmond.[54]

Another of the passengers was Wendell Fertig. Since being commissioned as a captain (reserve) in the U.S. Corps of Engineers in 1941, Fertig had been promoted twice and was now a lieutenant colonel. He had worked hard and efficiently. MacArthur continued to need his knowledge of the Philippine Islands, his engineering skills, and the results of some confidential reports he had been completing at the time of MacArthur's departure. Wendell's luck had not run out.[55]

With a roar of engines, the two seaplanes safely lifted off the waters of Manila Bay. They would be the last American aircraft to leave Luzon for the next two and a half years. Wainwright was now alone with his battered survivors and the excruciating decision of whether to fight on or to surrender.

Wainwright would not have to wrestle with his decision for long. General Homma decided to launch an amphibious assault upon the tadpole tail of Corregidor late on the night of May 5. To prepare for this, Homma's artillery unleashed its most brutal barrage of the campaign on May 4, raining sixteen thousand shells upon the island over a twenty-four-hour period. Corregidor now took on the appearance of no man's land in World War I. Trapped in trenches, caves, and tunnels, the remaining men and women fought to retain their sanity.

Sergeant Ben Waldron was a nineteen-year-old gunner from Colorado assigned to C Battery on Morrison Hill. In the midst of the intense shelling, Waldron was hunkered down in a fortified dugout next to his good friend, Sammy, a veteran soldier. Pressed against each other, Ben felt Sammy begin to shake "as though he had malaria. Soon he was sobbing and crying and then he began to scream."

Waldron grabbed Sammy and slapped him hard across his face, yelling, "Snap out of it, Sammy!"

Sammy choked out the words, "I have this feeling that I'm going to die and nobody will be able to help me."

Waldron shot back, "Look, you know that's a bunch of shit! As long as we stick together, everything'll be okay."

Later that night Sergeant Waldron remembered his own words and scribbled in his diary, "I was saying this for Sammy's sake, but inside of me . . . well, I didn't really believe it."[56]

During the same barrage Corregidor's last major gun emplacement, Battery Geary, sustained a direct hit, detonating its magazine and blasting ten-ton mortar barrels high into the air. By sunset on May 5, only three 155mm guns remained in operation. Knowing that the American force was virtually helpless, General Homma ordered a two-wave amphibious assault to land on Corregidor near midnight.

As a bright moon appeared high in the sky and midnight approached, the guns fell silent, and an eerie stillness enveloped the smoking island. Still in his fortified dugout on the side of a hill, Sergeant Waldron remembered:

It got so quiet you could have heard a pin drop. It wasn't but a minute later, that Captain Amery yelled out, "Everyone

take your small arms and hand grenades to your foxholes!
HERE THEY COME!" . . . I placed two belts of ammunition across my chest, my own .45 and its ammunition, a
canteen and first-aid kit. I heaved a .30 caliber machine
gun onto my right shoulder and took off. We arrived at
what was left of our foxholes, some of which had been
completely obliterated by the shelling. . . . Everything was
still quiet and eerie in the darkness. Then all hell broke
loose down below us [on the beach]. Somehow one of our
Search Light Batteries was capable of getting two search
lights back in operation and we could see hundreds of
barges loaded with thousands of Japs approaching Corregidor.[57]

Though to Sergeant Waldron it appeared that the entire Japanese army was afloat, the amphibious assault comprised only
two battalions with total troop strength of two thousand men
transported by nineteen landing craft of various sizes. Defending the extended shore of Corregidor were the remnants of the
Fourth Marine Regiment. Though this regiment numbered four
thousand troops, only one-third were marines, with the rest a
ragtag assortment of army and navy personnel.[58]

The Japanese assault approached Corregidor's shoreline
between Infantry Point and North Point, a distance of about
eighteen hundred yards guarded by the First and Second Pla-
toons of Company A, Fourth Marine Regiment. Though the
Americans were stretched thin, the Japanese paid dearly for a
small plot of beach. As the dark barges approached land and
their bow waves became clear, they were illuminated by the
bright moon and buffeted by a strong current. Floundering toward the shore, Japanese troops were cut down in swathes as
American defenders let loose with everything they had left.[59]
Looking down from a hillside, Sergeant Waldron remembered
that "Battery Way was soon in action and lobbing their 12-inch

mortars onto the barges. When one of their shells exploded over the barges, it would take out six or seven of them at a time. Then Denver Battery went into action with their 3-inch AA guns as they leveled them to a horizontal position and cut the fuse short enough so it would explode over the tops of the barges. With the help of the search lights we could see that the Japs were being slaughtered by the hundreds."[60] Only about eight hundred of the two thousand Japanese assault force lived to see sunrise.[61]

The American and Filipino defensive forces fought tenaciously, losing between six hundred and eight hundred men that night. However, by dawn on May 6, the determined Japanese were able to establish a tenuous beachhead, and were soon reinforced. The Americans and Filipinos then launched three counterattacks but failed to push the Japanese back into the ocean. Finally, about five hundred armed sailors attacked and successfully drove the enemy back until they ran into a Japanese machine gun crew they could not wipe out. Both sides were exhausted.[62]

Just as the American counterattacks waned, the Japanese realized that they were nearly out of ammunition. On Bataan, General Homma cursed and exclaimed, "I have failed miserably in this assault!"[63] However, at that critical moment, the Japanese successfully landed three tanks—one a captured American M3 Stuart tank—and fought their way to within a few hundred yards of the entrance of Malinta Tunnel.[64] With no antitank guns, and knowing the slaughter the tanks would create among the nurses, hospital patients, and unarmed civilians inside the tunnel, Wainwright was cornered. He later recalled, "I had to make up my mind—a mind then reeling with the task of trying to find ways and means of averting the inevitable. I went over our position in my mind. . . . But it was the terror that is vested in a tank that was the deciding factor. I thought of the havoc that even one of these could wreak if it nosed into the tunnel, where lay our helpless wounded and their brave nurses."[65]

Wainwright decided to surrender Corregidor. He first sent a previously prepared radio message of surrender to General Homma—read in English and Japanese—and then ordered a white flag to be raised above Corregidor at noon. As the white flag flapped in the breeze, the Fourth Marines burned their regimental colors. Colonel Howard placed his face in his hands and wept openly, exclaiming, "My god, and I had to be the first marine officer ever to surrender a regiment."[66]

For several hours Wainwright waited for a response while the Japanese shelling continued unabated. In these final moments before going to arrange terms with General Homma, he sent two cables to his superiors. To President Roosevelt he wrote, "With broken heart, and head bowed in sadness but not in shame, I report to Your Excellency that today I must arrange terms for the surrender of the fortified islands of Manila Bay. . . . With profound regret and with continued pride in my gallant troops, I go to meet the Japanese commander. Goodbye, Mr. President." And to MacArthur, Wainwright's words were tapped out, "We have done our full duty for you and for our country. We are sad but unashamed. I have fought for you to the best of my ability from Lingayen Gulf to Bataan to Corregidor, always hoping relief was on the way. . . . Goodbye, General, my regards to you and our comrades in Australia. May God strengthen your arm to insure ultimate success of the cause for which we have fought side by side."[67]

With his messages sent, Wainwright grew impatient. He ordered a marine officer to raise a white flag, brave the enemy fire, and go find a Japanese officer—any officer who could wield authority. An hour later the marine returned, saying he had found a Japanese lieutenant who spoke English, but he had refused to come meet with Wainwright. "He won't come to see you, General," the marine exclaimed. "He insists that you go and meet him."[68]

Wainwright and members of his staff left Malinta Tunnel to

find the lowly lieutenant. Intermittent shelling continued, and the journey was dangerous. Finally, Lieutenant Uramura was located, and before Wainwright could utter a word, Uramura shouted, "We will not accept your surrender unless it includes all American and Filipino troops in the whole archipelago." Wainwright blanched. Now he knew what the Japanese ultimatum would be. Not just the surrender of Corregidor or even Luzon, but the entire Philippines.

Demanding to see General Homma, arrangements were made to transport Wainwright by launch to Bataan. As Wainwright and his staff walked to the north dock, the shelling continued, and Wainwright lost his temper. Ashen with anger he shouted at his Japanese escort, "Why the hell don't you people stop shooting? I put up my white flag hours ago." Crouching for protection from shrapnel, a Japanese colonel shot back, "We have not accepted any surrender from you as yet." Wainwright realized that Japanese pressure and manipulation would be relentless.[69]

Arriving on Bataan, Wainwright and his staff were driven by car to a private home. They waited for Homma to arrive for over an hour. Wainwright later described the moment: "He drove up dramatically, in a beautiful shiny Cadillac, flanked by three overdressed aides. Behind the Cadillac was a car filled with staff officers, and following them was a car for Jap war correspondents. General Homma stepped out of the car, and I think all of us were a little astonished by his size. He stood nearly six feet tall, was heavily built, and must have weighed close to two hundred pounds. He wore an olive-drab tropical uniform [and] was bedecked with several bright rows of decorations and campaign ribbons, and carried the inevitable sword. How they worship those damned swords!"[70]

Ignoring the Americans, Homma walked to a long table on the porch of the house and sat in a chair at the middle of the table. Wainwright was motioned to sit facing him. Though Homma spoke fluent English, he refused to converse in English. Using an interpreter, Homma stated that the surrender would not be accepted unless all American and Filipino troops in the Philippines were surrendered. Wainwright bluffed and countered that he did not have the authority to accept such terms. Homma stood and angrily decreed that Corregidor would be pounded into dust until his unconditional terms were accepted. Fuming, Homma strode back to the Cadillac and drove away. Wainwright returned to Corregidor.[71]

Arriving back in the darkness of night, Wainwright was shocked to discover that the Japanese front line was now within a hundred yards of the entrance of Malinta Tunnel. Orders were being barked by Japanese officers to resume the attack. Wainwright suddenly knew that he had to agree to Homma's terms or every man, woman, and child would be slaughtered. Wainwright turned to a Japanese interpreter and snapped, "Take me to your commander." Brought to a stocky Japanese colonel, a surrender document was written quickly detailing Homma's nonnegotiable terms. On the night of June 6, 1942, the Philippine islands became a Japanese possession.

General MacArthur was furious when informed of Wainwright's decision. Safe in Australia, MacArthur could publicly polish his own reputation as an unconquered warrior—at the expense of the brave subordinate he had left in the Philippines to surrender in his stead. Wainwright became MacArthur's scapegoat. Immediately MacArthur contacted General Sharp, who was commanding the Mindanao Force, and declared, "Orders emanating from General Wainwright have no validity. If possible separate your force into small elements and initiate guerrilla operations. You, of course, have full authority to make any decision that immediate emergency may demand." MacArthur then sent a message to his superior, General George Marshall, in Washington stating, "I believe Wainwright has temporarily become unbalanced and his condition renders him susceptible of enemy use."[72]

After further assessing the situation on Mindanao and in the Visayas, General Sharp agreed with Wainwright's decision to surrender and replied to MacArthur on May 10, "I have seen Wainwright's staff officer and have withdrawn my order releasing commanders on other islands and [instead have] directed complete surrender. Dire necessity alone has prompted this action." With this terse message Sharp ordered the Visayan-Mindanao Force to surrender. Though many small military units throughout the Philippines were reluctant to comply, General Homma had achieved the formal surrender of American and Filipino forces throughout the islands.[73]

On Panay, Colonel Albert Christie surrendered his American and Filipino troops on May 20. However, prior to his surrender fully 90 percent of his soldiers—five thousand men—disappeared into the hills, taking equipment with them, and formed guerrilla units under the command of their ranking Filipino officer, Lieutenant Colonel Macario Peralta. Panay's would soon become one of the most effective guerrilla forces, constantly harassing the outnumbered Japanese invaders and denying them control of the island.[74]

Coincidentally, while American and Filipino forces were formally surrendering in the Philippines, the U.S. Navy was gaining its first major victory against the advancing Japanese. By the middle of April 1942, Japan had established bases south of the Philippines, in the New Guinea–New Britain–Solomon Islands region. From these island bases they could stage attacks on Melanesia and Australia. On May 4—two days before the fall of Corregidor—a powerful Japanese fleet, including three aircraft carriers, plied its way south toward the Allied air base at Port Moresby on the southeastern tip of New Guinea. If successful in taking Port Moresby, the Japanese would gain air superiority over the Coral Sea—including the Solomon Islands—and would establish air bases close enough to strike Australia.

In reflecting on the significance of this moment, Fleet Admiral Ernest J. King later wrote, "It should be noted at this point that during the first five months of the war, nearly every engagement with the enemy had demonstrated the importance of air-power in modern naval warfare. . . . As yet, however, there had been no engagement between enemy carrier forces and our own [carrier forces], and although we had reason to believe that most of our naval aircraft were of good design and performance, we had no basis for comparison."[75]

Against this Japanese armada the United States dispatched her unproven naval task forces 16 and 17, including the carriers *Lexington*, *Yorktown*, *Enterprise*, and *Hornet*. When the first conflict between opposing aircraft carriers took place, between May 4 and 8, military history was changed radically and naval strategy rewritten.

The Japanese and the Americans each lost a carrier and sustained major damage to other important vessels, resulting in a tactical draw. However, the Battle of the Coral Sea blunted the Japanese threat to Port Moresby and provided the war's first significant halt to further Japanese expansion.

Reflecting on this crucial victory, Admiral King wrote that the Battle of the Coral Sea was "the first major engagement in naval history in which surface ships did not exchange a single shot."[76] Rather, the U.S. Navy proved that her aircraft and pilots could hold their own against Japanese carrier forces. From this point forward Allied forces in the Pacific would wrest the offensive momentum from Japan, soon cripple her naval airpower at the Battle of Midway, and begin their steady and methodical push northward toward the liberation of the Philippines and the defeat of Japan.[77]

Hiding in the shadowed depths of Hopevale, the missionaries and the gold miners heard of the fall of Corregidor and the formal surrender of all American armed forces in the Philippines.

However, they could not know of the American victory at the Battle of the Coral Sea. They could not sense that at the moment American forces on Panay surrendered, Japanese military fortunes had reached their zenith. All they knew was that their future was grim. That something had gone terribly wrong. Their faith in both God and country was fragile.

Chapter Eight

June–October 1942,
Hopevale, Panay Island

It was finished. With the formal surrender of United States and Filipino troops, a traumatic chapter ended and a more dangerous one emerged. Now the Japanese controlled the Philippines, and all Americans were either prisoners of war or hunted prey. And no one knew when—or even if—the Philippines would be liberated by Allied forces. For the American refugees isolated in Hopevale, the dominant theme of this new chapter was expressed in three words: concealment, evasion, and survival.

The miners and missionaries had arrived in Hopevale on Saturday, April 18, 1942, after the fall of Bataan on April 9 and the Japanese invasion of Panay on April 16, but before the fall of Corregidor and the formal surrender of all American and Filipino troops throughout the islands. The gravity of their situation had at first been lightened by a sense of adventure. Looking at their lush jungle surroundings in Hopevale, many reflected on favorite childhood stories such as *Robinson Crusoe* or *The Swiss Family Robinson*. Some in Hopevale may have felt a twinge of such childhood suspense late at night, when the jungle grew quiet, or in the waking moments of dawn. But in the case of the fictional Crusoe, the ink on the page had dried and his ending was good. The fortunes of the Americans at Hopevale were still uncertain.

With every day that passed, the missionaries and miners realized that they had placed their lives not only in the hands of God but in the compassionate care and loyalty of many Filipinos. Without their Filipino friends—mostly fellow Baptists in a predominantly Catholic culture—these Americans could not survive for long. They were totally dependent upon their neighbors for food and an early-warning security system. The threat that someone would be tempted by a Japanese bribe to reveal their location was a constant and realistic worry. Even in the seeming peace and quiet of their isolated existence, safety was tenuous.

The canvas floor of a tent pitched on the bank of a rocky streambed quickly grows intolerable. Asleep on ground level, one becomes fair game to snakes, rats, iguanas, roaches, centipedes, and even monkeys. After a few days of tent dwelling, each American family was urgently contracting with Filipinos to build them more permanent and comfortable shelter. Using the materials at hand, these Filipino neighbors constructed indigenous nipa and cogan-grass dwellings similar to the ones that had housed their families for centuries.

Most nipa huts are approximately 400 to 600 square feet in size. Within each hut there is usually a *sala* (or den) and two or three small bedrooms. Usually the thatch wall partitions rise only three quarters of the way to the roof, thus limiting privacy. Every room has at least one open window that can be covered by a nipa shutter. The native beds are either a woven mat rolled out on the bamboo floor or a raised platform made of cross strips of bamboo. The front door of the hut is high above the ground and accessed by a bamboo ladder, which can be withdrawn at

night for security. Cooking is often done outside or in a separate
communal kitchen to reduce smoke and fire hazard.

Building something similar to an American bathroom was
more difficult. Initially, everyone simply bathed in the stream.

Sketch of Dr. and Mrs. Meyer's hut in Hopevale, Emmanuel Glen.

Milton Meyer

Fortunately, Francis Rose was farsighted enough to bring a
wooden toilet seat with him to Hopevale. It quickly became the
most popular imported item. A deep hole was dug, a thatch hut
built around it, and the wonderful toilet seat erected in place.
This communal privy was placed within walking distance of
most of the secluded nipa huts.[1]

Though primitive, the grass houses were comfortable and
serviceable. Ultimately, eleven nipa huts were tucked away under the trees and along the hillside that descended to the stream
that meandered through Hopevale. The community was close
and compact, and blended well into the jungle foliage, providing
camouflage from Japanese aircraft.[2]

As Laverne Fertig and Louise Spencer moved into a house

shared with another gold-mining family—Henry and Laura Schuring and their twelve-year-old son, Clifford—they were growing anxious about their husbands. For the previous month, Spence had been working on the construction of an airfield at Pilar. Claude was more mobile, supervising several engineering projects. When General Christie surrendered his sixty-first Panay division to the Japanese at Baloy, Claude and Spence should have been among the American officers with him, unless they had refused orders and gone into the jungle with the guerrillas. In the three days since the surrender, no one had seen or heard from them, and Laverne and Louise were becoming frantic.

News that filtered into Hopevale was sporadic and often inaccurate. Though the Rio family in Katipunan owned an old radio, it could only receive news from local broadcasts. All newspapers and radio stations in the Philippines were now controlled by the Japanese, and the news was heavily censored. Reliable news from the outside world grew more and more difficult to obtain. And the *poac*, or bamboo telegraph, was usually exaggerated and inaccurate.

Both women tried to stay busy, optimistically preparing their new home for their husbands' return, but thoughts of being abandoned and alone in a war without Claude and Spence overwhelmed them. One afternoon Louise found Laverne bawling her eyes out near a secluded bend of the stream. Louise hugged her, all the time wishing that she could dissolve into tears, too. But somehow, one of them always managed to be strong when the other needed support. Good friends were slowly becoming as close as sisters.

On Sunday, May 24, four days after the surrender, Louise stayed home from worship service, depressed and worried sick, and nursing an abscessed ankle wound. Standing at an open window washing dishes in a dirty dishpan, she gasped and squinted, and saw Spence's tall, slender frame ducking out of the jungle. Scrambling through the front door and down the bamboo ladder, soap suds and all, she gave Spence the biggest hug of his life. Soon Laverne joined them, desperate to hear news of Claude, only to be disappointed. Spence and Claude had been separated while working on different projects prior to the surrender, and Spence did not know where Claude was.

The next night an ominous thunderstorm blew in while some of the Hopevale crew were huddled in a grass house playing bridge by a dim kerosene-lantern light. Though nearly deafened by the deluge, they heard a man's voice bellow, "Laverne!" Throwing their cards down, they looked up to see Claude's silhouette emerging out of darkness as he clambered up the ladder and stood in the open door frame. He was soaked to the bone, chilled, and exhausted, after hiking in the rain all day and dodging the Japanese.

After Claude changed clothes and devoured some hot soup and crackers, everyone gathered to hear his story. Numb with fatigue, he could share little. But what he did say was that he and Laverne would not be staying in Hopevale. Then he collapsed into sleep.

Though it was his first visit, Claude Fertig had never liked the location of Katipunan and its surroundings. He believed that the region was not remote enough to hide from Japanese troops, and was vulnerable to attack. The missionaries had far more trust in the ability of Reverend Dianala's sentries and listening posts, and felt that if a Japanese advance toward Hopevale was made, they would be alerted in time to take evasive action. However, Claude doubted that a loosely organized collaboration of loyal Filipino neighbors living in surrounding barrios could give prompt and sufficient warning should the Japanese learn of Hopevale and decide to capture the Americans. So, Claude decided that he and Laverne would move to the more distant, secluded slopes of Mount Igabon, near an abandoned army cache

of canned goods that would provide food for six months to a
year.

Claude invited the Spencers to move with them. However,
Louise's ankle was still infected and she needed Dr. Meyer's

Foothills surrounding Hopevale.   *Milton Meyer*

medical attention. She could not endure a three-day hike
through rugged mountainous territory. Spence was familiar
with the trek and knew it would be impossible for her. The
Spencers decided to temporarily take their chances in Hopevale and let the Fertigs go alone. They would join them later if
they could.[3]

As the Fertigs disappeared along the trail to Mount Igabon,
Louise sent word for Dr. Meyer to come and examine her ankle.
Dr. Meyer and his remaining medical staff had set up their housing a kilometer farther upstream from the rest of the missionaries
and miners, on Ulaugan brook. Dr. Meyer was of an independent
disposition and liked "command of his own ship." He wanted
what remained of his medical team—Mrs. Meyer, Jennie Adams,

and any visiting Filipino nursing students—to have their own quarters. They named their small dwelling place Emmanuel Glen.[4]

Trudging back down the streambed to the main camp, Dr. Meyer found Louise in pain, her ankle swollen and tinted gangrenous green. With no surgical tools to operate, Frederick improvised. He found a box of toothpicks, a pocketknife, a swab of cotton, and a small bottle of Mercurochrome, and set to work. Lancing, probing, and draining the wound without anesthesia was primitive and painful, but the procedure was successful. Within a few weeks, Louise could walk without limping. Even though the army had burned his instruments and medications, Dr. Meyer could still work his healing magic.[5]

Whenever miners and engineers gather, they cannot sit still for long. Soon the emerging camp at Hopevale was one mass-improvement project. The first priority was running water. Carrying water in buckets from the stream had become more than a chore. Soon hollow shoots of bamboo, cut and spliced together, became natural piping. Using the power of gravity, stream water flowed to the grass houses.

Spence and Ben Zimmerman built a jury-rigged shower. After Louise Rounds and her son, Doug, braved their first shower in weeks, she reported, "[The shower head is] a margarine can with holes . . . and bamboo tubes bring the water from the creek. . . . We felt like we [were at] the Ritz Carlton!"[6] Spence and Ben also built bamboo drainage lines so that dirty dishwater could be carried away from primitive kitchens to the creek.[7]

Chickens were bought from Filipinos to provide meat and eggs. Special elevated coops were designed to protect both from large snakes, rats, ants, and other jungle marauders. The chickens were soon safer than they wanted to be.

Jungle critters still harassed the Americans. One day an iguana darted under the Roundses' elevated grass hut. Worried about their chickens, mild-mannered Erle went on the offensive. Louise jotted in her diary, "Erle went after it with a *bolo* [machete] and hammer and much to his surprise he really killed it! It was a small one—only about three feet long!"[8]

Henry Schuring, a gold miner, made his engineering contribution when he decided that he could face the terrors of war and the fear of the unknown—but not without an occasional nip of alcohol. Of course, conversation about this matter with the teetotaling Baptist missionaries was out of the question; so, discussion was wisely ruled out.

Henry bartered with a local Filipino to smuggle raw grain alcohol into Hopevale in used five-gallon kerosene cans and covertly became a master distiller. Temporarily borrowing kitchen bowls and containers—often from Mrs. Rose—Ben experimented in making a rotgut brew that was both safe and palatable. Reverend Dianala was asked to find a container of charcoal, never suspecting it would be used as an alcohol filter. Muscovado sugar was added to the elixir, as well as many mystery ingredients. Henry's first public sampling, on July 4, Independence Day, resulted in Louise Spencer declaring, "Our first try at drinking cane alcohol was almost enough to cure us of all desire for a drink!" But Henry was far more determined than offended. Within a short time he devised a recipe that both was tasty and lifted spirits. Though the hidden distillery reeked of alcohol, the missionaries never let on that they smelled a thing.[9]

While Henry Schuring brewed his liquor, Dr. Rose designed and built a small outdoor cathedral on the outskirts of Hopevale, laboring alone on his project. With his boundless energy and creativity, he reshaped a narrow, rock-studded gorge topped with tall, draping trees and beautiful foliage into an outdoor center for worship. He named it Cathedral Glen.

At one end of the gorge was a towering tree. Beneath this tree Dr. Rose built an elevated stone altar with a rough wooden cross placed in the center. Mirroring a European split-chancel cathedral, on one side of the altar he crafted a stone pulpit and on the other side a small, stone reader's lectern, both with slab tops. To the far left of the altar he built his greatest surprise—a semicircular raised terrace that formed an organ loft. That an organ could be found in a wartime jungle defies belief. However, for years Erle Rounds had transported a small, portable foot-pump organ in the back of his car on his circuit rides among rural churches. It was sturdy and could be folded into the size of a packing trunk. Erle had rescued the organ from destruction in Capiz and brought it to Hopevale. Dr. Rose quickly appropriated it for his cathedral, carefully packing and storing it between services.[10] Mrs. Rounds, Dr. Meyer, and Dr. Rose all took turns playing it at Sunday services.

As viewed from the pulpit when facing the congregation, stone benches followed the narrow sides of the gorge and then curved across the middle, forming an intimate semicircle of seating for worshipers. Dr. Rose laid a stone aisle between the benches leading to the altar. Beneath the altar he placed a rectangular block of stone upon which a small sacramental fire was built by twelve-year-old Clifford Schuring before each Sunday service. Surrounded by lush beauty, Dr. Rose's cathedral was intertwined with nature and provided a beautiful haven for meditation, prayer, and worship. Cathedral Glen became the defining symbol of God's presence for all who lived in Hopevale.[11]

One thing that the missionaries brought to Hopevale in adequate supply was books. If nothing else, they imagined that they could catch up on reading and professional studies. But like a patient who takes a book to the hospital to read after surgery, sometimes pain is too intense to enjoy it, and the mind is numbed by trauma, sickness, or hunger. Hopevale, though beautiful, was anything but idyllic. It was not a sequestered place for a focused sabbatical but a fragile refuge from war and capture.

Part of what made life difficult in Hopevale was a pervasive sense of claustrophobia. Living in the bottom of a river gorge covered over by thick vegetation often caused Hopevale's occupants to feel trapped and hemmed in. This was particularly true for older adults and single women, who could not break the monotony by hiking to Katipunan or visiting a distant guerrilla camp, as some of the men and younger couples occasionally did. Most spent weeks and months without leaving. This confinement was intensified during the six months of the rainy season, when frequent typhoons trapped them in their small grass huts for days. Mud became knee deep, mildew covered everything, and clothes were always wet. Such conditions bred depression, and depression triggered anxiety. Hopevale could be both a refuge and a prison.

Nurse Jennie Adams found writing poetry to be her solace. One of three single missionary women at Hopevale, she was forty-six years old and well-adjusted to living without a marriage partner. But the loneliness of Hopevale and her inability to lose herself in medical work sometimes overwhelmed her. Having grown up on the broad, open plains of Nebraska, where a clearly defined horizon gave her a sense of place and perspective, she was now enclosed by dense and oppressive jungle hills and felt smothered. It was hard for Jennie to find her bearings when she could not see a horizon and dense trees hid the evening stars.

Nurse Jennie Adams.
Courtesy American Baptist Historical Society, Atlanta

Jennie was not an accomplished, professional poet. But her feelings were keen, and the simple expression of her lyrics powerful. One day when the jungle closed in, Jennie grew defiant and her poetry sparked.

I shall not let these hills imprison me,
Where for refuge I've been forced to flee;
Like walls they shut me in on ev'ry side
While offering a sheltered place to hide. . . .
In wooded hills we chose to hide away
And not in concentration camp to stay.

These words helped Jennie to remember that Hopevale was her deliberate choice, and better than imprisonment, but they did not erase her homesickness for Nebraska and her family:

My thoughts turn homeward to a sunny plain—
The sun emerging from the fields of grain
And sinking into meadow land again,
For I am prairie born where wheat fields grow,
Where prairie grasses wave when breezes blow.
With eyes that yearn to gaze on distant scene,
Must I be cloistered in a small ravine?

Then, looking up and glimpsing tropical birds flittering in the overarching trees, Jennie concluded with a determined credo:

I shall not let these hills imprison me.
The birds are not shut in, nor shall I be. . . .
I must be looking up if I would see
What love and goodness God has given me.
I must look up beyond life's walls and bars
If I would see the brightness of the stars.
Mine eyes I must lift upward unafraid,
Remembering on Whom my strength is stayed.
Each day I must more grateful learn to be,
Remembering with joy that I am free,
The freedom God alone can give today
None other gives, and none can take away. . . .[12]

As Jennie Adams used her poetry to lift her despair, so did Ben Zimmerman use hammer, saw, and shovel to numb his grief. Ben was thirty-one years old, and he had been a miner on Masbate for six years, living at the same sites as the Fertigs and Spencers. He was the only Democrat and Catholic at Hopevale, and proud of it. He was married and had two little girls but had wisely sent his wife and children back to the United States before the war began. Though grateful for his decision, he missed his family terribly. His long face often reflected the pain of his separation. He coped by being the "fix-it man" at Hopevale, keeping himself busy with building and repair projects, and in doing so, deepening friendship with his Hopevale companions.[13]

In Hopevale faith was challenged, bruised, and refined for missionary and miner alike. Hopevale could be both freedom and captivity, often both on the same day. Each person's tempered perspective made all the difference.

In early July 1942 a crisis arose among the missionaries. Since the American surrender, Japanese planes had crisscrossed Panay, dropping leaflets announcing that all Americans must surrender—supposedly without reprisal—to Japanese forces within four months or be executed if later captured.[14] The Americans at Hopevale were aware of this ultimatum, and yet each had determined not to surrender. For some this decision was based upon their advanced age and poor health; they feared that prolonged imprisonment under extreme conditions would kill them. Others desired freedom and would rather die than be at the mercy of the Japanese. Still others, because of their previous connections with the American military and guerrilla groups, suspected that they might be punished for their associations. As a result, the missionaries and the miners at Hopevale had weeks before elected to evade the Japanese.

Writing after the war, Milton Meyer reflected on his parents' decision: "Frederick's and Ruth's reasons for evacuating, rather than surrendering, were never written down. One can only surmise their motivation. To those who saw the doctor at this time, Frederick was never so full of fight as he was then; he apparently never even remotely considered the idea of surrender. Moreover, he had been too deeply involved in army work; he probably thought that he could be of greater help in his medical work to the Filipino guerrilla group."[15]

However, the American Baptist missionaries interned forty miles south in Iloilo had grown concerned about their fellow missionaries in Hopevale. They evidently had been questioned about Hopevale's location. Fred Chambers recounts in his memoirs:

> A Japanese Chaplain who had studied in Japan under [Jimmy] Covell came into camp one day to see if contact could be made with our colleagues who were hiding in the Panay Hills to encourage them to surrender and come into camp. None of us knew whether it was a bona fide offer or a trap. With all our concern, we could only say that they had left before we were interned and we did not know their whereabouts. A Filipino minister also tried to effect their surrender. We suggested to him that he tell them what he had seen and heard while visiting us and then leave it to them to decide.[16]

Finally, the missionaries in Iloilo smuggled out a letter to Hopevale and evidently urged the Hopevale camp to surrender before the four-month ultimatum expired.[17] Though a copy of this letter did not survive the war, Louise Spencer remembered that the Iloilo internees "were begging our missionary friends to give themselves up to the Japs. If they did not do this, their friends in the Iloilo concentration camp were afraid of the consequences for all concerned."[18]

There were multiple possible reasons for this letter. First, the missionaries in Iloilo probably did not believe it was possible for the missionaries in Hopevale to evade the Japanese for long, and feared the consequences of their capture. Second, there was concern that the Hopevale missionaries' dependence on Filipino neighbors for food and security would endanger the very people who were helping them. Finally, it was possible—though no supportive evidence exists—that their colleagues imprisoned in Iloilo might be held for ransom or harmed if the Hopevale party did not surrender. Whatever the reason, the missionaries interned in Iloilo requested that the missionaries in Hopevale at least review their decision.[19]

One of the missionary couples in Hopevale who perhaps had the keenest insight into the gravity of their decision to avoid imprisonment was James and Charma Covell—the same Jimmy Covell who had taught the Japanese chaplain who was inquiring about him in Iloilo. Jimmy Covell and Charma Moore had both been appointed as missionaries to Japan in the early 1920s, when they were young and single. They met on an ocean liner sailing to Japan and were married less than a year later, while attending language school. Jimmy, a graduate of Brown University, and Charma, a graduate of Ohio State University, were both teachers, and for the next twenty years were assigned to Kanto Gakuin University, in Yokohama.

James and Charma Covell, Peggy, David, Alice, about 1933.
Courtesy American Baptist Historical Society, Atlanta

Within their first six years of marriage, they had three children: Margaret (Peggy), David, and Alice. Jimmy taught Bible and English at Kanto Gakuin while Charma managed their household, tutored students, and was active in the Japanese community. Their life was happy and fulfilled but increasingly marred by the rising militarism in Japan.

Jimmy Covell abhorred violence and war, and was committed to inspiring international peace and goodwill. He believed that participation in war was incompatible with Christianity. He was particularly concerned as he noted Japan's war preparations affecting his students and encroaching on life at the university. Never a hothead or an extremist, he was still a man of strong and irrepressible convictions.

Jimmy began to quietly protest against how the Christian church in Japan was acquiescing to the strident militarism of Japan's government. He wrote slogans such as "Friendships Not Battleships" on the envelopes of his personal letters. When the administration of the university allowed military training courses for their students, Jimmy showed up at the parade ground dressed in black funeral clothes. The chairman of the board of trustees, Hajime Watanabe, saw him and asked, "Whose funeral is it today?" Jimmy looked him in the eye and said, "It is Kanto Gakuin's funeral."

Later there came a day when the emperor's picture was hung in a special ceremony at Kanto Gakuin. The government required all students and faculty to attend, but Jimmy Covell refused. His absence was both expected and noted, and pressure for him to acquiesce mounted. In the spring of 1939, eighteen months before Pearl Harbor, the American Baptist Foreign Mission Society reassigned the Covells to the Philippines to teach at the Central Philippine University in the city of Iloilo in southern Panay. It was a safer environment for a man who could not "bend his knee to Caesar."[20]

After they arrived in Iloilo on June 7, 1939, their seventeen-year-old daughter, Peggy, and fourteen-year-old son, David, were sent to attend the Bordner High School in Manila. When Peggy was graduating in 1940 and preparing to go to college in the United States, Jimmy and Charma feared war in the Pacific was imminent. They decided to send all three of their children back to the States for school, and planned to join them when their furlough was scheduled, in 1942. Now, in the summer of 1942 when they should have been on an ocean liner bound for home, they were instead hiding in Hopevale mired in war. What would happen if they turned themselves in? Did the Japanese *Kempeitai*—the dreaded secret police—now in Manila have Jimmy Covell's records in their vast files? Would he be interrogated and tortured if he surrendered?

All of the missionaries at Hopevale continued to be plagued by questions like these. If they surrendered, would they be treated as civilians or as guerrillas? Would their status as missionaries be respected and honored? Would their previous involvement with the military now harm them? Would they prefer to spend the war years in the dangerous freedom of Hopevale or in captivity, where personal control was forfeited? The Hopevale contingent—missionaries and miners—became unified in their decision not to surrender. Against the urging of their fellow missionaries in Iloilo, they reaffirmed their decision to stay in Hopevale.

June–October 1942,
Santo Tomas Internment Camp, Manila

The greatest pain that the Roundses and the Meyers endured in Hopevale was their inability to receive news from their teenage sons, Donal Rounds and Richard Meyer, trapped in Manila. Mrs. Rounds noted in her diary that during the early days of the war, before the evacuation to Hopevale, several Filipino friends who fled Manila and reached Panay had reported that they had seen the boys in Manila on a street near the Red Cross building and also at a church service at Ellinwood Church. But there had been no further news in months.[21] In fact, the boys were now interned in the Santo Tomas prison camp in Manila.

When the Japanese attacked on December 8, 1941, both Donal Rounds and Richard Meyer were living in the American Bible Society building, a boarding home for missionary children attending Bordner High School. As the first Japanese bombs crashed down, the missionary children crouched in the stairwell of the building, feeling the terror of war for the first time. When the bombing ended, they dashed outside to see the destruction and to gawk at fierce dogfights between outclassed American P-40 fighters and superior Japanese Zeros. Later, when the Cavite naval base was bombed and razed, and Manila harbor was closed to commercial shipping, cold fear seized their young hearts. The boys realized that they were cut off from their parents and on their own.[22]

Donal Rounds, about 1945.
Dodie Borroughs

To escape further bombing, the missionary children boarding in Manila were transported south of Manila to an agricultural university in Los Banos. Later, as the Japanese made amphibious assaults south of Los Banos, and infantry troops began to push north toward Manila, the missionary children returned to Manila seeking safety.[23]

Several weeks later, when Manila was declared an open city and the first Japanese troops arrived on New Year's Eve 1941, the missionary children were again living in the American Bible Society compound with their dorm parents, Mr. and Mrs. Fonger. Sometime during the first weeks of January, Japanese soldiers appeared one morning at the compound and hammered on the door. The missionary children were ordered to pack one suitcase each and load up on a troop truck. Gathering up his courage, Donal Rounds asked a Japanese officer if he might also take his prized possession, his trumpet, which was separate in a leather case. Glaring at him, the officer tensed and then nodded a grudging assent. Donal did not yet realize how reckless his request had been. Soon he would see Americans slapped and beaten for uttering a word.[24]

With armed guards riding on both ends of the tailgate, the students were driven toward an unknown destination. Within five miles the truck slowed to a crawl and entered the gates of the University of Santo Tomas campus. Brusquely unloaded, they stared wild-eyed as Americans, Canadians, Australians, British, Poles, Dutch, French, Norwegians, and other internationals were herded into captivity. Santo Tomas would be the scene of their intense teenage years, their years of growth and maturation, in the midst of privation, hunger, and insecurity.[25]

The University of Santo Tomas was founded by Spanish missionaries on April 28, 1611, and is one of the oldest existing universities in Asia. Located on a sixty-acre campus in the Sampaloc district of Manila, it was selected by the Japanese to become the largest civilian internment camp in the Philippines.[26] In the initial weeks of 1942, roughly 3,200 internees converged on the campus: Approximately 70 percent were American, 25 percent were British, and the rest were of other nationalities. By February there were 2,000 male and 1,200 female internees. Married couples numbered some 450, and there were 400 children under fifteen years of age.[27]

These international civilian internees were unprepared and traumatized by their sudden deportation into prison camp. A. V. H. Hartendorp—an internee and leading historian on the Santo Tomas prison camp—remembers that his fellow prisoners

were thrown into camp stripped of virtually all their possessions, without the commonest necessities and conveniences; many of them without other clothing than they had on, without bedding, without food, without money. Even those among them with money in the banks had been unable to draw out any. . . . Many of them were ill. All of them were worried, apprehensive. Their businesses had been destroyed, their homes looted. Many of them had already lost everything but their lives. . . . But individual tragedy was lost in the general disaster, and they were thankful to be still alive, to have their loved ones with them—those who had. That was all that mattered.[28]

The most direct and intentional maltreatment that the Japanese directed toward their civilian prisoners was not torture or execution—though the Japanese guards could be cruel, tough, and physically abusive. Rather, their true crime can be summed up by the phrase "intentional and willful neglect." After corralling the civilian internees into the confines of the Santo Tomas campus, the Japanese assumed no responsibility for their feeding, housing, sanitation, medical care, or child care. They had not prepared an organizational structure in advance for the internees. Therefore, the most urgent and immediate task for the internees was to form a civilian Central Committee to create order out of chaos. Within the first few days of confinement, the hastily formed Central Committee appointed numerous subcommittees and work teams to address such vital tasks as the procurement and preparation of food, dormitory organization, sanitation, medical care, an education system for children and teenagers, and any other aspect of communal living that would affect a camp that would grow to over seven thousand internees in the subsequent twenty-four months.

Without prior preparation, a four-story administration building, a three-story education building, and a gymnasium were soon transformed into crowded dormitories. The average living space per person varied between sixteen and twenty-two square feet. It was discovered that the entire university offered only

fourteen bathrooms for all the internees. Amid the long bathroom lines the common joke was "close your eyes if you want
privacy!"[29] The most coveted and hoarded possession was toilet
paper.

Husbands and wives were initially separated. All the men
were placed in the gymnasium and the three-story education
building. Boys over the age of twelve were quartered with the
men. Donal Rounds and Richard Myers were assigned to an up-
per story of the education building and placed in a room designated for teenage boys.[30] Donal described the boys' room:

> [Each small room] housed about thirty people. . . . Each
> person had a cot with slats or some had mattresses or
> canvas cots—whatever we could put together. Eventually
> every bed had a mosquito net. These came from Chinese
> traders who became quite a help to internees. Mosquitos
> were everywhere and such an annoyance. . . . Bedbugs
> were also present. . . . Each section with single boys or
> girls had a house person to keep order. Our [house father]
> was a Mr. Leek who had been head of the Boy Scouts in
> the Philippines.[31]

Soon, most healthy men and women were given a specific job by
the central committee; each teenager was also given an assignment. Donal Rounds was fortunate to be designated for kitchen
duty, serving as a runner to bring food to the dining tables or
food lines. At first food was meager but adequate for survival.
However, in the late months of the war, when food rations were
cut to starvation levels, Donal's job gave him access to extra
food.[32]

Donal's memories of kitchen duty were forever vivid: "I got
up with the light, then dressed in shorts and went to the kitchen
for my assigned job. . . . When the cooks gave the OK to start, the
runners carried very large pots with two handles—one runner on

each handle with equal distance between them. . . . Our imple-
ments for eating consisted of a tin can in which we put holes to
create handles of wire. These we carried all the time on our
belts along with a large spoon."[33]

The diet at Santo Tomas was meager, and it grew worse as
the war progressed. Donal recalled:

> Menus were mainly rice and corn; also talinom, which
> was a large green leaf; rarely chicken or pork, corn bread
> and hard tack out of wheat. Once and a while a truck load
> of left over fish was delivered and dropped on the con-
> crete. We picked them up in wheel barrows and took them
> to the kitchen and washed the load down. These were
> cooked whole but later ground including fish heads and
> tails—what a feast. My body weight had stayed the same
> for three years [during my internment] even though I had
> grown five inches. Adequate food was hard to come by.
> But when the [rare] Red Cross packages came, I traded
> my cigarettes for cans of Spam. These I saved under my
> bed, eating only a spoonful at a time. . . . We started a
> garden in the soccer field. We cultivated it with care until
> the Japanese saw how great it was and took over. We were
> forbidden to enter the area. . . . [34]

Within weeks, a school system was begun for children and teenagers. Attendance in school was required on every day except Sunday. Crowded for space, classrooms were often outside or in a
university laboratory. The teachers were drafted from among the
adults in the camp, and they formed an impressive and capable
faculty. Dodie Peters Borroughs was twelve years old and in the
sixth grade when she entered Santo Tomas. She later wrote:

> School was held for approximately 700 students and
> staged by qualified teachers and experts in the technical

field. Classroom space was limited as well as text books, which were one for every five students. . . . The Classes were fairly small and teachers had an easy time as far as discipline. Some of the teachers were Catholic Seminary fathers who lived at the Seminary next door. They were excellent teachers. We also had Internee professors, mining engineers, scholars and scientists to guide us through, and at the end of camp, everyone received a diploma. They did so much with so little![35]

Donal Rounds also remembered his school experience as excellent. As an adult he would write, "When we finished with the first meal of the day, it was time for school. We were very fortunate to have excellent teachers. One lady was a writer who taught English, another was an engineer for Pan Am and his job was teaching physics. It seems we had high quality and very professional professors for three years."[36]

In addition to school and required jobs, the children and teenagers participated in organized social and sports activities. Donal had grown up on Panay without contact with many children his age and was a late bloomer. Emerging into adolescence, he was strikingly handsome and soon had the girls flocking to him. Though conservative Baptist missionaries took a dim view of dancing, it was not long before he was cutting a rug at school dances and discovering that he loved it. He also relished playing poker by candlelight at night with a carefully preserved deck of cards, and using treasured cigarettes for antes. Most of all, he was discovering the allure of young women. Remembering one evening, he wrote, "Sexes were kept separate, so it was very difficult to 'make out.' One evening my girl friend and I decided to take a blanket into the football field and give it a try. But that was the night the Japanese were shooting anti-aircraft guns [into the sky for practice, and the spent shells were falling back] into the camp. Our rendezvous came to an abrupt halt." Young

Mr. Rounds was a long way from his missionary parents on Panay. And it was not all bad.[37]

Donal also joined a teenage touch football league. Awkward and new to competitive sports, he played offensive end. What he remembered most was: "Almost always I missed the ball, until one day my status elevated to hero when I caught the pass and ran for a touchdown." Donal was coming of age in the most unusual and dangerous surroundings, but life had not jolted to a halt. On the surface he maintained a smooth, calm veneer, but in unguarded moments anxiety would break loose and engulf him, however. What Donal Rounds and Richard Meyer uniquely lacked—and most of their interned teenage peers possessed— were parents there to support and protect them. More than their own welfare, however, they feared for their parents' safety.[38]

Two hundred and fifty nautical miles south of Manila, on Panay, the Roundses and the Meyers decided that they could not cope without further news concerning Donal and Richard. Dr. Meyer had a Filipino friend, Mr. Alcolentaba, whose life he had once saved when the man was badly burned in a gasoline explosion, leaving both of his hands crippled. Mr. Alcolentaba had accompanied the missionaries on their initial journey to Hopevale, and subsequently had helped many of Dr. Meyer's student nurses slip through Japanese lines and return to their homes, often by *banca* to nearby islands. Though crippled, he was an adventurer and a veteran guide, and had often traveled from Panay to Manila.

Frederick decided to talk with Alcolentaba to see if he would be willing to journey to Manila and seek information about Donal and Richard. Alcolentaba agreed to do so, refusing payment, and left on his mission on August 18, 1942. He disguised himself as a beggar, acted as if he had palsy, and used a hollow cane in which he inserted the money that Dr. Meyer and Erle Rounds were sending to their sons. Arriving in Manila, he soon discerned that the boys were interned in Santo Tomas University. Whether he was able to see the boys and talk with them personally is not clear. But what is known is that he successfully transferred the money to them, and confirmed that they were faring well under the circumstances.

As he returned home in October, Alcolentaba did not realize that the Japanese navy had blockaded Panay in an effort to curtail interisland guerrilla activity, and that they were not allowing *bancas* to approach. As he sailed with other Filipinos in a cluster of three *bancas* and drew near the northern shore of Panay, a Japanese destroyer suddenly appeared and raked them with machine-gun fire. Two of the *bancas* were ripped apart and the occupants killed. Only Alcolentaba's *banca* evaded the destroyer and landed safely.

Making his way overland to Hopevale, Alcolentaba arrived on October 20, 1942, to bring the Meyers and Roundses the hard-earned news that their sons were alive and doing well. The joy of the parents was exceeded only by Mr. Alcolentaba's loyalty and love for a doctor who had saved his life.[39]

The Fertig Brothers

Another family was anxious about missing members. Since the fall of Bataan, Claude and Wendell Fertig had heard nothing from each other. Each brother feared that the other was wounded, dead, or imprisoned. Though Wendell might suspect that Claude was on Panay, Claude had no idea that Wendell was alive and living on Mindanao.

Wendell's survival had indeed been remarkable. Escaping from Corregidor on one of the last two PBYs to leave for Australia, the two large flying boats headed to Mindanao, where they would be refueled before winging out over the Pacific for Darwin. The seaplanes landed on Lake Lanao in west-central Mindanao, and the passengers unloaded and bedded down for the night.

The next evening, as the planes were refueled and reloaded, one of the PBYs drifted onto a submerged rock in the darkness, and the thin fuselage was punctured in several places. Water poured in, and the craft taxied back to shore, signaling the waiting PBY to take off without them.

All night and the next day the men worked furiously to patch and repair the damage. Finally, after jury-rigging the gaping hole with a blanket and a wooden tray wedged between the stringers, the PBY was ready to attempt flight. However, the structurally weakened plane could only support the weight of half of the passengers. Women, the elderly, the sick, and high-priority officers were given preference, and the remaining passengers were told they would be picked up later by a B-17.

Wendell Fertig   *Kathy Fertig*

Not making the flight list, Wendell Fertig gave the pilot some staff studies to be delivered to MacArthur and scribbled a hasty letter to his wife, Mary, who was now living with their two daughters in Colorado. Knowing that his letter would be strictly censored, he wrote a cryptic salutation: "Dearest! Pineapples for breakfast!" He hoped that Mary would understand that he was writing near the pineapple plantation at Del Monte on Mindanao. Handing the letter to the navy pilot to mail in Australia, he was comforted that Mary would at least know that he was alive.

From the edge of Lake Lanao, Wendell watched the damaged PBY strain and lumber into the air, barely missing a looming mountaintop. Wendell sensed that his luck had at last run out. The promised B-17 never showed up, and he was stranded in Mindanao for the duration of the war.[40] Fertig was wrong, however, for his luck held fast.

When it was obvious that no more planes were coming to Lake Lanao from Australia, Wendell went into the hills and moved northwest, intent on forming an effective guerrilla force composed of abandoned American military personnel and fragmented Filipino guerrilla bands. He established his base of operations near the coastal town of Misamis in the province of Misamis Occidental, in northwestern Mindanao. This province was far from Japanese activity and had been largely ignored by their offensive operations.

As he settled in Misamis, he discovered that small Filipino guerrilla units already had formed within the province but that there were often political tensions between them. Fertig was soon able to unite them effectively behind his leadership and strengthen them through his organizational abilities. Within a short time he had become the dominant guerrilla leader in Mindanao.

What quickly became obvious about Fertig's character was that while he appeared easygoing and amiable, he was also aggressive in seeking command and did not hesitate to pull rank. Perhaps the one singular act that enabled Fertig's success, defined his personality, and aroused the most severe criticism was his self-promotion to brigadier general.

Fertig held the rank of lieutenant colonel when he was evacuated from Corregidor and transported to Mindanao. It did not take him long, however, to realize that all Americans with the rank of brigadier general and higher were in prison camps. Knowing the respect and fascination that many Filipinos had for rank, Fertig decided to commission himself as a brigadier general. He paid a local Moro silversmith to fashion silver stars for him, wore them proudly on his uniform, and decreed that he was the highest-ranking American officer still free. It proved a great public relations ploy to impress rank-and-file Filipinos and attract them to follow him. However, it irked the hell out of his fellow American officers. Nor did it escape the notice and the ire of

MacArthur. But until American forces returned, Fertig ran his own show and remained "General Fertig."[41]

With his self-proclaimed authority, Fertig issued a general order on October 1, 1942, announcing the activation of the United States Armed Forces in the Philippines (USAFIP), Mindanao-Visayas Command, with Brigadier General Wendell Fertig in charge. The order was circulated by word of mouth. Soon individuals and representatives of scattered resistance forces on Mindanao traveled to Misamis to confer with Fertig. When they arrived, they were impressed to see veteran soldiers training and drilling new guerrillas. They observed Filipino women busy in tailor shops making uniforms. Fertig gave them rides in a commandeered staff car, and he made sure they saw the two powerboats he had "borrowed" for coastal operations. Rural Filipinos, isolated Americans, and local politicians were awed by such effective organization and savvy.[42]

Slowly the size and credibility of Fertig's guerrilla movement grew. As MacArthur would later write in his published reports, "By perseverance and diplomacy Colonel Fertig gradually won the respect of the other guerrilla leaders [in Mindanao], and by October 1942 he had built up a fairly cohesive guerrilla organization."[43] In the ensuing months MacArthur would be impressed by Fertig's moxie and effectiveness and would designate Fertig "to command the Tenth Military District (Islands of Mindanao and Sulu)." By 1945, Colonel Fertig's command would total a troop strength of thirty-eight thousand men, the largest guerrilla force in the Philippines.

The rugged mountains of Central Panay and the coastal city of Misamis on Mindanao are only two hundred nautical miles apart. Yet the Fertig brothers were a world apart in terms of the conditions they faced. Mindanao was an island large enough for Wendell to evade a weak Japanese force for months. Panay was much smaller and confined. While Wendell Fertig ran his own show,

Claude Fertig was trying to find his place in a guerrilla movement that was primarily directed by competent and professional
Filipino officers. And while Wendell's wife and children were safe
in Colorado, Claude felt heavy responsibility for his young wife
and the small American community hiding in Hopevale.

Two brothers from rural Colorado never could have imagined that their lives would lead to such dramatic circumstances.
But in less than a year the world had turned upside down for mil-
lions of people around the globe. It was a time when dynamics
that made and shaped men and women, cultures and nations,
destroyed them as well.

As the final months of 1942 approached, there was much to
be thankful for in secluded Hopevale. Nearly a year of warfare
had passed and the residents of Hopevale had not experienced
serious illness, death, or significant lack of food or other essential
provisions. But with each passing day there was increasing fear
that their luck was being strained. Most significant, the Japanese ultimatum of a four-month time limit to surrender had
passed. The Hopevale community had made its decision: They
had chosen to live in freedom, a dangerous freedom, but freedom nonetheless.

Chapter Nine

November–December 1942

Nineteen forty-two had been filled with costly but crucial turning points for American and Allied forces around the world. In the Pacific, the strategic victory of the U.S. Navy at the Battle of the Coral Sea, May 4–8, 1942, had blunted the southernmost advance of the Japanese toward Australia. One month later, at the Battle of Midway, June 4–7, the U.S. Navy crushed a Japanese naval attack against Midway Atoll, destroying four Japanese aircraft carriers and a heavy cruiser. This battle critically weakened Japanese naval aviation due to their loss of over two hundred veteran pilots. After Midway, Allied forces in the Pacific moved from a defensive stance to a rapidly escalating offensive operation.

On August 7, 1942, the U.S. Marines assaulted the Japanese-occupied Solomon Islands, twelve hundred miles northeast of Australia. From August 7, 1942, through February 7, 1943, one of the most savage land and naval campaigns raged, ultimately leaving Japanese infantry forces defeated and beginning a slow northern retreat toward Japan. Simultaneously, American and Australian forces waged a grueling offensive in New Guinea that would still be sputtering when Japan surrendered three years later. Slowly, American forces edged closer to the Philippines.

On the other side of the world, the British Eighth Army in Egypt stubbornly held back Field Marshal Erwin Rommel's Afrika Korps from capturing the Suez Canal while American troops invaded northwest Africa, starting Operation Torch. The result was that Rommel was wedged between the British in Egypt and Libya and the Americans advancing from the west across Morocco, Algeria, and Tunisia. German forces were squeezed out of North Africa, allowing an Allied invasion into Europe through Italy in 1943.

In the Soviet Union, Russian troops finally stopped Hitler's relentless eastern advance at the siege of Stalingrad and successfully counterattacked in November 1942. Hitler's overextended army retreated until Russian troops captured Berlin in 1945.

In hindsight, the worldwide events in the final eight months of 1942 formed the turning point for the Allied victory in World War II. But from the darkness of the jungle on Panay and other Philippine islands, there was no awareness of an emerging Allied victory. The only news from the outside world came from snatches of information filtering through the jury-rigged radios of guerrilla units. Amid the global silence they watched as the Japanese continued to land more troops on the major islands in the archipelago, strengthening and consolidating their hold on the Philippines. For most Americans there, hope dwindled and faded as 1942 drew to a close.

Yet even in the Philippines, fortunes were beginning to turn. On Panay, Lieutenant Colonel Macario Peralta, a dynamic and aggressive career officer in the Philippine army, refused to obey orders and surrender. Instead, he retreated into the rugged interior of Panay and rapidly unified and reorganized remnants of

the surrendered Sixty-first Division and other fragments of local guerrilla resistance. Peralta established three guerrilla regi-
ments under his unified command: the Sixty-third Regiment in
Iloilo province, the Sixty-fourth Regiment in Capiz province, and
the Sixty-fifth Regiment in Antique province. Having effectively
stockpiled large amounts of salvaged American supplies and
weapons before Japanese troops could secure the island, Peralta's
emerging guerrilla force was well equipped to wage war. Within
ten weeks of the surrender, Peralta had solidified command of
the resistance movement on Panay. Such rapid unification was
rare among guerrilla movements, and it resulted in an unusually
potent and effective resistance to the Japanese occupation of
Panay.[1]

A top priority for Peralta was to establish contact with Mac-
Arthur in Australia for the purpose of future resupply and moral
support. He was determined to construct a radio station capable
of reaching Australia.[2] Upon assessing the communications resources on Panay, he contacted Mariano Tolentino, who before
the war was the chief radio operator and head of the Bureau of
Posts radio station in Iloilo. As the Japanese approached Panay,
Tolentino stripped his station of a radio transmitter, three re-
ceivers, spare parts, gasoline, oil, batteries, and wiring and hid
them away. Now he donated these supplies to Peralta's guerrillas. Accompanied by fourteen former employees of the radio
station, Tolentino joined the guerrillas and reported to Peralta
at his headquarters in Sara, a small municipality thirty miles due
east of Hopevale. On October 18, 1942, Tolentino's crew secretly
reassembled the radio station at a remote waterworks reservoir
outside Sara. However, Tolentino's transmitter proved too weak
to reach Australia.[3]

Fortunately, a British freighter abandoned in Iloilo harbor
had a marine radio transmitter, which was taken by guerrillas
and brought to Sara. Soon Tolentino's station WPM—Radio
Free Panay—was receiving signals from KFS, a radio station in

San Francisco, California. On October 30, 1942, WPM attempted to contact KFS across thousands of miles of Pacific Ocean. Staff Sergeant Tolentino recounts, "At 9:00 p.m., we began the transmission of the 950 word message to General MacArthur and . . . a 650 words radiogram to President Quezon."[4] Colonel Peralta's message to MacArthur read:

> We wish to report on the reorganization of the Visayas free Forces into the IV Philippine Corps. . . . Panay Island is fully reorganized into the Sixty First Division. Total men now on active service about eight thousand. Japanese occupation troops in this island have been limited to provincial capitals. . . . Badly need arms and ammunition caliber thirty. This is a matter of life and death with us. In Panay we control the interior in general and most of the coastline. . . . Civilians and officials ninety percent loyal. . . . Please relay this message to President Quezon, MacArthur, and General Valdez. . . . Later messages will be short to avoid possible enemy goniometric detection.[5]

Not having current code books, this message was sent "in clear" (not in code), a dangerous but unavoidable risk. Station KFS in San Francisco received Peralta's message and relayed it to radio station KAZ in Darwin, Australia.

After receiving the message, MacArthur's signal corps was faced with a dilemma. Because Peralta's message had been sent in clear, it was not known whether this was an authentic message from Peralta or a Japanese attempt to infiltrate American intelligence. On November 5, 1942, KFS replied to Peralta in clear, "Your message to General MacArthur has been received and forwarded to him in his GHQ in Australia. . . . Do you have any code or cipher system query?" Peralta replied that all code books had been destroyed before the surrender.[6]

Several tense weeks passed with no further contact from

KFS. Then a cryptic in clear message was received from KFS, forwarding a transmission from the War Department: "Break the coded message using as key word in combination cipher device M-94 followed by double transposition the name of place where President Quezon and Governor Confesor [the prewar governor of Panay] last dined together?"[7]

Peralta and his staff were stumped. Even Governor Tomas Confesor, now gravely ill, was not sure where he had last dined with President Quezon. Finally, after several weeks of intense search, Lieutenant Anicio Ykalina learned of the quest for the answer to the cryptic question and reported that he had been present at Quezon and Confesor's last meeting, and it was at Panubigan on Negros Island. Quickly the word "Panubigan" was inserted as the key word into the cipher, or decoding device, as instructed. Everything clicked. The enigma was solved. A decoded message emerged: "Can you rendezvous a submarine query if so give five places in order of preference. War Department." This succinct sentence not only solidified communication with MacArthur, but also instantly established a priority for operations on Panay. Submarine rendezvous points had to be established to enable support and resupply of guerrilla war matériel.[8]

Peralta's guerrillas became the first resistance force in the Philippines to establish two-way contact with MacArthur. Soon Major Ralph B. Praeger, in northern Luzon, and Lieutenant Colonel Wendell Fertig, on Mindanao, were also able to have two-way communication with MacArthur's headquarters. The long silence was lifted and contact with distant Allied forces encouraged isolated guerrilla forces in the Philippines.[9]

As Peralta turned his attention to developing the first submarine rendezvous point, he sought out Major Claude Fertig, who had been secluded with his wife on remote Mount Igabon since the formal surrender of American troops. Peralta directed Fertig to become district engineer officer of the guerrilla organization on

Panay. His first assignment was to work with Major Cirilo Garcia, the director of planning and operations. Shortly thereafter, Claude would be given the critical assignment of assisting in the development of the submarine rendezvous point MacArthur had requested, and specifically of constructing a radio station near the landing zone. This operation was top secret and was not shared with other ranking officers.[10] Fertig accepted Peralta's order and prepared to leave Mount Igabon.

Unknown to the Fertigs, the Spencers in Hopevale had decided it was time to contact the Fertigs. Normally relaxed and confident, Spence had become anxious about Claude and Laverne's safety as days, and then weeks, passed with no communication. Finally, Spence decided to hike to Mount Igabon and locate the Fertigs. After a long and difficult trek, Spence found the Fertigs in good health, but was surprised to discover that they were preparing to return to Hopevale. Responding to Peralta's summons, Claude had decided that until he could complete his assignments for the submarine landing point on the northwest coast, it would be safest to leave Laverne temporarily at Hopevale. Spence helped Claude pack much of the canned food that was left from the prewar army cache, and then they set out for the foothills, reaching Hopevale just as the first storms of the rainy season descended. Arriving on November 4, 1942, they were greeted warmly by miners and missionaries alike.

Waiting only a few days, Claude departed from Hopevale on a thirty-mile hike due east, to Lieutenant Colonel Peralta's headquarters at Sara, entrusting Laverne to Spence's care in Hopevale. Traveling across open country was risky, but most Japanese forces were still garrisoned on the coast or in large towns. This false sense of safety would soon change.

As Laverne Fertig moved in with the Spencers and settled back into a more communal life in Hopevale, she was glad to see that Dr. Meyer was still healthy and active; he was usually seen walking about in shorts and a large, floppy straw hat. Frederick particularly loved to slip away occasionally and go to the Ford camp, which was a one-and-a-half hour raft trip down the lush Panay River, over twelve picturesque rapids. Mr. and Mrs. Thomas J. Ford were wealthy owners of the large Asturias Sugar Central company, which had had locations at San Juan, Dumalag, and Capiz. Mr. Ford was an American who had married Maria Garcia, a Filipina mestiza.[11] Prior to the war they had constructed a secluded but comfortable retreat center named Casa Blanca that paralleled the Panay River. When the Japanese attacked, the Fords turned their retreat center into an emergency hideaway, and it was amply stocked with food and supplies provided by their scattered farming enterprises and *bodegas,* or storage facilities.[12] Their accommodations were comfortable, including beds with mattresses and food served on china. Of most importance to Dr. Meyer, the Fords had a battery-powered radio able to receive news from beyond the Philippines. Dr. Meyer would float down the river to the Fords, enjoy their hospitality, and return to Hopevale eager to share any news he had obtained. The trips helped him regain perspective and escape the claustrophobia of camp.[13]

Frederick also occasionally walked the two and a half miles to Katipunan to see an old friend, Reverend Tomas Conejar, who was the Filipino pastor of the Baptist church in Capiz. Conejar had also retreated to Katipunan, and he had agreed to hide some of the Meyers' personal possessions in his temporary home. These trips always carried risk, as Japanese scouting parties were drawing closer to Katipunan. However, risk was now a way of life, and Frederick cautiously took his chances. While visiting Reverend Conejar, Frederick would inspect the locked trunk that held his prized stamp collection, a hobby that had provided pleasure for years. Frederick sadly noted that humidity and mildew were causing his collection to deteriorate.[14]

Ruth Meyer also stayed busy, by giving weekly voice lessons to Frances Rose, James Covell, and anyone else who was interested. However, she was hampered by serious dental problems. When her pain grew unbearable, Frederick and Ruth risked a hike to a nearby guerrilla base at Igi, where there was a medical team with a dentist. The paths up the jungle slopes were so steep and muddy that Ruth often had to crawl on her hands and knees. But the dentist was able to relieve her suffering temporarily.[15]

Though Dr. Meyer turned down a commission as a major, and declined to assume active duty with the guerrilla medical units, he did offer his medical services as a civilian. Frequently he gave assistance to both Filipino civilians and guerrillas. Scribbling on a rare piece of paper, he wrote, "My hospital personnel is scattered, a few bed patients however scattered in different hill clinics with plenty of consultations, long hikes, keep us thin but happy to be of service even though surrounded by hostile forces."[16]

Mrs. Rose wrote about Dr. Meyer, and about his nurse, Jennie Adams: "Our doctor and nurse have done a wonderful piece of work in this region watching out for the health of all in our camp, and in addition attending to the sick and injured of all nationalities in outlying camps and districts. They deserve a medal of honor."[17]

However, Dr. Meyer was losing weight and aging noticeably. The stress of long years in the tropics coupled with the trauma of the war was taking its toll. Frederick was now fifty, but he looked much older.

One thing that elevated spirits, however, was a determination among all in Hopevale to celebrate special occasions. Birthdays and anniversaries never went unnoticed. In this spirit the first Thanksgiving at Hopevale was approached with great anticipation and preparation.

Laverne Fertig was assigned to create a festive atmosphere for the 1942 Thanksgiving banquet. She pulled together mismatched tables from each hut, covered them with green banana leaves, and highlighted them with fruit centerpieces. Then, with meticulous planning, a large turkey had been obtained and guarded zealously for weeks. The old gobbler had been fattened and primed for the seasonal sacrifice. When the grand moment came, the turkey was roasted on a spit over an outside fire. The last of the carefully hoarded canned goods were contributed to the feast by all Hopevale residents. The turkey was stuffed with rice mixed with a can of traditional stuffing that Laura Schuring had saved. Giblet dressing was created using native saba flour. Native *camotes*, or yams, were transformed into sweet potato casserole. Canned peas, carrots, and even cranberry sauce were opened, and a jar of bottled pickles magically appeared. Finally, a concoction similar to Indian pudding was created for dessert, using dates, nuts, and canned cream that the Roses had brought into the hills. The sumptuous meal was finished off with coffee that was ground from native beans.[18]

The dinner was a splurge, a moment to cast off care and open the gates to the savored past. In this spirit, two bottles of wine, donated by the Ford camp, were chilled in the streambed for after-dinner toasts and enjoyment. The missionaries did not drink alcohol. However, the Roses loaned the miners their special communion chalices for the toasts, telling Louise Spencer that "wine from our terrible old tin cups would be unthinkable."[19] The Thanksgiving celebration ended with the singing of "Praise God from Whom All Blessings Flow" and a hearty but off-key rendition of "God Bless America."

Miners and missionaries had come together as a family. Though at times an odd and diverse assortment of individuals, they had found that they shared far more in common than they had differences. The communion chalices served as a powerful symbol of their growing unity. Louise Spencer fondly wrote, "The missionaries and the miners were poles apart in many respects, but both groups were intensely interested in each other. . . . I think we found the missionaries much more broad-minded than we expected, and perhaps they found us better Christians than they expected, I don't know."[20]

With the ending of Thanksgiving, the deluge of the rainy season and violent typhoons swept into Hopevale. Such continuous rain often triggers depression. The sky is dark, clothes stay wet, humidity is inescapable, mildew is everywhere, and mud is the color of life. The typhoons are life-threatening. Hurricane winds, flash floods, falling trees, and landslides abound. The Thanksgiving feast was the last bright spot before they descended into a season of darkness.

While the residents of Hopevale made their way through the month of November and celebrated Thanksgiving, they were unaware that military conditions were rapidly changing thirty miles south of them in Iloilo. As the rainy season began, Japanese military activity rapidly accelerated. Until November 1942, the Japanese had concentrated their troops primarily in Panay's provincial capitals and a few other essential outposts, sending out occasional combat patrols into the province to inspect their perimeters of operation.[21] However, on November 10, 1942, the Japanese began their first aggressive, battalion-size offensive, fanning out of Iloilo City and spreading in a north and northeastern direction.[22] The objective was to destroy guerrilla units operating in the southern and central regions of Iloilo province and to intimidate and punish the civilian population that supported them.

The Japanese in Iloilo province had a troop strength of an estimated fourteen hundred combat soldiers. The guerrillas greatly outnumbered them. However, the Japanese dominated the guerrillas in firepower, transportation, and air support. As the Japanese moved into the countryside, they brought with them light and heavy machine guns, light and heavy mortars, and ample field artillery. They also used bombers based out of Mandurriao landing field near Iloilo City for reconnaissance and bombardment. For transport the Japanese had trucks for rapid troop movement, and where the topography was suitable, they could support these troops with tanks and armored vehicles. Most important, their ability to resupply and reinforce their offensive was excellent.[23]

Though the guerrillas put up a spirited defense, inflicting many Japanese casualties, they were forced to remain mobile and to fall back toward central Panay and the foothills of the Cordillera, a mountain range along the island's west coast. By the end of November the Japanese army had gained control of the southern half of Iloilo province, and was simultaneously pushing due north toward Hopevale and northeast toward Peralta's headquarters at Sara.[24]

At this critical time Claude Fertig left Peralta's headquarters and made a rapid thirty-mile hike back to Hopevale to check on Laverne. Arriving on December 2, he brought with him an assortment of early Christmas gifts, which he had scavenged from the guerrilla camps and supply depots. Unloading his pack, he produced a demijohn of local Sara rum, two bottles of crème de menthe, Manila cigarettes, a bottle of Spanish olives, notebooks, and a precious new stock of matches. He delighted Louise Spencer with the gift of a much needed new pair of shoes. But most of all he brought the incredibly wonderful news that his brother, Wendell, had escaped from Bataan and was alive and well in Mindanao.

Claude had just been told this news by Colonel Peralta, who had received a letter by courier from Mindanao informing him that a Wendell Fertig had successfully attacked the Japanese garrison in Zamboanga City, and had assumed command of the majority of guerrilla forces on Mindanao. Now Peralta and Wendell Fertig would be working collaboratively in the guerrilla efforts in the central and southern regions of the Philippines.

Claude quickly wrote a return message to Wendell and sent

it by Peralta's courier, informing Wendell of their activities on Panay. Now, for the first time in eleven months, the Fertig brothers were united in the knowledge and spirit of each other. There was a sense of marvel that two brothers from rural Colorado both had become guerrilla leaders in war-torn islands thousands of miles from home. These glad tidings during the Christmas season of 1942 would never be forgotten by either brother.[25]

While Claude was in Hopevale, he talked with Spence and urged him to officially join the guerrillas and assist Claude with special projects. On December 5, Claude and Spence left Hopevale to return to Sara, not knowing how long they would be away. Claude directed Laverne to evacuate immediately to Peralta's headquarters if the Japanese continued to move closer to Hopevale. Knowing that they would likely miss Christmas with their wives, glum good-byes were said, and Claude and Spence trudged back to Sara. Peralta soon commissioned Spence as a captain and ordered him to accompany Claude on his assignment to assist in establishing a submarine landing zone.[26]

Hiking over difficult and mountainous terrain, Claude and Spence were to proceed approximately sixty miles to the extreme northwest corner of Panay, a region known as the island's "panhandle." The panhandle was a large spur of land that jutted out into the western Sulu Sea, was sparsely populated, had little Japanese presence, and could be accessed by only one poorly maintained highway that could be easily defended from motorized Japanese attack. The terrain was characterized by high mountains and broad rivers cascading down to the sea. This wild coastline offered deep, sheltered coves that were perfect for a secret submarine rendezvous and also provided adequate room for a submarine to maneuver if attacked. Upon selecting a suitable site, Claude and Spence were to set up a radio station capable of communicating with submarines, Australia, and Peralta's mobile headquarters. While they worked, a defensive perimeter

would be provided by two guerrilla rifle companies. The submarine rendezvous point was code named HUBAG.[27]

Accompanied by Filipino guides and *cargadores* (baggage
carriers), they left Peralta's headquarters in Sara and disappeared into the Western Cordillera, heading toward the panhandle. They faced formidable terrain that had to be crossed
entirely by foot. This was no Boy Scout hike. They forded turbu-
lent rivers, which had been swollen and made dangerous by torrential monsoon rains. They clambered up steep volcanic ridges,
inched along dizzying cliffside paths, and crossed the heights of
the Western Cordillera, which were fifteen miles wide at the center. Though the Japanese had not infiltrated these remote inland
areas to any significant extent, dangers from falling, snakebite,
and disease were abundant. Despite these difficulties, Claude
and Spence were happy to be engaged in an important project
and no longer idle. They sensed that they were regaining control
of their destiny. Their biggest problem was that they could not
tell Louise and Laverne that they had departed from Sara and
were on a secret mission. How long they would be gone was unknown.

While Claude and Spence hiked northward, Japanese planes
bombed Calinog on December 8, approximately ten miles south
of Hopevale on the national highway. Significantly, this was the
one-year anniversary of the Japanese bombing of Clark Air Base
and Manila. Clearly able to hear the bombing in Hopevale, Ruth
Meyer scribbled in her diary, "When will we have peace? . . .
Many bombs were heard near Calinog, with danger near."[28]

As the bombing increased, so did the constant monsoon
rains, hampering the Japanese offensive. However, by December
11, Calinog was occupied by the Japanese, who transformed it
into a strong infantry outpost and a staging ground for further
advance. Now Japanese troops would be based within a day's
march of Hopevale.[29]

At the same time that Calinog was captured, the Japanese drove northeast toward Peralta's guerrilla headquarters at Sara, thirty miles east of Hopevale. Though the guerrillas made hit-and-run attacks on the Japanese, inflicting over 176 verified deaths, Sara was soon in danger, and Peralta retreated on December 23, 1942, moving his headquarters to the west.[30] Reaching the safety of the same mountain range and foothills that sheltered Hopevale, Peralta estabished his new headquarters in the barrio of Daan Norte, near the town of Tapaz in Capiz province. Daan Norte is less than ten miles northwest of Hopevale. Peralta would keep his headquarters at Daan Norte until the final weeks of 1943.[31] As Christmas of 1942 approached, Hopevale was caught between Japanese troops ten miles to the south in Calinog and Peralta's guerrilla forces camped less than ten miles to the northwest.

In Hopevale, the holiday season did not bring good cheer. Louise and Laverne were depressed and worried as Christmas neared with no news from their husbands. Not knowing that Claude and Spence had been sent on a secret mission to the northwest coast, their wives assumed they were with Peralta's retreating troops, somewhere between Sara and Daan Norte.[32] From December 8 through December 20, the women watched each day as Japanese bombers flew over Hopevale supporting Japanese troops driving to encircle Peralta. Growing desperate, they asked Laverne's house servant, Solomon, if he would make his way to Peralta's headquarters and inquire about Claude and Spence. Solomon replied with a smile and began his journey.

The missionaries' stoic faith was jarred by the nearby bombing. Jennie Adams coped by scribbling rough poetry in her notebook:

> *Planes, planes,*
> *Enemy planes*
> *Incessantly droning over my head*

> *Soaring planes,*
> *Roaring planes,*
> *Distressingly filling my senses with dread*
> *Expressing a warning to small and to great,*
> *Queerly, but clearly,*
> *"Annihilate."*[33]

Ruth Meyer's terse entries in her diary during December also reveal frustration:

> Everything is mildewed; doctor bitten by scorpion . . . I also found a scorpion in the greens, well cooked. . . . Rain, plenty of it, clothes will not dry; takes five days in weather like this to dry clothes in the forest. Centipede in my sewing bag. . . . Bombers over us every day this week on a mission of destruction. . . . Rain all day. Played anagrams after supper. Usual pastime of Doctor, Jennie and myself.[34]

Losing herself in books or naps, Ruth tried to shut out the deluge and not worry about her children. She knew that her oldest son, Buddy, should have completed his studies at Yale and was probably in medical school. Milton was a sophomore at Yale, while Dick remained a prisoner at the Santo Tomas internment camp in Manila. How each of her sons would spend this Christmas, she did not know. But the pain of separation from her children—and fear for Dick's safety—would not subside.

Money and food were also becoming a problem in Hopevale. The Americans depended on Mr. Rio and Reverend Dianala in Katipunan to acquire food in local markets and quietly transport it to Hopevale. They also supplied a limited guard system to give early warning if Japanese search patrols approached. A modest salary was provided by the missionaries and miners, but money was not these good men's motivation for service. No amount of money could compensate for the risk that the Filipinos aiding the Americans were taking. If caught, they and their families would be butchered and their homes and barrios burned. Nothing but love and fierce loyalty could have engendered their fidelity. It was compassion that trumped self-preservation.

As Christmas approached, funds ran dangerously low. The missionaries were flat broke, and the miners had been helping them from their meager cash reserves for several weeks.[35] Finally, the money nearly ran out. Calling a meeting with Mr. Rio and Reverend Dianala, the Americans explained that they could no longer pay their salaries and must discontinue their services. Both Filipino men understood better than their American friends that the Americans could not survive without their help. Rio and Dianala insisted they would continue to support their fellow Christians on a volunteer basis. No greater symbol of the Christmas spirit could have come to Hopevale.[36]

On Christmas Day the Fords invited all twenty-three of the missionaries, miners, and children at Hopevale to float down the Panay River and spend Christmas at their hideaway. The miners accepted the invitation, and the Fords sent outriggers for them. The missionaries, however, chose to gather at the Roundses' nipa hut in Hopevale for Christmas dinner and invited many of their Filipino friends from Katipunan to join them. It was a time for the missionaries to draw their Baptist family together, to remember their purpose for being in the Philippines, and to deepen their spiritual unity with their Filipino brothers and sisters.

Before the miners left for the Fords' camp, Christmas gifts were exchanged among the residents of Hopevale. For weeks, missionaries and miners had made the simplest but most meaningful gifts for one another from tatters of cloth, strands of wire, carved wood, or whatever else was at hand. There was no extravagance, but also no lack of thought and love. Few gifts were ever more meaningful than these.

As New Year's Eve closed the chaotic year of 1942, Louise Spencer sat in dim lantern light and gazed at the yellow-pad calendar she had made in her home on Masbate before escaping to Panay. Each day of every month in 1942 had now been boldly crossed out. Spence's confident words echoed in her memories: "You won't need that thing for a full year!" But 1942 had come and gone, and no end to the war was in sight. As midnight approached, Louise listened to the pelting rain and gazed through tears as water leaked through the thatch roof and dribbled through the slats of the damp bamboo floor. She was terribly alone without Spence. Refusing to think that he could be anything but alive, she picked up her tattered calendar and tossed it into the small kitchen fire. Thoughtfully, she unwrapped the aged newspaper that held her new 1943 calendar, which twelve-year-old Clifford Schuring had made her for Christmas. She clutched it to her chest, wondering what the next twelve months would bring.

Chapter Ten

January–March 1943,
from Hopevale to Bunglay

As 1943 began, Lieutenant Colonel Peralta was adapting to new orders from General MacArthur that reshaped his guerrilla strategy. On December 18, 1942, MacArthur sent a firm directive to all guerrilla commanders in the Philippines. To Peralta, the general wrote:

> For Peralta. Your action in reorganizing Philippine army units is deserving of the highest commendation and has aroused high enthusiasm among all of us here. You will continue to exercise the command. Your primary mission is to maintain your organization and secure maximum amount of information. Offensive guerilla activity should be postponed until ordered from here. Premature action of this kind will only bring heavy retaliation upon innocent people. As our intelligence unit covering maximum territory you can perform great services. . . . We cannot predict date of our return to the Philippines but we are coming. MacArthur[1]

MacArthur clearly wanted all guerrilla units in the Philippines to cease offensive action against a superior Japanese force. Instead, guerrilla forces were primarily to gather critical intelligence information and build an infrastructure to undergird the future American invasion of the Philippines. The Filipinos coined this strategy the "lie low policy."

At the same time that Peralta received his new orders, the Japanese were reinforcing and enlarging their troop strength on Panay. At the end of 1942, Peralta's intelligence reports estimated that there were 1,500 Japanese troops on Panay to police a population of approximately 1.4 million Filipinos and a growing guerrilla force exceeding 8,000 men. However, between January 6 and 8, 1943, 2,000 additional Japanese soldiers landed at Iloilo, more than doubling their strength, to 3,500 infantrymen.[2]

With these additional troops, the Japanese decided to seize control of the rice-growing sections of Panay, thus denying adequate food to the guerrilla units and their families. Because January is a prime rice-harvest month, Peralta immediately ordered his guerrillas to prepare hidden food caches in the mountains and to acquire as much rice as possible during the first weeks of 1943.[3] Though successful in obtaining temporary rice reserves, the guerrillas were not able to stop the Japanese from occupying most of the towns in the traditional rice-growing regions across the entire island.[4]

While Peralta was adjusting to his new strategy in December and January, Claude and Spence successfully reached the remote Aklan region of Capiz province and began to build a radio station and prepare suitable submarine rendezvous points.[5] Developing the submarine rendezvous points was not difficult. It required locating acceptable sites along Pandan Bay on the northwest coast of Panay that met certain specific criteria. Landing zones needed to have deep water close to the shoreline. The

beach area must be able to be secured by guerrilla rifle companies; transportation must be available to remove the submarine
cargo inland; and a primitive visual signaling system had to be
erected to let the submarine crews know that it was safe to surface at the landing site.

Building a radio station was more difficult. Until submarines
could transport portable and powerful radio equipment to Panay
from Australia, Claude and Spence would have to piece one together from dated parts and equipment that had been scavenged
from all over Panay. The radio station had to be secluded and
placed at a high elevation for adequate reception and security.
An antenna had to be erected that could not be spotted by Japanese air and land reconnaissance. To meet these requirements,
the radio station was located inland, several hours away from
Pandan Bay and closer to the northern coast of Panay.

Working rapidly, Claude and Spence completed work on the
radio station in a few weeks, and it was officially designated
HUBAG. On December 30, 1942, Lieutenant Colonel Peralta
sent his first radio message from his headquarters in Daan
Norte to HUBAG: "For Major Fertig—Are you ready? For Major
Garcia—Stand by radio and report enemy situation everyday."[6]
With the successful reception of Peralta's orders, the most difficult part of Claude Fertig's assignment was completed. Now he
and Spence must monitor the airwaves and help Peralta plan for
the first American submarine to land on Panay.

Back in Hopevale, the new year brought escalating danger. Laverne and Louise had still not heard from Spence and Claude.
Finally, on January 4, Solomon trudged in from Daan Norte to
report that though he had not seen their husbands, he was assured by guerrilla headquarters that they were safe. Proudly he
presented them with two letters and a package from Claude and
Spence, delayed mail that should have been delivered by military

courier long before Christmas. In the letters the men explained that they were on a secret mission that required at least a month's absence. Though they gave no insight into their mission or where they were located, Claude again explicitly instructed Laverne to move to the guerrilla camp in Daan Norte should the Japanese advance closer to Hopevale. Opening the package, the women discovered their belated Christmas presents, bars of soap and talcum powder, simple gifts that would have seemed insignificant a year earlier but now were gifts from the gods. However, gifts did not compare to the good news that Claude and Spence were alive.[7]

Hopevale continued to be deluged by rain. Dr. and Mrs. Meyer and Jennie Adams were isolated in their huts at Emmanuel Glenn, a kilometer upstream from Hopevale. Though Frederick and Jennie were nimble enough to plow through the mud and navigate the swollen streambed, Ruth was trapped there for weeks. Frederick visited patients and coped with his restlessness through his medical practice. However, rumors were flying that the Japanese were closing in on Hopevale. With Peralta's main guerrilla base now only ten miles northwest of them, the Japanese were approaching from the south and the east.[8]

On January 18, Ruth Meyer counted as thirty-two bombs exploded northeast of Hopevale, probably on guerrilla positions near Daan Norte. Laverne and Louise immediately packed to be ready to retreat north to Peralta's headquarters at Daan Norte. Late on the night of January 19, Solomon burst into the women's bedroom, wild-eyed and stuttering that the Japanese were at Katipunan, only forty minutes away. However, Solomon's news proved false. Reverend Dianala immediately increased the guard service and waited. On January 22, he and Mr. Rio rushed to Hopevale and insisted that all missionaries and miners immediately evacuate or hide out in the forest.[9] They, too, were now convinced that the Japanese were advancing close by, and that their discovery of Hopevale was imminent.

Louise, Laverne, the Schurings, and Ben Zimmerman quickly evacuated on jungle paths leading north toward Daan Norte. The missionaries chose to hide in dugout shelters called *camaligs* that they had prepared in the jungle only a few hundred yards beyond Hopevale. Any determined enemy patrol would likely discover the nearby *camaligs*, and the miners had objected strongly to the missionaries' escape plan. However, the older missionaries, as well as the Clardys' and Roundses' young children, would have had trouble walking rapidly along long and difficult escape routes through the woods and jungle. Louise Spencer— and perhaps other miners—felt that the missionaries held onto the hope that if captured, the Japanese would place them in a prisoner-of-war camp, given their religious profession and humanitarian work. Thus, for multiple reasons, the missionaries chose to hide in their *camaligs* rather than evacuate, even if the risk of discovery was high.[10]

For four miserable days the Meyers and the other missionaries hunkered down in their scattered *camaligs*. Primitive in design, these subterranean dugouts looked like small World War I bomb shelters. The roofs were flush to the ground and constructed of logs camouflaged by earth and foliage. The muddy floors were covered by logs or bamboo slats and softened by matting. With the incessant rain, the log roofs leaked and the wood-slatted floors oozed pungent mud. These quarters were dank and claustrophobic. Ruth Meyer scribbled in her diary, "With little to eat, and logs [floors] hard to sleep on . . . back aches plenty."[11]

After four days, the missionaries returned to Hopevale. Yet, over the next few weeks, Japanese patrols were often glimpsed on hilltops nearby. On February 10, 1943, the missionaries returned to their *camaligs* for eight days. Then again from February 22 to 25. For the missionaries the first two months of 1943 were horrendous due to this constant hiding and terror.

In the darkness of her *camalig*, Jennie Adams naturally feared betrayal by someone among the hundreds of Filipinos

who were aware of the Americans in Hopevale. By candlelight
she scribbled in her poetry notebook:

> *I am weary of war and its worries*
> *The life in a forest wild,*
> *The haunts of a lonely hermit,*
> *A captive too long exiled,*
> *Ever ready to flee still farther*
> *When the warning cry is heard—*
> *Whether that cry be official*
> *Or proves but a rumored word—*
> *The vigilance ever required*
> *When enemy troops grow bold,*
> *Or when thieves begin molesting,*
> *Or the termites, mildew and mold.*
>
> *I am weary of war and hatreds,*
> *When a friend may become a foe;*
> *A nation, a neighbor, or brother*
> *Into a traitor may grow.*
> *Need presses hard upon people,*
> *One grasps from another's pain;*
> *Out of some poor man's misery*
> *A neighbor grows greedy for gain. . . .* [12]

It was, indeed, a miracle that someone did not inform the
Japanese of the Americans at Hopevale. And though the Japanese visited Katipunan on several occasions in the early weeks
of 1943, they never stumbled upon the hideaway.[13] The missionaries were beating long odds.

Meanwhile, the miners hiked rapidly toward Daan Norte. They
spent the night at a guerrilla hospital center in the barrio of Igi,

sleeping in one large infirmary room with over forty Filipino guerrillas recovering from wounds, surgery, and tropical diseases such as malaria. The next day, January 23, Louise was stunned and elated when Spence wandered into camp. She had not seen him since the fifth of December. Though overjoyed to see Louise, Spence was desperately looking for medical care for his bare feet, which had been cut and ulcerated from walking miles on mountain trails without shoes. His infection would soon be serious.

While lying down in the medical clinic and having his feet washed and bandaged, Spence explained that while on their secret mission, he and Claude had learned of the danger in Hopevale. Spence immediately left Claude to find Laverne and Louise and bring them back to the radio station. Over the next six weeks, he had walked more than two hundred miles, mostly barefooted. He mistakenly went first to Sara, only to discover that Peralta had evacuated inland to Daan Norte. Then he hiked toward Hopevale but found the region crawling with Japanese soldiers. Nearing Hopevale, he heard rumors that Louise and Laverne were on their way to Daan Norte. He then followed their trail, reaching the guerrilla hospital camp in Igi only hours after the women arrived.

Spence was a seriously ill man. In addition to his infected feet, he also had amoebic dysentery, and was weak, dehydrated, and feverish. Though desperate to spend time with Louise, he insisted that Laverne and Louise hike on to Daan Norte while he remained at the infirmary in Igi to rest and receive treatment.

The next day the women, Ben Zimmerman, Solomon, and six Filipino *cargadores* left for Daan Norte. Reaching the Panay River two days later, they met the leading elder, or *teniente*, of that region fleeing with his wife from the direction of Daan Norte. He vehemently insisted that the Japanese were between them and Daan Norte and that they must not proceed farther or else be captured. Though the information later proved to be false, the *teniente* obviously believed his report and was convincing. Laverne insisted that they change direction, forget Daan Norte, and hike to the Fertigs' old hideout on Mount Igabon. There was still canned food stashed away, and it would be safe from the Japanese. So, unable to inform Spence of their sudden change of plans, the women and their party set out for Mount Igabon in the Baloy district, a tough six-day hike.

Arriving exhausted at the Fertig hideout on January 29, everyone collapsed. Though worn-out, they were safe, alone, and could finally rest. Louise, however, was distraught that Spence would not know where they were when he discovered that they had not arrived in Daan Norte. In the midst of her worry, Claude Fertig suddenly walked into the hut. Amid Laverne's excited screams, sleep and worry disappeared.

When Claude could finally tell his story, he related that he had also taken temporary leave of the radio project. Now that the station was operational, the guerrilla guards provided security. He had then hiked for days to Daan Norte in search of Laverne. Not finding her, he guessed that she and Louise were at Mount Igabon, and he had trailed them for several more days. Now, for the first time in two months, Louise and Laverne both knew where their husbands were and that all were safe.

For the next two weeks everyone slept, ate the precious canned food, and regained strength. Claude and Laverne were both crippled by badly cut feet and ankle abrasions from walking barefoot. Hardly able to hobble about, Claude sent a message to Spence assuring him that Louise was with them at Mount Igabon and urging him to join them. Spence replied that he was still sick and that Peralta wanted him to return to the radio station as soon as possible. Claude decided that he, too, should return to the station, and that the women and Ben Zimmerman must go with him. He assured them that they would find safety in northwestern Panay and at last shared with them the nature of his secret mission.

Traveling in the rugged back country of Panay, where roads and highways did not exist, was best accomplished by following streams and rivers through deep mountain ravines and valleys rather than hiking steep paths across mountains. However, in the rainy season, flooded rivers were dangerous and often forced hikers to take indirect routes. One of the biggest difficulties that the Americans now endured was their lack of shoes. Laverne Fertig often remembered the Russian woman who had told her in the first weeks of the war that if she did nothing else, she should stock up on shoes. Laverne now wished that she—and everyone else—had taken that veteran advice. Walking mountain trails barefooted, or with the final pieces of shoes lashed together with vines, was a torturous experience.

Claude did not tell anyone their exact destination. He knew that if they were captured and interrogated, it would be best for them not to know. So the women trudged off into the unknown. What should have been a three-week trip would soon become a six-week trek, as swollen rivers surged over banks, forcing the group to take many detours.

Tracing the Aclan, Dumalili, and Ibajay rivers, the small group of Americans slowly moved northwest toward Aklan. Once, when forced to leave the river trail of the Aclan due to flash flooding, Louise and Laverne were terrified when they had to slowly edge their way along a narrow goat path on a rock ledge high above the raging river. Clinging to exposed roots and vines and praying that their bare feet would not slip or the pathway collapse, they gritted their teeth, fought vertigo, and tried not to look at the raging torrent cascading around large boulders far below them. It was a nightmare scene from which they could not awake.[14]

As frightening to the women as the surging rivers and narrow mountain paths was the constant presence of insects, leeches, snakes, scorpions, and other jungle predators. One night the Americans squeezed into a small hut that was infested with giant cockroaches. Louise remembered that "the walls were black with cockroaches and I shivered . . . The results in the morning were terrible. Our first task was, literally, to shake the cockroach turds out of our eyes. My head felt like a dirty sandpile, and when I shook my hair the turds came out in a shower."[15] Never did washing one's hair in the river feel so good.

Slowly the rainy season turned dry, and the rivers receded and pathways became passable. Making their way northward along the shallow Ibajay River, Claude finally led the group to their destination near the end of March 1943. They settled into a large house nestled safely along the bank of the Ibajay and several miles removed from the ocean near Bunglay. Most important, the surrounding region was free of Japanese troops. Their new house was built of wood and had beautiful hardwood floors; the roof was grass. The house had two stories, and the women selected rooms on the second floor. After the tiny nipa huts in Hopevale and the horrid conditions along the mountain trails, Louise and Laverne felt as though they had found their mansion in heaven.

A trail disappeared behind the house and led to the secret radio station, a two-hour hike to the top of a small mountain. Spence, though still quite ill, had already returned and was running it. Claude soon left to join him and take stock of his friend's health, and of the activity at the station.

On March 26, Spence came down for an elated reunion with Louise after another two-month separation. He was gaunt and still plagued by dysentery and diarrhea. But there was laughter in his voice and brightness in his eyes, and Louise knew that there were better days ahead.[16] For the next two months the

Spencers and Fertigs would be together at a safe distance from the Japanese. It was a much needed respite.

Spring 1943,
The United States

The adult children of the missionaries in Hopevale who were now living in the United States were also being affected by the war, but in very different ways. In addition to being anxious about their missing parents, Uncle Sam was knocking at their doors, requesting their services in the war effort.

Frederick "Buddy" Meyer, age twenty-two, had recently graduated from Yale University. He was now attending Rochester Medical School and was in the Navy V-12 program. This program would allow Frederick to complete his medical studies and then serve as a doctor in the navy.[17]

Milton Meyer, age nineteen, was a sophomore at Yale when he was jolted into adulthood by receiving his draft notice. In February 1943, as his mother and father were hiding in dugouts in Hopevale, he was inducted into the army and shipped off to serve in the China-Burma-India campaign with the Office of Strategic Services.[18] Though he constantly worried about his parents on Panay, and wondered whether his younger brother, Dick, had escaped from Manila, the rigors of boot camp and the constant travel and relocation diverted his anxiety and kept him focused on the tasks at hand.

David Covell, Jimmy and Charma Covell's son, was only eighteen in the spring of 1943 when he received his army draft notice. A skinny teenager, he flunked his physical for being underweight and color-blind. However, when he visited a Marine recruiting office and they learned that he had been raised in Yokohama, Japan, and spoke fluent "street" Japanese, they forgot about physical requirements and signed David up before he could change his mind. Because of his linguistic skills, he was assigned to intelligence and trained as an interpreter and interrogator of prisoners. In 1944 he would be involved with the Fourth Marine Division in four amphibious assaults—at Kwajalein, Saipan, Tinian, and Iwo Jima.

In combat David was often used as a "cave caller." He was taken to Japanese caves shortly before they were detonated, or "torched," by the marines. He would call into the caves in fluent Japanese and, using his cultural knowledge urge the young Japanese soldiers to surrender. Many times he was successful in saving their lives.[19]

While David was experiencing combat, his older sister, Peggy, graduated after majoring in social work at Keuka College in Keuka Park, New York. Also fluent in Japanese, she volunteered to serve as a social worker in a Japanese relocation center in Colorado, helping Japanese Americans who had been interned by the United States government.[20]

As a cave caller or social worker or young private—and from the army, navy, and Marines—the adult children of the missionaries in Hopevale were playing their own roles in the world war. The young adults and their lost parents knew that it would not be until the end of the war that contact would be regained. And the war seemed to be fated to go on forever.

March–June 1943,
Hopevale

Once the Japanese had gained control of the major rice-growing section of Panay, their offensive momentarily paused. With only three thousand troops on Panay, the Japanese could terrorize the countryside and hope to keep the guerrillas off balance, but they did not have the troop strength to conquer, subjugate, and control the majority of the people in all three provinces. What they could do effectively, however, was control the "rice basket" that fed the Filipinos. By doing so they would slowly lower the morale of the poor villagers who supported the guerrillas with food and provisions. Rebels with empty stomachs will soon lose their will to fight, and will hoard their meager resources.

Content with the success of their November and December operations, the Japanese pulled back behind secure lines to regroup and plan their next offensive. With the Japanese no longer sending aggressive patrols out of Calinog, the level of danger in Hopevale diminished, and the missionaries breathed easier. They came out of their burrows and returned to Hopevale and Emmanuel Glen.

On March 25, Ruth Meyer walked the two-and-a-half miles to Katipunan with Frederick for the first time in nearly a year. Suffering from chronic dental infection and cooped up by the rainy season, she had not been able to exercise or enjoy nature. The fear of Japanese patrols had also kept her on a short leash. But this excursion to Katipunan released her from her prison and opened her soul to a larger world. Then Ruth and Frederick floated down the Panay River to the Fords' camp and spent some days in what seemed like luxury, eating fresh food and listening to music and news from San Francisco on the radio. By Easter Sunday, Ruth was back in Hopevale and singing "The First Easter Morn" at the service at Cathedral Glen.[21]

Afterward, with Ruth still suffering from gum and tooth pain, she and Frederick hiked to the same guerrilla medical camp at Igi from which Spence had recently departed to return to the radio station. A dentist was available, and Ruth endured primitive but successful dental work. Frederick continued to make medical rounds and give expert help and consultation in guerrilla hospitals and clinics. Erle Rounds was also visiting the scattered guerrilla camps, serving as the Protestant district chaplain with the rank of lieutenant.[22] By now the guerrillas had set up a printing press and were printing their own currency. Though not on an official payroll, the missionaries would sometimes be paid small sums or given needed supplies for their services to the guerrillas. This in turn helped them to pay Reverend Dianala and Mr. Rio for food and security at Hopevale.[23]

On May 17, 1943, Frederick wrote a letter to the American Baptist Mission Union. This was a risky action, for the chance of a letter getting out of the Philippines and to the United States was almost nil. For weeks this letter was passed from hand to hand along the guerrilla circuit. How it ever found eventual passage to the United States is not known, though likely by submarine. But before the war was over, the much worn letter did arrive at its destination. It was the last letter to emerge from Hopevale during the war years. Frederick wrote:

> The ways and means of communication through you to our families may open up here, though we are in forests deep somewhere on Panay. . . . [We are] hale and hearty, mountaineers, thin, but well supplied with food.
>
> The story of the past year is [too] lengthy for a letter of this type. . . . Capiz province (except Aklan district) is scorched. Capiz city is gone, but most of our [Emmanuel Hospital] compound buildings were standing in January, used by the enemy as a fort.
>
> My hospital personnel is scattered, a few bed patients however are scattered in different hill clinics with plenty of consultation, long hikes, keep us thin but happy to be of service even though surrounded by hostile forces. . . . Miss Adams, Mrs. Meyer and myself, residue of Emmanuel [Hospital], have been of daily service to the district; medical missions can carry on even in the very trying surroundings. Some day peace will come and bring you the whole story.

Emmanuel Hospital, therefore, with no equipment, hardly any medicines, with its missionary residue of personnel in grass hut buildings in jungle sends our home folks loving greetings. We carry on, because of Emmanuel, God with us.[24]

Dr. Meyer's repeated reference to Emmanuel Hospital reveals where the passion of his life still lay. World War II was a temporary obstacle to be endured and overcome. This healing institution was his life's work. And he did not intend to walk away and turn his back on his dream.

Despite the Japanese camped in Calinog only ten miles away, there was an unrealistic feeling of safety in Hopevale. On June 13, Frederick and Ruth led Sunday services for Reverend Dianala's congregation in Katipunan. More than seventy-five Filipinos attended to listen to Frederick preach and Ruth sing. Afterward the women's society of the church served a large and festive luncheon. Though the fact that the American missionaries were hiding in Hopevale had always been a loosely guarded secret, there was little pretense of secrecy now. Only the love and commitment of the Filipinos for the Americans—and their patriotic resistance to the Japanese invaders—had kept lips closed tight and the Hopevale secret hidden for over a year.[25]

More encouraging than any other news, the Meyers and the Roundses received word through Filipino friends traveling from Manila that their sons, Richard and Donal, were healthy and adjusting well at the Santo Tomas internment camp. In many ways the boys were safer at Santo Tomas than they would have been at Hopevale. And at Santo Tomas they were able to go to school, meet girls, play sports, and continue their adolescent growth. It was probably a blessing, though painful, that Richard and Donal had been trapped in Manila and had not returned home for Christmas in 1941.[26]

April–June 1943,
Aklan, Northwest Panay

Three weeks after arriving back at the radio station, Claude Fertig received unexpected orders from Lieutenant Colonel Peralta's headquarters, on April 15, 1943, relieving him of command of the radio station and further participation in the submarine landing projects. Fertig was redirected to other critical engineering needs in the vicinity of Sara. Now he would build airstrips, bridges, and other facilities—in preparation for MacArthur's return.

Claude and Spence were extremely disappointed. They both wanted the first American submarine to "land on their watch." They had planned and worked for this momentous event. But there were probably other guerrilla officers lobbying for the same opportunity and honor. Politics is seldom absent from military decisions.[27]

Most disheartening, both men had just settled in with their wives in some semblance of safety and stability. Now the new orders would separate them again and keep them constantly on the move. Both Claude and Spence, though strong and young, were not physically well. They needed time to recoup and gain strength. But orders were orders, and they did not protest.

Captain Spencer immediately requested a two-week leave with Louise, and it was granted by his commanding officer, Major Fertig. The Spencers escaped to the nearby coastal city of Ibajay, now nearly deserted. Renting a beach-side cottage, they felt like honeymooners. Each day they swam in the ocean, basked in the sunshine, and watched their sallow skin grow tan and healthy.[28] As they stared at the far distant horizon where the sky meets the sea, they did not know—indeed, no guerrillas on Panay seemed to know—that the first American submarine was already on its way to Panay. On April 15—the same day that Claude had been relieved of his command of the radio station by Peralta—the

Gudgeon (SS-211) left Fremantle, Australia, on its eighth war patrol. Commanded by W. S. "Bill" Post Jr., it carried six thousand pounds of equipment for Peralta's guerrillas.[29]

The *Gudgeon*, a new Tambor-class submarine, was launched on January 25, 1941, and already had an envied reputation. Four days after the surprise attack by the Japanese on Pearl Harbor, the *Gudgeon* sailed from Hawaii on the first offensive American patrol of World War II. It soon became the first American submarine to patrol along the coast of Japan and the first to sink a Japanese warship, the Japanese submarine *I-73*. On its sixth war patrol it transported an elite six-man intelligence team from Australia to Mindanao, arriving on March 13, 1943. Now, only a month later, on its eighth war patrol it was returning to the Philippines to land supplies and a specially trained Filipino intelligence team under the command of Second Lieutenant Torribio Crespo, U.S. Army, on the northwest shore of Panay.[30]

Shortly before reaching Panay, the *Gudgeon* gave unsuccessful surface chase to a Japanese tanker and then sank a huge troop transport, the *Kamakura Maru*. This intense combat activity severely depleted the sub's batteries. On April 29 the *Gudgeon* reached the Aklan coast of Panay and sailed submerged along the southern coast of the panhandle, approaching Pucio Point. Taking station 1.5 miles off the town of Pandan, Commander Post spent the entire day running at periscope depth between Pandan and Pucio Point, conducting submerged reconnaissance. It was decided that the best landing spot was 3.7 miles east of Pucio Point.

On the night of April 29 the *Gudgeon* surfaced 1,800 yards off the coast, and Lieutenant Crespo and Sergeant Orlando Alfabeto rowed ashore in a rubber raft to make contact with guerrilla units. Because no one seemed to be aware that the *Gudgeon* was arriving, it took Crespo and Alfabeto until dawn to make contact with a guerrilla shore patrol. As the sun came above the horizon, they saw the silhouettes of armed men walking down the beach. When they realized that they were Filipino and not Japanese, they stepped out on the beach and identified themselves to the stunned guerrillas. They were hurried to the nearby landing-zone headquarters, where a celebration broke out.

Unable to return to the submarine until nightfall, Crespo and Alfabeto spent the day interviewing the guerrillas and taking notes on vital information. That night, April 30, they signaled the *Gudgeon* to surface and paddled back to the submarine. Quickly, two seven-man rubber boats and two five-man boats, were loaded, and they transported the sub's cargo safely to land before dawn. The cargo consisted mostly of ammunition, medical supplies, radio supplies, ten Thompson submachine guns, cigarettes, boots, and ninety-thousand prewar pesos in a sealed can. But the most important thing brought ashore was the knowledge that the guerrillas were no longer fighting alone.[31]

After successfully unloading the cargo and putting Second Lieutenant Crespo's intelligence unit ashore, Commander Post turned his submarine northward to approach his assigned hunting ground. In the process he likely made one evening very exciting for the Spencers, who were still on furlough in Ibajay.

On that night Spence and Louise were asleep in their bungalow on the beach when they were jolted awake by the sound of a loud diesel engine just a few hundred yards off the coast. Spence immediately identified the sound as a submarine on the surface recharging its batteries. Not expecting an American submarine, he was convinced it was a Japanese vessel. Spence immediately made Louise get up, and they packed their bags and beat a hasty retreat through the darkness back toward Bunglay and the radio station. The next day, rumors were everywhere that an American submarine had landed somewhere along the southern Aklan coast. Spence refused to believe it until a Filipino offered him a fresh Camel cigarette. Then he knew that the submarine he had heard was an American one recharging its batteries to go on combat patrol.[32]

When the Spencers and Fertigs finally got back together in Bunglay, the news of the submarine landing filled their conversation. This event was what they had been working for, hoping for, and dreaming of for months. Both men were elated by their success and yet disappointed not to be present when the submarine surfaced. But this news was upstaged by one further bit of news. Laverne shared with Louise that she feared she was pregnant.[33]

Laverne knew what pregnancy felt like: She had conceived twice before the war began. Once she had a miscarriage and once the baby was stillborn. Her doctor in Manila had told her that for her next pregnancy, her child must be delivered by Caesarean section or she would run a high risk of bleeding to death. For the last eighteen months, these words had haunted her. Now she was often queasy, and she suspected that she was in the first eight weeks of pregnancy. Evading capture by the Japanese was no time to have a baby.[34]

Immediately all thoughts turned to Dr. Meyer in Hopevale. He was the only doctor that the Fertigs knew on Panay with the competency and experience to deliver Laverne safely, or to bring her through another miscarriage. Hopevale was a dangerous place. But Laverne's return there was now a risk that must be taken.

As Claude and Laverne adjusted to the news and made plans to hike to Hopevale, Spence and Louise got into a huge argument. Louise was determined that she, too, was going to Hopevale to help Laverne through her pregnancy. Spence told her that she was not returning to Hopevale. Words flew and tempers flared. Spence snapped and said, "No, Louise, you can't just give your life to Laverne. She will manage all right with Dr. Meyer and Miss Adams. It's all right for you to be on hand if we are near anyway, but I don't want you tying yourself to anybody at all, even the Fertigs."

Spence then told Louise that he wanted them to escape

from Panay as soon as possible and sail to Mindanao. From there he had dreams of somehow finding passage to Australia. Louise refused to listen to Spence's bold plans. She was committed to being with Laverne in her crisis. Spence and Louise went to bed upset and angry at each other. They had reached an impasse.[35]

After a good night's sleep, Louise knew that she had won the argument. A rested Spence had returned to his old big-hearted self. His intensity had eased, and he was more open to the idea of Louise spending some time in Hopevale if he deemed it safe.

The Fertigs and the Spencers stayed at the radio station for one more month, to tie up details and rest, and then set off for Hopevale together. Laverne often felt nauseated, had little appetite, and was losing weight. Such a rough trek through the interior of Panay was not good for her. Fortunately it was the dry season, and the receding rivers provided a much easier riverbank pathway through the mountain valleys than they had during their previous trip. Halfway down the Aclan River, Claude left Spence with the women and detoured to their old food cache at Mount Igabon. He wanted to pick up supplies for Laverne and then find Lieutenant Colonel Peralta and talk with him about Laverne's health situation.

Spence led the women down the Aclan River, then to the Malinao River, and finally down the Panay River. As they moved closer to Hopevale, a Japanese presence became palpable, and every Filipino they passed seemed to be afraid that the Japanese were close by. While stopping by the Fords' camp on the Panay River, Spence learned that the Fords had already evacuated farther inland twice due to recent Japanese incursions along the river. Things were much safer at the remote radio station in Aklan, and Spence now wished they had stayed there. Finally, on June 20, 1943, the exhausted threesome staggered into Hopevale. They had been gone from this hidden community for nearly six months.[36]

After the initial excitement of being warmly greeted by the missionaries, they were amazed to see how overgrown the once neat camp had become and how everyone appeared older and worn down. Though grateful to be together again, there was an intuitive awareness that things in Hopevale were not the same. They sensed a silence that precedes a violent storm.

Chapter Eleven

July–December 1943,
Hopevale and Katipunan

The Fertigs and Spencers could not have returned to Hopevale at a worse time. Within days of their arrival, the Japanese army began an intense series of what the Filipinos called "penetrations" into specific regions of Panay. A former guerrilla officer, Gamaliel Manikan, remembered: "Every time a sizable enemy force went out of their garrisons and ventured into the rural areas, the warning cry of the civilians was '*Penetration!*' . . . [It was] a colloquial barbarism that became a common expression of both the military personnel and the civilian inhabitants on Panay."[1] And the colloquial barbarism of penetration meant rape and murder.

During the summer of 1943 the Japanese army had increased its troop strength in the central Visayan islands in order to patrol larger areas of the islands and suppress guerrilla resistance. Guerrilla intelligence on Panay estimated that there were now between 2,800 and 3,200 Japanese soldiers there, compared to approximately 16,400 guerrilla officers and enlisted men. The total civilian population on Panay in the most recent 1939 census was 1,348,721. Because the guerrillas greatly outnumbered the Japanese on Panay, the Japanese decided they must resort to terrorizing the local Filipinos to inhibit their support of guerrilla efforts. They reasoned that only such tactics would frighten them into submission.[2]

To carry out such terrorism, a special squad of eight hundred soldiers led by a Captain Watanabe (Tai-I) was established. The guerrillas often referred to these squads as "punitive forces," or punishment teams. These teams began their grisly work on Panay on July 3, 1943, in the central region of Iloilo province. Their official task was to capture Governor Tomas Confesor, who was in hiding. They also intended to locate and destroy the guerrilla printing press that they knew was being used to produce currency. However, their real purpose was to intimidate the civilian population. Watanabe failed to find Confesor or the printing press, but he excelled at raw brutality.[3]

He followed a set pattern. He would enter a town or barrio with a punishment squad and, not finding guerrilla forces, would immediately arrest the first available citizens for interrogation—men, women, and children. Watanabe then publicly tortured them to gain information about the local guerrilla groups. If, as was usual, he did not receive the information he wanted, he would randomly select men or women and behead, bayonet, rape, or burn them as a public example of the power of Japan. Then his troops would execute all captives and leave the village in flames. The purpose of such violence was not only to unnerve the average citizen but also to turn them against the guerrilla movement that the Japanese insisted caused such reprisals.[4]

In the small barrio of Taban near the town of Alimodian, the citizens fled to the foothills when the Japanese entered their region in August 1943. A week later some returned on market day to buy food and restock supplies. Anticipating this, the Japanese surrounded the barrio and entered the market. Arresting every man present, fifty were bound, and their hands tied behind their back. Accused of being guerrillas, each was forced to stand at attention with his back against a coconut tree. Every Japanese soldier took his turn pinning the "guerrillas" against the tree with a bayonet. Finally, the dying men were beheaded, and their heads were scattered around the barrio. It was a terrifying lesson about the cost of associating with guerrillas.[5]

On Guimaras Island, a coastal island separated by a narrow strait from Iloilo province, over one thousand Filipinos were killed by Watanabe's punishment squads during the last week of August. In the barrio of Salvation, fifty women of varying ages were publicly stripped and raped. They were forced to lie naked in the scorching sun all day without water, and then were bayoneted at sundown.[6]

One guerrilla officer, Lieutenant Colonel Leopoldo Relunia, wrote to Lieutenant Colonel Peralta, revealing the quandary that the Japanese punishment squads had created for Filipino guerrillas: "Is it any wonder that the people go over to the Japs? There is a limit to human endurance. The people do not know why we do not defend them. They do not know of our 'lie low' policy. Yet they get punished and killed for helping and obeying us. . . . The people must be hating the [guerrilla] Army. For one year and a half they have given their foodstuffs to the Army without getting paid. . . . Now the Japs kill them for this."[7]

Watanabe's terror tactics were effective. They shocked everyone into confusion, striking fear in the bravest hearts and undermining—though also often reinforcing—civilians' commitment to the guerrilla cause. Though some Filipinos chose to play the Japanese game and profess loyalty to their "fellow Asian" conquerors, most Filipinos remained quiet, stayed out of the way, and tried to live inconspicuously. Inside, however, most hated anyone of any nationality invading their land—Spanish, American, or Japanese. While they could better stomach a benevolent big brother, as the Americans had painted their presence, the ruthlessness of the Japanese could not be tolerated. Most Filipinos chose not to support the Japanese, prayed for MacArthur to return, and waited for a better day, when their independence would at last become reality.

In Hopevale, the miners and missionaries heard of the atrocities in the Iloilo region to the south. Then, in August, the focus of the Japanese operations shifted to the east of Hopevale, into eastern Iloilo and Capiz provinces. This change in direction was due to the fact that Peralta had once again moved his headquarters staff, this time from Daan Norte, ten miles north of Hopevale, to the Barotac Viejo–Sara–Passi triangle, approximately thirty miles east of Hopevale. This triangle covered 240 square miles and comprised rolling hills and small dense forests and jungle. Eighty percent of Peralta's field-grade officers were currently found in this area.[8]

At this same time, Dr. Meyer set off on a barefooted medical mission that would take him directly into the path of the new Japanese penetration. Leaving on July 23, 1943, he headed northeast toward the Sara-Ajuy region on the coastal plain of Iloilo province. He had agreed to tour the guerrilla medical camps and treat the more complex wounds and diseases. His last pair of shoes had worn out weeks before, and he found that a fifty-year-old American could not easily toughen soft, flat feet. He sent a letter by courier to Ruth, saying that he was safe, though he was battling chronic diarrhea and losing weight. Of most concern, he had developed an abdominal hernia that made it painful to walk or exert himself.[9]

While he was gone, Frederick missed celebrating his fifty-first birthday and his twenty-fourth wedding anniversary. Alone in Emmanuel Glen, Ruth and Jennie Adams ran out of kerosene and resorted to coconut oil to give them dim lighting. In the doctor's absence, someone robbed the meager medical dispensary, leaving the medicine but taking the small cash reserve. Ruth found living without Frederick to be frightening and destabilizing.[10]

Frederick returned five weeks later, having dodged the Japanese. By now Spence and Claude had left Hopevale to return to duty with the guerrillas, and it was good to have Dr. Meyer back with the women and children. Spence was working near Sara, and had been assigned to upgrade maps of Panay for the anticipated American invasion. Claude worked on engineering projects.[11]

Both Claude and Spence were elated when they learned that a second American submarine, the *Grayling* (SS-209), had surfaced on July 31, and again on August 23, at the landing zone they helped prepare near Pucio Point on Pandan Bay.[12] The *Grayling* delivered thirty tons of critical supplies, primarily arms and ammunition. Claude's and Spence's work had been effective, and it was clear that MacArthur intended to send more submarines.[13] However, there was a high cost. The *Grayling* proceeded north on its war patrol from Panay to Luzon, stalking Japanese ships approaching Manila Bay. After sinking a Japanese passenger-cargo ship on August 27, the *Grayling* was not heard from again. On September 30, it was officially reported as "lost with all hands" somewhere along the western coast of Luzon. Seventy-five sailors perished. Of all branches of the American armed forces in World War II, submarine crews in the Pacific had the highest fatality rate: almost 23 percent.[14]

Dr. Meyer continued to monitor Laverne's pregnancy and found everything normal. He estimated that the baby would be born in late December or January. Nutrition was a worry, but Laverne had recovered from her morning sickness.

Both miners and missionaries continued to be low on funds, though guerrilla officers were beginning to receive small stipends. Spence was currently receiving a captain's salary of sixty pesos (thirty dollars) a month from "emergency money" printed by hidden guerrilla printing presses. The Filipinos in Katipunan continued to send food to Hopevale, paid or not. Such generosity reveals a basic virtue that runs deep in Filipino culture that will not allow one member of a family to turn his or her back on another who is in need. The Filipino Baptist Christians in Katipunan considered the Baptist missionaries—and now the miners—to be such family. Without this bond of commitment, the Americans at Hopevale could not have survived.[15]

After only five days' rest from his extensive hike to Sara, Frederick received a request from Peralta's headquarters to rush to a remote guerrilla camp and operate on a patient with complex appendicitis. While he was making this trek, Frederick's hernia became acute. He could barely walk. Though he completed the mission, returning to Hopevale on September 16, his traveling days were over.[16] From this point on, Frederick's health deteriorated rapidly. Louise Spencer observed: "[Dr. Meyer's] illness was a terrible blow to him, for he wanted so much to give his services to the fight. His heart seemed broken, and in almost no time he had aged so that he looked like a man of eighty, I thought, instead of fifty-one, his real age."[17]

Needing rest and diversion, Frederick and Ruth slipped out of Hopevale for a few days and risked drifting down the Panay River to the Fords' camp. The Fords had recently returned from hiding farther inland and were again receiving visitors. The Meyers relaxed in more comfortable quarters, listened to news on the radio, and enjoyed real coffee, not the wartime substitute.[18]

In the Sara triangle, things were collapsing at guerrilla headquarters. The Japanese penetration was gradually surrounding the guerrillas. Finally, many of the guerrillas evacuated and dispersed to other areas. Claude and Spence first retreated back to Hopevale to join their wives. Then Claude set up his engineering command post on a secluded mountaintop several hours from Hopevale. His headquarters was nothing more than a large cogan-covered shelter and small huts to protect the guerrillas who assisted him.

As Spence and Claude took stock of Hopevale, neither man was happy. There was clear danger and vulnerability. Japanese terror squads could walk in at any time. That they had not done so already was a miracle. Probably at least half of the Filipinos in a fifty-mile radius knew that there were Americans hiding outside Katipunan. Many of them—if pressured, paid, or tortured—could lead the Japanese directly to Hopevale.

Spence called the men in Hopevale together to make contingency plans. The first priority was a better security or guard system. More Filipino sentries were stationed at stragegic points approaching Hopevale.[19] At night the American men took turns walking the immediate perimeter and making sure that guards were awake. Quickly, the alert system within the vicinity of Hopevale was raised to a higher level.

As he developed the security system, Spence was haunted by horrible news he had heard while retreating from Sara, about a fellow American guerrilla officer, Captain Joe Herman, with whom he had worked in the engineering department. Once Herman told Spence that he would not allow the Japanese to take his family alive and be tortured. He kept his word. As Sara collapsed, he and his family were surrounded in their hideout. Drawing his pistol, Herman shot his wife, his child, and three Japanese soldiers, and put the last bullet through his brain. The desperate circumstances of the Americans on Panay could not have hit Spence any harder.[20] As Louise Spencer wrote in her diary, "[We are] now living on the edge of terror."[21]

Feeling the same mounting danger, Claude had a tense talk with Laverne and insisted that they move out of Hopevale, perhaps back to Mount Igabon. Laverne adamantly refused to leave Dr. Meyer. Now they were talking about the health of a baby, and all of her motherly instincts held her in Hopevale. At the same time, Louise was committed to staying with Laverne no matter what happened. Claude and Spence grimaced and quietly made contingency plans.

Spence called another meeting of the men in Hopevale and proposed that they not remain bunched up within the small confines of the camp. He suggested that they disperse as family units farther away from Hopevale—yet close enough to assist one another—increasing their chance of escape if the Japanese suddenly appeared.

After deliberation, the missionaries decided they should not leave Hopevale but rather stay close together as a mission family. They still seemed to cling to a hope that if they were captured, their lives would be spared. Whether their position was outright denial or reasonable thinking can be debated. But at this time there had been no known execution of American Protestant missionaries on Panay or any other Visayan island. The bottom line was that no one knew what would happen should the Japanese advance into Hopevale and capture the Americans. Those at greatest risk might not be the Americans but the Filipinos who had supported them.

Unlike the missionaries, the miners decided to disperse and build new huts. Already Claude had built a new nipa hut for Laverne twenty minutes removed from Hopevale and higher in the hills. She was close enough to be in touch with Dr. Meyer but far enough away to get a running start should Hopevale be surrounded. Claude had also built servants' quarters and asked their prewar helper, Federico Condino, to again live with them. Federico brought with him his wife, daughter, and Laverne's Airedale terrier, Debbie.

The Schurings moved forty minutes away from Hopevale, and to the other side of the Panay River. They built a nipa hut on top of a high hill that had a view for miles around. Henry

Schuring had army field glasses and monitored the surrounding area. Liking this location, Spence decided to build a new nipa hut for Louise near the Schurings.

The Clardys had two small children: seven-year-old Terry and five-year-old John. Both boys had begun school in Hopevale, along with eight-year-old Douglas Rounds. The Clardys decided that the safest option for their family was to move to the outskirts of Hopevale near Laverne Fertig's new hut. The Roundses, wanting to keep the boys together, decided to move in with the Clardys allowing the children to continue their play and school lessons together.

Remaining directly in Hopevale and Emmanuel Glen were the Roses, the Covells, the Meyers and Jennie Adams. These seven missionaries were in the greatest danger, trusting in their hidden dugouts to save them.

While Spence was having his new hut built near the Schurings, Louise moved in with Laverne. Claude and Spence were still busy with the guerrillas and were seldom at home. Louise also wanted to be close to Laverne in case she went into early labor. Concerned that in a crisis they might be separated from Dr. Meyer, Louise took birthing lessons from Jennie Adams. She also helped Laverne sew for the baby, using any scrap of cloth they could find. Diapers were made, and a crude medical kit put together for the delivery. All the baby supplies were kept in an emergency bag ready for sudden evacuation.[22]

To break the tension, the women in Hopevale often visited one another to talk and drink native coffee or herbal tea. One afternoon Louise Spencer dropped by to chat with Louise Rounds. Louise Spencer loved her cigarettes, and by now felt comfortable enough around Louise Rounds to smoke. The Roundses' youngest son, Douglas, had been seven when they moved to Hopevale and in November would be nine. A handsome, blond boy, he was inquisitive and energetic, but he had always suffered from asthma. As Louise inhaled her cigarette deeply, she noticed Douglas watching her with great curiosity, as if he were learning how to properly smoke a cigarette. He had reason to do so. Doc Meyer had decided that the best way to treat the boy's asthma was by a native remedy. The leaves of a certain tropical tree were harvested, dried, and then ground into fine powder. The potent powder would then be placed in a cigarette paper and rolled. When this medicinal cigarette was smoked during an asthma attack, it brought children relief. Young Douglas had been trying to perfect his smoking technique and Louise Rounds was a good model.

After Douglas ran out to play—or to smoke, perhaps—Louise Rounds became reflective and began to talk personally. She told Louise Spencer that if the war had not come, she and her family would have been in the United States on furlough at that very moment. Walking over to a suitcase, she opened it and pulled out a folded suit that she had bought before the war for Douglas to wear on the ocean liner going back to the States. Even though Douglas's current clothes were now threadbare, the special suit for the trip home had never been worn. She then held up a beautiful dress and a matching pair of shoes that she had bought for herself to wear on the trip. Though she was now barefoot and had no shoes for daily use, the special shoes remained unused.

Trying to cheer her up, Louise Spencer chuckled and asked, "Well, Louise, what ship are you sailing on?"

Louise Rounds replied wistfully but firmly, "I just know that there will be a ship for us. And I want to look decent when it comes."[23]

On another afternoon in October, Louise Spencer noticed that Laverne was feeling very low. Claude was gone, and now six months pregnant, she was more and more anxious about the last trimester of her pregnancy. Louise briskly stood up and told Laverne to get dressed and look pretty, whether she wanted to or

not, because they were going on a walk. Laverne decided to cooperate, and she put on her one nice pair of slacks and a blouse.
Lipstick was a rare and treasured commodity, but Laverne splurged
and put some on, even though the men were away. Louise laughed
and followed suit, and they headed out on a ten-minute walk to
visit Fern Clardy and Louise Rounds.

After sending Terry, John, and Douglas outside to play, the
women sat in the *sala* and talked. Louise Spencer noticed Louise Rounds staring at Laverne. Louise Rounds was a beautiful
woman, but modest and conservative. For personal and religious
reasons she had never worn makeup or lipstick. Suddenly Louise Rounds blurted, "You know, I must tell you girls how nice
you look with your lipstick on . . . I've never used lipstick myself, but after this war I think I will. It's one of the things I've
made up my mind about."[24]

Of course the other women were elated to hear this and immediately offered to share their lipstick with Louise right then.
But, a little embarrassed, she declined, saying that she wanted
to wait until she could buy her own lipstick, choose her own
color, and wear it on a special occasion.

The war continued to change both miners and missionaries.
These women were sisters now. They had rubbed off on one another, and they needed one another to bring warmth and laughter into their bleak world.

Rainy season returned in October 1943, and with it the misery of
constant mud and typhoons. But the Japanese incursions did not
relent. Having already sent major punishment teams into southern and eastern Iloilo province, the Aklan region (near the submarine landing zone), and northern Capiz province, the Japanese
were now converging upon the central heart of Panay, where
Katipunan and Hopevale were located.

Five different times in October and November the Japanese

entered Katipunan.[25] On October 19, Ruth Meyer scribbled in her journal, "The headman [from Katipunan is going] to the district administration center of nearby Tapaz town to surrender the village, to fly the white flag, and to be prepared to receive Japanese visitors anytime. We folks are all jittery, under tense situation."[26]

Following a short entry for October 20, Ruth's diary abruptly ends. This is because the Meyers decided that they needed to move their most personal possessions out of Hopevale to be stored with friends in Katipunan. Ruth's diary, her sheet music collection, some of Frederick's stamps, and Jennie Adams's tattered notebook of poetry sewed inside a pillow were all sent by courier to Katipunan for safekeeping.[27]

Chronic anxiety and fear were eroding everyone's health. Depression became a way of life, and several young women, including Louise Spencer, discovered their menstrual periods had ceased. She dealt with her fear by taking walks during which she memorized the location of little-known escape routes and paths made by wild pigs. She also made a form of native peanut butter and placed it in containers in her emergency bag, in case she had to flee suddenly. She had no intention of being caught by the Japanese.

As Thanksgiving approached, the missionaries were huddled in their *camaligs*, and the miners, living at a distance from Hopevale, were poised to run at any time. Finally, the day before Thanksgiving, the missionaries left the *camaligs* and returned to their huts. In contrast to the year before, there was no communal celebration. Each cluster of people living in a single hut planned their own simple celebration.

Claude managed to return for Thanksgiving, but Spence was not present. Louise Spencer was determined to decorate Laverne's small hut and used ferns, wild berry bushes, native flowers, and whatever else she could find of festive color. The Fertigs' cook, Federico, produced a wonderful Thanksgiving meal with only meager food supplies. In place of a pumpkin pie, he surprised everyone with a squash pie. Each person tried to stay upbeat and happy.

However, Claude was clearly down and worried sick. He was scared of losing Laverne during a difficult delivery. And he, more than anyone else, knew the intensity of the present Japanese penetration. Every instinct told him to escape this region. But Laverne had to remain close to a skilled doctor. And that meant staying in Hopevale with Dr. Meyer.

The day after Thanksgiving, Claude reluctantly left Hopevale for his command post several hours away in the mountains, promising to be back within a few days. However, soon after arriving, Claude developed a large boil on his leg that made walking nearly impossible. Now he could not return to Hopevale easily. Then, on the first of December, a strong typhoon blew across Panay, knocking down Claude's headquarters building, injuring staff members seriously, and destroying food stocks. The next day word came that the Japanese had overrun the guerrilla base at Igi, destroying the medical infirmary and the printing press. Most alarming, though, was a widespread rumor—believed by many Filipinos and guerrillas—that the Japanese intended to round up all Americans remaining in central Panay between the fifteenth and twentieth of December. Claude was desperate to join Laverne, but the boil on his leg grew worse.[28]

On Thursday, December 16, Spence returned to Hopevale from working with the roving guerrillas, calming Louise's and Laverne's fears. Spence had also heard the rumor about the American roundup, but he discounted it. On December 17, a Japanese reconnaissance plane flew over Hopevale barely above the treetops. It seemed an omen. On that same day Reverend Dianala and his wife hiked in from Katipunan, bringing the missionaries ten bundles of bananas. Mrs. Dianala did not feel well and went to see Dr. Meyer. He diagnosed her case as acute "Japanese fear."[29]

On December 18, Louise Spencer hiked the twenty-minute pathway from the Fertigs' hideaway to Hopevale to visit the missionaries. Food stocks were low because most Filipinos believed the roundup rumor and refused to go near Hopevale. Stopping by the Meyers' in Emmanuel Glen, Louise picked up some ointment to send to Claude for his boil. She found the doctor and his wife intensely worried about the roundup rumor.[30]

In Hopevale, Louise Spencer was surprised to meet for the first time two single missionary women, Signe Erickson and Dorothy Dowell, who had arrived there only the day before. Signe, age 45, and Dorothy, age 54, were both teachers. Dorothy was from Colorado, a graduate of Brown University, and had lived in the Philippines for twenty-three years. Signe was a native of Pennsylvania, a graduate of Gordon College, Bethel Seminary, and Columbia University, and had arrived in the Philippines eleven years before World War II. Both women were independent, adventuresome, and loved their work as missionaries and educators. But they were both exhausted and sick after their trek to Hopevale.

Dorothy Dowell.
Courtesy American Baptist Historical Society, Atlanta

As they talked, Louise discovered that when the war engulfed the Philippines, Signe and Dorothy had been living together at the Woman's Training Department of the School of Theology at Central Philippine College in Iloilo. This department offered a professional diploma for women who had not completed high school but wanted to study religious education. Signe and Dorothy taught many young Filipinas how to teach the Bible, establish Sunday schools, and minister to the special needs of women in rural barrios.

When the Japanese invaded Panay, Signe and Dorothy exerted their fierce independence. Much like the gold miners, they determined that they would not surrender to the Japanese nor would they go to Hopevale. Rather they retreated into the hills and became itinerant ministers to rural churches and congregations. As Signe wrote in a letter that was smuggled out of Panay by submarine in May 1943, "We have occasionally played hide-and-seek with the Japanese. When it is safe we make occasional evangelistic visits to nearby barrios."[31]

Signe Erickson.
Courtesy American Baptist
Historical Society, Atlanta

As Louise talked with Dorothy, she realized that she was in great pain. For years Dorothy had suffered with chronic and debilitating arthritis. As the rainy season enveloped her in 1943, her joint inflammation became more acute. Dorothy and Signe decided to pay a visit to Dr. Meyer in Hopevale and to spend Christmas with their fellow missionaries. Braving the Japanese advance into central Panay, Dorothy was literally carried by Filipino friends into Hopevale on a stretcher.[32]

Impressed by the pluck and spunk of these two new friends, Louise then went to visit the Covells. They were not in their nipa hut but had retreated again to their *camalig*, worried about the roundup rumor. Louise found the Roses also distressed and not their usual bright and positive selves. As Louise trudged home, she realized that the missionaries were really struggling.

Later that afternoon, Erle Rounds visited with Spence. He figured that Spence might have more information from the guerrillas and a better grasp of the situation. As they talked, it was clear that Erle—usually resilient and upbeat—had hit bottom, too. He could no longer conjure up hope.

By sunset on Saturday, December 18, it seemed that everyone in Hopevale needed a Sabbath rest and a meaningful worship experience. As Louise Spencer readied for bed, she watched her husband pack his bag, preparing to leave Sunday morning to return to the guerrillas before the new year began. This sight was oddly the most encouraging thing that she had seen all day. Spence was not giving into rumormongers and his own fatigue. He always believed that there would be a better day tomorrow, and this war would be won.

Sunday morning broke lazy and sluggish. Struggling to get up, Louise craved coffee. Spence was dressed and Laverne was rustling around when Pilo, Spence's Filipino aide, rushed in. Trying to stay calm, he blurted, "Sir, the Japs are on this side of the Panay River running in this direction." Spence bolted from the hut, binoculars in hand, and sprinted up a low hill beside the house. Returning, his blanched face told the story. They had only minutes to flee.

Spence knew they could not follow a trail out of Hopevale. Every approach would be blocked by the Japanese. Sticking his .38 revolver in his belt, he threw his favorite .22 rifle under brush, knowing it would only get in the way amid thick jungle foliage. Grabbing the very pregnant Laverne by the hand, he warned her that breaking through the Japanese encirclement would be almost impossible. But they had to try. It would take everything that she could physically endure to escape.

Laverne faced the decision of bringing her dog, Debbie, or shooting her. Left alone, the Airedale would guide the Japanese to Laverne. She put the dog on a rope leash, and Pilo grabbed her green emergency bag, which contained her important papers, scissors, and a small vial of pituitrin that Dr. Meyer insisted

Laverne carry to inhibit post-birth bleeding. Louise was horrified by the thought that the trauma might induce Laverne's labor. She brought up the rear carrying a three-pound can of Klim powdered milk for the baby and her midwife kit.

Pilo, Spence, Louise, and Laverne formed a foursome splashing up a narrow mountain stream, sliding and falling but not leaving footprints. If they could sneak past the Japanese, they would then make their way into the higher mountains to Claude's command post. However, to do this, they must first cross a steep, open hillside densely covered with thick *tigbao*—head-high shoots of razor-sharp mountain grass.

Falling on their hands and knees, they crawled up the long, sloping hill, grasping at the roots and stalks of the *tigbao*. If they stood, the Japanese would see the grass weaving and detect their escape. For many agonizing minutes they clawed their way up the slope, Laverne's swollen stomach scraping the stubbled ground. Halfway up, Laverne collapsed, exhausted and spent.

Spence paused and wanted to let Laverne rest. But he had seen the Japanese in operation before. All it took was one match and the *tigbao* grass, though damp, could ignite into an inferno. Rather than beat the grass to find them, the Japanese would burn them out. Silently shaking his head, Spence signaled Laverne with narrowed eyes and tight lips that they must go on. They could not stop now.

After finally reaching the summit of the ridge line and edging out of the *tigbao* grass, all four collapsed, exhausted. Gazing back at the valley below, they gasped. Dr. Meyer's nipa house at Emmanuel Glen was a flaming torch. The Roundses' and Clardys' hut on the outskirts of Hopevale was also burning. The popping and crackling of burning nipa grass and bamboo could be heard across the distance. Laverne fought back panic. How could she ever deliver her baby without Dr. Meyer?

Crouching on the ridge line, Spence drew his .38 and cocked it. They had to cross an open plot of land and descend to another stream. Scrambling across the ridge single file, they reached the stream safely and plodded up the streambed toward Claude's command post. Spence sent Pilo ahead to alert Claude to the Hopevale disaster.

Louise later remembered that they climbed steadily for an hour, fear goading them on over boulders, along ledges, and straight up nearly vertical slopes. After an hour of relentless climbing, Spence risked taking a break. Rummaging in her shoulder bag, Louise found a jar of native peanut butter and passed it around.

While Laverne gasped for breath and rested, Spence whispered to Louise that as they were leaving Hopevale he had seen Fern Clardy with her youngest son, John, running down a path headed straight for an approaching Japanese squad. Just the day before, while they were walking, Fern had blurted suddenly, "I'm afraid someday I'll walk right into the Japs, and then what would I do?" Visibly wincing, Louise tore herself away from that terrible memory. Fighting tears, she stood up. It was easier to scramble up hills than to think.[33]

In the early afternoon, Claude and another American guerrilla were sighted charging down the trail toward them. Claude was hobbling on his wounded leg, but was ecstatic to see all of them safe. They quickly continued up the mountain to his command post. However, safety had not been reached. Too many Filipinos from Katipunan had served as *cargadores*, carrying supplies to the command post. Under duress they could lead the Japanese there in a few hours.

Everyone changed clothes, coffee was made, and they decided to risk spending the night before moving on. Spence stayed on sentry duty, keeping an eye on the trail from Katipunan. The sun could not rise fast enough.

As the miners escaped, Captain Watanabe personally led his punishment squad toward Hopevale, surrounding the perimeter.

Reverend Dianala remembered: "The Japanese soldiers were very many, going down to Hopevale from many points. All adult Filipinos on their way were all captured and brought down to Hopevale."[34] These hostages possibly would be used for ransom or negotiation.

By Sunday evening, all of the missionaries and the Clardy family had been captured and rounded up. Some had been found in their dugouts and others caught while trying to escape. On Sunday night they all slept in one location, under guard. Sometime that evening, Captain Watanabe told them they would be executed the next day.

Jimmy Covell was the only hope the missionaries had. He spoke fluent Japanese, understood Japanese culture intimately, and was a persuasive speaker. Witnesses later reported that Covell spoke with Watanabe privately and pleaded with him to spare their lives. Watanabe wavered. Using a field radio, he contacted his superiors, who then wired their headquarters in Manila to request a verdict. On Monday, Watanabe was ordered by headquarters to execute all American prisoners. A Japanese officer could not disobey or alter a direct order.[35]

The details of exactly what took place then cannot now be reconstructed fully. How the missionaries and the Clardys were told of their fate and how they reacted is unknown. Perhaps some adults were stoic. But to stand beside their children— Terry Clardy, age five; John Clardy, age seven; Douglas Rounds, age nine—and know they would soon be murdered would have broken the strongest heart.

What is known is that the small band of Americans asked if they could meet alone for a time of prayer before the execution. At exactly 3:00 P.M. they were summoned. Their final communal act was to boldly sing a hymn of faith as they walked back to the Japanese. The words and the tune do not now matter. Rather, it was the years of their lives spent caring for others that composed that sacred hymn, and now their deaths formed its loudest crescendo.

Standing before Watanabe, they were directed to walk toward one, and possibly two, nipa huts. The children likely were torn away from parents at this time, and carried away to be bayoneted to death. Amid the strangled screams of children and the anguished tears of parents, the first adults were motioned to enter the nipa hut door. Perhaps they were offered a blindfold. Perhaps their hands were tied. Perhaps they went forward as married couples or entered singly. But each missionary mounted a bamboo ladder and walked beneath the cogan grass roof. Ordered to kneel and bow, their necks extended, a Japanese soldier raised a long sword, careful not to scrape the blade on the low roof beams. With practiced precision, the blade split the air. It was a quick death. Blood convulsed and dripped through the slatted bamboo floor to the earth below. Then it was time for the next victim. Those who were executed first were those to whom mercy was extended.[36]

Following the executions, the children's bodies likely were placed inside the slaughterhouse with those of their parents. Then a match was struck and the cogan grass and nipa palm erupted into flame. A charnel house became a funeral pyre. Japanese soldiers—stunned, elated, nauseated, exhausted from the killing—gasped for breath in the heat of the fire and the stench of burning flesh.

The killing had not ended. Many Filipinos died as well. Claude and Laverne's house servant, Federico, his wife, Catalina, and their little daughter, Bienvenida, had also been captured in or near the Fertigs' hut. When interrogated and asked where the Fertigs and Spencers were fleeing, Federico refused to answer. He was strung up by his heels from a bamboo beam in Laverne's kitchen and tortured. He was forced to watch his wife beaten to death, her face crushed. His little daughter was also

slaughtered, and finally the nipa hut was set on fire and Federico burned to death. Some other Filipinos who had been ab-
ducted as the Japanese approached Hopevale were also reported
to have been killed, but their stories are not known.[37]

While the Japanese entered Hopevale, Reverend Dianala, his
wife, and their youngest daughter remained in Katipunan. Late
on Sunday his frightened church members gathered and asked
him for advice. He replied, "Every man to himself! But don't forget to pray. Only prayer can save us now. You must understand
that all of us in Katipunan are involved with the Americans for
keeping and feeding them." By nightfall Katipunan was deserted
except for the Dianala family.[38]

Reverend Delfin Dianala and
Mrs. Dianala. *Elmo D. Familiaran*

On Monday at midday, Reverend
Dianala did not yet know the fate of the
missionaries. He later recalled: "The clouds
began to gather at noon. At about two
o'clock p.m. it was showering, and the barrio was again very quiet. Looking towards
the west from my house, I pointed out to
my wife who stayed with me, some red
clouds hovering over Hopevale. Surely
those red clouds were ominous. A cold feeling ran through my body. . . . My heart
was filled with anxiety because of the red
clouds."[39]

Later on Monday night Dianala saw
a flickering torch bobbing down the pathway from Hopevale. "This is it; the Japa-
nese are coming down," he whispered to his wife. Wanting to
protect her, he ran to meet the Japanese at a distance from his
house. In the darkness he heard voices speaking in his dialect.
They were not Japanese. Rather, they were citizens of Katipunan who had been held hostage. Seeing Dianala, they said, "All

of us from Katipunan are set free. But all the Americans are finished." This was the terrible moment when Reverend Dianala knew the missionaries he had loved and protected for eighteen months were dead.

Then the torchbearer looked through the shadows at Dianala and said, "The Japanese are asking for fifty men from Katipunan tomorrow morning. Failure to comply means annihilation, including animals, and all houses will be burned."

Stunned, Dianala asked why the Japanese wanted the men. They replied that the Japanese would use them to hunt for the Fertigs, Spencers, and Schurings. Dianala immediately sent them into the foothills to see if they could gather fifty men by the next morning.

Dianala called that Monday night the "night of weeping"—weeping for the loss of his friends and weeping because he knew it would be impossible to convince fifty men to return to Katipunan and subject themselves to the Japanese. But at daybreak the men began to appear. By eight o'clock over fifty had arrived, and Dianala could see the Japanese troops on the ridge of the hills, ready to come down and raze the barrio if the men had not obeyed.

The men left with the Japanese, and Dianala sent the rest of his family to hide. At three that afternoon Watanabe's search patrols were ambushed by guerrillas, slowing the Japanese down and inflicting casualties. Dianala was sure that the Filipinos of Katipunan—the friends of the Americans—would also be seen as conspirators and the village would be destroyed.

At dawn on Wednesday, two of Reverend Dianala's deacons came to his house and begged him to flee. He refused. Seeing the Japanese returning with the villagers walking behind them, Dianala again ran to meet them at the edge of the barrio. The Japanese were angry, and Watanabe sternly cross-examined him concerning the Fertigs and the Spencers. Then Watanabe said that the guerrillas had destroyed his portable radio. Obviously agitated, he was hurrying to his base camp to get another one so he could return to pursue the Americans. Watanabe did not come back to Katipunan.[40]

As the Japanese disappeared, Dianala could not bring himself to go to Hopevale. He sent five boys to scout the burned community and to report back. In two hours they returned, physically sick at seeing the burned and decaying bodies of the missionaries and the Filipinos. With no mortuary facility, Dianala let the bodies remain where they were for two weeks, decomposing. Then he and Reverend Engacio Alora, the general secretary of the Panay Baptist Convention, went to Hopevale with large burlap bags and gathered the charred remains and hid them above Cathedral Glen. Later, influenced by a dream, Dianala brought the skeletal remains to Katipunan and buried them under the altar of the Baptist church. He kept the burial location a secret until the end of World War II.[41]

Chapter Twelve

**December 1943–April 1944,
Panay**

On Monday, December 20, 1943, the day of the missionaries'
executions, Claude and Spence knew they must leave Claude's
command post. They needed to relocate to a more hidden place
that no one from Katipunan had seen before. Claude knew a Filipino captain who had prepared a hideout for his family higher
up in the mountains. The hut was vacant and the captain had
previously offered it for Claude's use. Traveling lightly and without *cargadores*, the two couples and Spence's helper, Pilo, accompanied by Laverne's Airedale waded in streams all day, concealing
their trail from Japanese scouts. They were sure that Watanabe
was in fast pursuit.

Arriving near the end of the day, they found a larger than
usual cogan-roofed house with two separate rooms. The next
day, as Watanabe's terror squad was being ambushed by guerrillas near Katipunan, Claude sent runners out to find a competent physician and bring him to their hideout, even if he had to
be forced to come. Someone must stand in for Dr. Meyer.

On Christmas Eve day, the runners returned with a splen-
did Filipino doctor who had come willingly to help Laverne with
her delivery, projected for the first week in January. Like Dr.
Meyer, Dr. Teruel was a civilian doctor who was helping the
guerrillas. He was a graduate of the prestigious Santo Tomas
University Medical School in Manila where Richard Meyer and
Donal Rounds were now imprisoned. Leaving his own family at
Christmas, he came prepared to stay until Laverne's delivery.
He brought with him only basic medical instruments—a pair of
surgical scissors, catgut and a needle for stitching, a box of cotton, and a hypodermic needle. But he also brought experience,
expertise, and a wonderful spirit. The Fertigs breathed easier.

Christmas Day arrived and everyone was too exhausted
and numb to celebrate. Though it was good to be alive, the future seemed grim. On this day the first rumors of the massacre
at Hopevale reached the Spencers and Fertigs. Refusing to believe it, they suppressed their fears until there was confirmation.
Though he was separated from his own family, Dr. Teruel was
the only one with Christmas spirit. He noticed that the Spencers' clothing was particularly worn and threadbare. He reached
into his traveling basket and gave them two of his own shirts as
Christmas presents.

The small band of refugees rested from Christmas until New
Year's Eve day. Rumors that the Japanese were looking for them
and drawing closer were growing frequent. Spence and Claude
knew that they must move immediately. Several days before,
Spence had explored deeper into the mountains and had found
a small vacant hut. Just as they were packing to leave for this
house, Pilo arrived with a letter from Reverend Dianala con-
firming that all of the missionaries, the Clardys, and their children had been executed. Dianala also wrote that the Fertigs'
servants had been caught in their hut and cruelly murdered.

As the devastating news sank in, Louise Spencer was locked
into horrified silence and began shaking violently. Laverne broke

into sobs, instantly blaming herself for asking her servant, Federico, and his family to come to Hopevale and take care of her during her pregnancy. The terrible savagery of the murders combined with Laverne's weakened condition pushed her to the breaking point.

Claude and Spence were masked in intense silence, pale and drawn. Stunned, they used all of their energy to stay in control. Now they knew for sure what would happen if the Japanese caught up with them. The island was small and the Japanese presence was growing stronger. They could not run forever. They had to come up with a better plan.

While trying to cope with emotional collapse, they frantically packed and bolted for the trail. After two hours of rapid hiking, they arrived at the hut that Spence had scouted, just as the darkness of New Year's Eve descended on them. For once Louise entered a new year without a calendar, not even a scrap of paper. The future months in 1944 would be a totally uncharted course.

Though exhausted, nobody slept that night. Louise tossed and turned imagining how Mrs. Rose had reacted when she saw the first Japanese. She remembered the moment long ago when she was drinking coffee with Mrs. Rose and that normally stoic lady had looked out her bamboo window and suddenly blurted, "Louise, what will we do if we are here in the kitchen some day and the Japs come down that trail?" And Signe Erickson, petite and refined, who was the most sensitive of all? How did she react in those final moments before her execution? And the little boys and their helpless parents, and . . . ?

Louise couldn't stand to think and imagine and reflect any longer. Yet sleep would not come. The only merciful thing was the coming of first light, the crow of a rooster, the escape into activity and flight.

That dawning light brought New Year's Day of 1944. Before the sun was high in the sky, it was apparent that their new hideout was again not adequately protected. Curious neighbors were already dropping by, and the hut was exposed. Claude and Spence decided that they must move again. Over the next few days the men searched for a place that was remote and secure, where Laverne could have her baby in safety. Finally, Spence and Claude found an isolated spot near the barrio of Burri in southern Capiz province and made arrangements with a few Bukidnon tribesmen to hastily build a one-room hut. The location was secluded, difficult to approach, camouflaged by dense growth, and close to a clear stream. It was the best place—an increasingly necessary place—for the baby to be born.

On January 6, the stilts, floor, and roof of the hut were completed and the Spencers and Fertigs hiked two hours to the hidden site. No sooner had they arrived than it was reported that a Japanese patrol was nearby. The Bukidnon workmen fled, leaving the hut without walls and fully exposed to the afternoon rains. For the next few days Claude and Spence kept a vigilant watch on the approaching trails, and everyone remained hunkered down in the dense foliage. Finally, the Bukidnon workers returned, and Claude was satisfied that the Japanese were not in the immediate vicinity.

On Sunday, January 9, exactly three weeks after fleeing from Hopevale, Laverne awoke feeling very uncomfortable. Sensing that the baby might come that day, she walked to a nearby mountain stream, took a hurried bath, became chilled, and promptly felt her first labor pains.

The timing was right. Only the day before had the nipa palm sides been attached to the bamboo frame of the hut and the construction completed. Dr. Teruel ordered a kettle of boiling water, and Claude worried about the smoke from the open fire attracting the Japanese. As the sun set, it began to rain hard. Everyone, including the Filipino helpers, crowded inside the one-room hut. A sheet was draped across a section of the room to give Laverne some scant privacy, and Dr. Teruel timed her contractions.

As the room grew ever darker and the quiet whispers of Americans and Filipinos fell into a hushed harmony, Louise suddenly found herself becoming a midwife. She assisted the doctor, bathing Laverne's sweating face and often holding and directing the only source of light—an old tin can containing coconut oil and a floating wick burning dimly.

Laverne's delivery was blessedly short. With the last contraction and painful push, Dr. Teruel pulled forth a little girl into the flickering lamplight. When the doctor held her up and slapped her on the bottom, she let out a healthy cry. On cue, Laverne's Airedale, Debbie, began to howl, joining the celebration. Grown men shed tears, and bright smiles lit up a darkened room and an anguished world. Dr. Teruel had defied great odds and performed marvelously in the most primitive of circumstances. Mother and daughter were fine, and Susan Beatrice Fertig was born safely.

Susan was from the first a healthy baby and nursed well. For the next eleven days she was shielded by a typhoon and constant torrential rain that had become a blessing—the Japanese were kept from patrolling, Laverne was able to rest, and a fragile equilibrium continued. Dr. Teruel departed on the third day after the birth to return home. This good man had shown skill and compassion not only in delivering Susan, but in hiking halfway across Panay and dodging Japanese patrols for over two weeks. He was dearly loved and never forgotten.

Shortly after Dr. Teruel left for home, Claude grew feverish and delirious. Alarmed, Spence sent one of his Filipino helpers to look for another doctor. With incredible luck the young man found a Filipino doctor near Buri and returned with him. This doctor spoke little English, but he examined Claude, gave him three hard to acquire sulfa tablets, and prescribed a liquid diet. As he prepared to go, Spence asked him if he would also check on

Louise. Recently her legs had been swelling and her face looked puffy. Spence feared kidney disease. After a quick examination the doctor looked Spence in the eye, and in broken English said, "Sir, the senora is pregnant." Spence turned ashen. When the doctor left, he flopped down and exploded, "Where is the Army and Navy? We have to have a good doctor, nurses, a hospital! I have to have help!" Spence had finally reached his limit. Laverne laughed and Claude moaned in his sickbed. Now it was the Spencers' turn to experience what the Fertigs had endured for the last nine months![1]

As the first week of 1944 flew by and the United States entered its third year of war, American infantry and marines were slugging it out with the Japanese on New Britain; the Americal division was relieving the Third Marine Division on Bougainville in the Solomon Islands, and American and Australian troops were defeating the Japanese on New Guinea. Slowly the Allied forces were edging north toward the Philippines. But progress was never as fast as MacArthur expected. The general would celebrate his sixty-third birthday on January 26, and he was beginning to wonder if he would live long enough to return to the Philippines at the present rate of progress.

What really enraged MacArthur, however, was that he had received a coded message from Colonel Peralta detailing the slaughter of American missionaries and civilians at Hopevale. This was likely the first time that a large number of American civilians in the Philippines had been slaughtered by the Japanese. The fact that they were missionaries made the situation even more grave. MacArthur realized that once such a precedent was set, more executions of American civilian might ensue. Indeed, within a few weeks the Japanese army in the Philippines made clear their intentions when an official policy was distributed widely throughout the islands that read, "The amnesty under which the Americans have been guaranteed safety and internment by the Imperial Japanese Government is about to expire. After 25 of January 1944 any American found in the Islands, whether unsurrendered soldier or civilian, will be executed without trial."[2]

With the Hopevale massacre and the reinstatement of Japanese policy and intent, the situation was dangerously clear. With the submarines' recent success landings in the Philippines, MacArthur decided to attempt to rescue as many American civilians on Panay and other islands as possible.[3]

On February 9, 1944, Laverne was strong enough to travel again. News of the birth of the American baby had leaked out and curious visits from neighbors were increasing. The security of their hideout was jeopardized. Spence, highly motivated by news of Louise's pregnancy, was hard at work constructing a more permanent and suitable camp a few hours away. When Susan Fertig was a month old, a move was made to Spence's new camp.

On the day the Fertigs and Spencers arrived, February 13, 1944, Claude received word that Colonel Peralta wanted to speak with him about an urgent matter. On February 17, he left the camp to talk with Peralta's courier. Returning at dark, he brought news that was fantastic and life changing. MacArthur had decided to attempt to rescue as many American civilians on Panay as possible in one submarine pickup. If the attempt worked, it would be an incredible feat. And if it didn't, a lot of people would likely be killed. But MacArthur knew that time was running out for Americans on Panay.[4]

The Fertigs and Spencers were beside themselves with joy. Laughter bubbled and tears flowed once again—now tears of joy. But there was also sober reality. They had three weeks and six days to cross a high and difficult range of mountains and descend to the appointed landing zone, all with a newborn baby, an exhausted mother, a pregnant woman, two men weakened and sick, and Japanese soldiers in pursuit.

Having traversed the northwestern mountains multiple times, from central Panay to the submarine landing zone, Claude and Spence knew the terrain and only needed to retrace their steps. But each trip was unique and carried its own danger and risks. Leaving Spence's new hideaway on February 24, they made their way northwest toward Aklan, certain that of all the Americans hiding out, they knew best how to find the rendezvous point. They also pooled their limited money to hire Filipino *cargadores* to guide them, translate for them, and carry such things as bags of rice, cooking utensils, and any other supplies they could scrounge together. Spence's assistant, Pilo, also came with them, forever faithful and indispensable.

Thankfully, it was near the end of rainy season and the trip progressed smoothly. Yet they were still haunted by the fact that Watanabe was looking for them. There was a sense of constant danger. Their biggest fear was that the so-called secret of the rescue plan would leak out to the Japanese. How do you preserve confidential information when dozens of people are aware of an opportunity to escape and are intensely excited? Especially when an unknown number of American civilians who had been hiding out for over two years were all converging on one landing zone? Logic suggested that the Japanese would discover the secret.

As the Fertigs and Spencers made their way, Laverne was still weak and feeling lousy. Baby Susan needed to breast-feed every three hours and have her diapers changed often. Laverne was afraid the physical demands of the long trip would cause her milk to dry up, and there was no baby formula. This young mother was moving into an experience she had never known before.

By now Louise was looking quite ragged and threadbare. She had no shoes, only one pair of slacks and one shirt to wear on the trail, and one dress crammed in a thatch bag to sleep in at night. As they climed to higher altitudes after several days on the trail, Louise Spencer grew breathless since her pregnancy made it difficult to adjust to the thinner atmosphere. By the end of each day both women were exhausted.

Stopping one late afternoon for everyone to rest, Claude and Laverne decided to take a brisk bath in a nearby mountain stream. Suddenly the Fertigs heard feet pounding up the trail above them. Frightened, they grabbed their clothes and struggled to get dressed. Peering through the brush, they were stunned to see not Japanese soldiers but rather Henry and Laura Schuring and their young teenage son, Clifford. Though they knew that the Schurings had escaped from Hopevale, they had not seen them since.

Stepping out of the jungle, they ran to embrace the startled Schurings. Words were not needed. Just squealing hugs and back pounding. It was a grand reunion that unleashed pent-up emotions. As the Spencers also emerged from the woods and ambled down the trail, Laura Schuring took one look and realized that Louise was pregnant, too. Their whole crazy and tragic world was laced with wonderful surprises.

The next day the three couples agreed to travel together on the same trail. However, for safety reasons they decided that they would leave separately over three days, so that if the Japanese discovered their whereabouts, they would not be grouped together and all captured. The Schurings traveled the first day, the Spencers delayed and left the second day, and the Fertigs brought up the rear.

As the Spencers continued their journey, the mountains grew steeper and Louise encountered greater difficulty. Hiking on unlevel ground had been difficult for this pregnant woman, now climbing up steep hills and descending nearly vertical slopes on narrow footpaths seemed almost impossible at times. Spence was always walking protectively in front of her or behind her, ready to catch her at any moment. Because of this their progress was slow and plodding.

Finally they reached Aclan River, and the gentle stream provided a natural water pathway. However, for several days it rained nonstop. The Spencers found it strange to wade in water above their knees and also have water falling out of the sky. Even in a tropical climate the rain chilled them if they did not move at a brisk pace and keep their body temperatures elevated.

Several days later the Spencers caught up with the Schurings. Laura Schuring's feet were lacerated and covered with ulcers. She had to travel slowly. Ahead of them was a large mountain and both women dreaded crossing it. Finally it was decided that the *cargadores* would transport Laura on a jury-rigged stretcher. She could not walk farther.

Making their way up the mountain's steep slopes, they were terrified that their feet and legs would become covered with blood-sucking leeches. Soon each carried a small knife with which to flick the leeches off before they attached themselves. The native Bukidnons rubbed tobacco leaves on their skin to repel the leeches, but nothing seemed to help.

As they neared the top of the mountain, they were enveloped by a thick fog that often covered the summit during early morning and late afternoon. Surrounded by the cloudy coolness, they felt like they were on top of the world. When the fog would briefly break, they could catch a glimpse of the horizon to the west and almost see the ocean. As they crested the summit and descended out of the mist, they knew they were crossing the great divide of Panay Island, leaving the province of Capiz and entering the province of Antique. The Sulu Sea was now much closer.

Despite the beauty, they worried that the Japanese were close. They soon found evidence that the Japanese had been there several months earlier. Even amid lush beauty danger lurked.

Several days later they began to descend the western side of the Cordillera and move toward the coast. The western slope was steeper and the descent more dangerous. Frequently they traversed paths so narrow that only one person could pass at a time, with drop-offs that descended to dizzying depths below. One fainting spell or one misstep would be fatal. Sometimes Louise got on her hands and knees and crawled instead of walked. Pilo and Spence doted on her and helped whenever possible. But there were moments when she was totally on her own, grasping vines and tree roots, surviving on sheer willpower.

Finally, the day came when they crested the summit of one more ridge and found the sparkling panorama of the Sulu Sea gleaming in the distance. Too tired to celebrate, they slowly descended toward the shoreline of Pandan Bay. Their mountain journey had been memorable days of unmitigated hell.

As they crossed the last series of foothills, the Spencers again caught up with the Schurings. The Schurings' feet looked like raw hamburger, and they were taking a much-needed rest. They were also the bearers of very bad news. Reports had come from the landing site that the Japanese navy had been patrolling the coastline along Pandan Bay for the past two days. It was likely that they had discovered MacArthur's plan for evacuation. If so, Japanese infantry would be appearing soon.

Crushed by this news, everyone was despondent. That night Louise had nightmares. Spence told her the next morning that she had spent half of the night running from the Japanese in her sleep, actually crawling on her straw mat as if trying to scale a steep hill. But the next day her mood was improved greatly when an American guerrilla officer hiked up to the barrio where they were staying with the news that the Japanese ships had moved down the coast and the landing zone was now clear. They could proceed. Perhaps it had just been a routine naval maneuver after all.[5]

Finally reaching the coastal highway, the Spencers were at least a day ahead of the Schurings and the Fertigs. Deciding not to wait, they plodded along flat ground for a change. Soon Spence realized that Louise was expending her last reserve of energy. At that moment, Spence had an inspired idea. Leaving Louise in the shade for an hour, he found a Filipino fisherman and hired him to sail them down the coast in his *banca*. He strutted back to Louise elated and rather proud of himself. The *banca* would pick them up that evening.

Late that afternoon, Spence learned that the Japanese ships had returned. Their sailing plans were dashed. Dejected, they found lodging with a Filipino family. Taking stock of their situation, they knew that they were a few days ahead of schedule. They decided to sleep through the next day and only travel in the coolness of night. Three nights later, they finally approached the stretch of Pandan Bay where previous submarines had unloaded, a few miles east of the small town of Libertad. They had made their rendezvous point with time to spare. Now, if only the Japanese navy would cooperate.

Shortly before the Spencers arrived at the coast, an American submarine commander received an unexpected change of orders. His name was Lieutenant Commander R. I. "Swede" Olsen, and he was not happy with his new assignment.

Swede Olsen was a product of the U.S. Navy. His father, Lieutenant Hjalmer E. Olsen, was a career naval officer, and all five of his sons graduated from the United States Naval Academy.[6] Olsen was an aggressive young officer in his early thirties and eager to prove his mettle. In the beginning months of the war, Olsen had been the executive officer serving on the submarine *Haddock*. Late in 1943 he was given command of a new attack submarine, *Angler* (SS-240), then under construction at the Electric Boat Company shipyard in Groton, Connecticut. *Angler* was commissioned on October 1, 1943, and was soon transferred to Pearl Harbor. Olsen began *Angler*'s first war patrol on January 10, 1944, and engaged an enemy convoy north of the Marianas, sinking the Japanese tender *Shuko Maru*. Olsen paid the price when depth charges dropped by Japanese destroyers damaged his vessel. As a result, the *Angler* developed major structural noises that prevented silent running. The submarine returned to Midway Island for repairs, arriving on February 15, 1944.[7]

In early 1944, eighteen submarines were transferred from Pearl Harbor to Fremantle, Australia, under the command of Rear Admiral Ralph Waldo Christie. *Angler* was tapped for this transfer, and Olsen received his orders from Christie for the *Angler's* second combat patrol in late February 1944. He was assigned to patrol Philippine waters, specifically the Mindanao and Sulu seas. Eager to make up for lost time and increase his tally of sunken vessels, he was disappointed when he received direct orders from Australia on March 18, 1944, to abandon the hunt and proceed to the northwest corner of Panay to rescue "about twenty" American civilians.[8]

Prior to this time, American submarines had evacuated some civilians in the Philippines while on secret missions to deliver equipment and weapons to guerrilla units. On November 15, 1943, the large supply submarine *Narwhal* had delivered forty-six tons of stores and two military landing parties at Nasipit, Mindanao. Upon arrival, a request was made to allow thirty-two people, including eight women and two children, to come aboard. The commander of the *Narwhal*, Lieutenant Commander Frank Latta, agreed and ferried them to Australia, setting a precedent for the rescue of American civilians in the Philippines. More recently, on March 2, 1944, the *Narwhal* had also delivered forty-five tons of cargo and evacuated twenty-eight women and children off the island of Negros. However, the smaller *Angler* now became the first attack submarine to be pulled off the line and specifically ordered to attempt the rescue of a large group of predominantly American civilians.[9]

Before Olsen's arrival, Colonel Peralta received a message from MacArthur's headquarters instructing the guerrillas to display a series of large colored signal panels that could be seen seaward for at least two miles. The coded panels should be displayed beginning March 20. The order concluded, "Upon the arrival and if signals displayed as indicated sub will appear at sunset at which time send all evacuees and baggage alongside immediately so as not to delay departure. Give matter utmost secrecy. Confirm understanding."[10]

Lieutenant Commander Olsen immediately proceeded toward Panay. At 9:00 A.M. on Monday, March 20, the *Angler* arrived at Pandan Bay and was making a submerged approach toward the landing site near Libertad. A mile from the shore, Olsen gazed through his periscope and could just barely make out a number of people walking behind the tree line of a narrow beach. The previously arranged three-paneled identification panels were hoisted in trees and the color code was correct. Olsen had to observe radio silence and could not confirm to the landing zone personnel that he had arrived. However, it looked like the "party was on," and he stood out to sea to wait for nightfall.[11]

The day before, March 19, the Fertigs and the Schurings had finally arrived at the landing zone and joined the Spencers. Then Mr. and Mrs. Ford and their daughters showed up. The Hopevale crew knew that the Fords had survived the Japanese penetration but did not know if they would also attempt the submarine evacuation. Now, with the survivors safely together, there was the feeling of the greatest family reunion in the world. Yet the submarine had not appeared. The Japanese navy could resume their shore patrols at any moment. None of the evacuees had been told on what day the submarine might arrive, much less what time. They experienced wild elation amid intense fear and anxiety.

That night the Spencers and most of the other evacuees slept in a primitive camp prepared for them within walking distance of the landing zone. Spence knew the expected arrival date of the submarine because he had been briefed by Colonel

Peralta at a meeting just days before. And he anticipated that the evacuation would be after dark. But honoring military security, he did not tell Louise. She did not need to know one more thing. Her pent-up excitement already had her thrashing and talking in her sleep.

The next morning, March 20, a simple breakfast was prepared, and at 10:00 A.M. the civilians were instructed to leave the camp, walk to the beach, and move down behind the sheltering tree line. Louise took off at a fast clip. If anyone was going to be first in line, it was going to be her. Spence, trotting along behind her, chuckled at his pregnant wife's spirit. Finally, he could stand it no longer, and whispered to her that the sub would surface at six that evening, precisely at sunset. There was no need to hurry.[12]

When they reached the shoreline, a cool breeze was blowing on the beautiful, bright day. The guerrillas manning the landing zone had prepared three shelters hidden in the trees, and had secured four large *bancas* to transport the evacuees to the sub, should the sub arrive and surface.[13]

Though the mood was joyful, Spence and Claude had not forgotten that this was no picnic. They knew that if the Japanese uncovered their plans, all hell would break loose. With furtive glances, the men looked for a place to escape should the U.S. Navy not arrive.

As people continued to filter in, there were many happy reunions. Old friends were reunited, and people assumed dead appeared in full life. It was a time of nervous handshaking and backslapping. Louise sat back and marveled at the bizarre scene. They looked like a convention of scarecrows—skinny frames covered with rags, tatters, and old straw hats—all mingling together. Shoes were a rare commodity. Some folks were so sick they were carried on home-made stretchers. While most of the Americans were "short timers" in the Philippines, some had been there for years. Many of the old-timers had Filipino wives and beautiful mestizo children. But all of them were eager for one thing: rescue from this hellacious war. They wanted out of these islands and passage to freedom.

Soon everyone was counting noses. Most estimated there were nearly sixty waiting to board. This was almost as many people as an entire submarine crew. Though no one spoke openly of the fact, it was assumed by most that not everyone could be loaded on the submarine. Some people would be left behind. How would it be decided who would go? Most likely, women, children, the aged, and the critically ill would receive top priority. Claude's and Spence's chances were not good.

Submerged in the Sulu Sea at periscope level, Lieutenant Commander Olsen had not seen Japanese ships or planes for hours, and he grew impatient. As evening approached, he lowered his periscope and slowly approached the shore still submerged. At exactly 5:45 P.M., armed Filipino guerrillas led the civilians down to the beach. Staring at calm waters, the moment of truth had finally come. There was no evidence of a submarine. And things became deathly quiet.

The sun touched the ocean horizon; the sky was reflecting radiantly on the calm waters. The "ghost grey" nose of the great sub broke the surface of the sea. An audible sigh of awe broke forth from the beach, and then a crescendo of applause and laughter and joy erupted. There was not a dry eye among the refugees, or even the guerrillas. Tears flowed proudly from the toughest of men, and frazzled women turned into frolicsome girls for a spontaneous moment.[14]

Olsen had made a sudden and dramatic "battle surface," lunging from the depths like a porpoise. He was in no mood to take his time and remain exposed for long. Now, with his crew at battle stations and decks awash, he edged to within one thousand yards of the beach. Soon a small *banca* bearing Colonel

Garcia, the Filipino commander of the landing zone, came alongside the *Angler*. Garcia hesitated and then blurted, "Captain, can you take aboard fifty-eight people?"

Olsen was standing with authority on the small bridge, "high on the sail." He was tall, much taller than most submariners. But even he seemed to shrink an inch or two in the face of this news. His eyes grew big and he swallowed hard. Slowly he nodded yes and gazed at his fellow officers. They would find a way to make it work. Tremendously relieved, Garcia turned and sent a signal to shore by flashlight for all the refugees to board the four *bancas* and proceed immediately to the submarine.[15]

Stunned and elated by the good news, the Fertigs and Spencers hurriedly gathered around Pilo, sharing an emotional good-bye with this brave and loyal man. Everyone was choked up, the women openly weeping. Laverne looked down at her beloved dog, Debbie, knowing that a pet would not make the head count. Quickly she handed the leash to Pilo and, shedding tears of grief and joy, moved quickly toward the *bancas*.[16]

As the *bancas* glided out from the beach, the Spencers' and Fertigs' thoughts were filled with the memories of the Meyers, Roses, Roundses, Covells, Clardys, Jennie Adams, Signe Erickson, Dorothy Dowell, and Federico and his wife and little daughter—people who had become closer than family. The eternal journey of the Hopevale dead was now beyond the sunset and the depths of the ocean. Beyond human imagination into the realm of spiritual mystery. But even profound religious faith did not take the edge off tragic sorrow.

Darkness was falling quickly as the *bancas* bumped against the swaying hull of the sub. Claude was still nervous and unsure of Olsen's earlier response to Colonel Garcia. He yelled up to Olsen, "How many of us are you going to be able to take?" Olsen, now composed, hollered back, "All! All of you, of course!"[17] Even with such assurance the good news seemed impossible.

It was difficult clambering from the shallow-hulled *bancas* up the elevated, slippery hull of the submarine, even for the healthiest. Young sailors lined the deck grabbing hands and arms and hauling people aboard. Most of the sick and elderly were dead weight. One large redheaded sailor reached down to help Laverne scramble up. First she gently handed him a cloth bundle, which he took roughly and then suddenly yelled, "Well, what have I got here!" Laverne shouted back, "It's my two-month-old child." Breaking out into a huge grin, he clutched her to his chest like a football. Susan Fertig was possibly the first baby his rough hands had ever held.[18]

With urgent speed, the *bancas* were unloaded and passengers rushed belowdecks One Japanese dive-bomber or fighter plane screaming out of the darkening sky would change this party into tragedy. Within minutes the *Angler* battened hatches, slid out to sea, and shaped course for Darwin. For an hour it sailed submerged, and then surfaced for a night run. The sub crew, though serious and professional in enemy waters, were delighted to play host to these dirty, scraggly, gaunt civilians.

As the submarine got under way, the Americans found the cramped, spartan sub luxurious. The galley ran overtime trying to feed this famished group. Simple sandwiches of white bread, ham, and cheese served with potato salad and pickles seemed like a gourmet meal to these survivors. When dessert was brought out, one American army captain—probably Spence—offered to buy a whole apple pie for one hundred pesos with cash he had personally printed from Colonel Peralta's printing press. Though rations were soon cut due to the large number of people on board and the length of the voyage, the quantity of such good food still seemed opulent to these evacuees, who had lived primarily on rice, fruit, sun-dried fish, and anything they could scavenge for two and a half years.[19]

Louise, baby Susan, and Laverne were assigned to the chief

petty officer's quarters due to their obstetric health needs. Soon they were drinking real coffee served in nautical silver with cream and sugar poured into china cups. Coveted American cigarettes—Camels, Chesterfields, Lucky Strikes—were handed out by the carton. Though they could not be smoked unless the sub was surfaced, just to hold the colorful cartons was reassuring.

But even though the Panay survivors felt like they were on a luxury liner sailing to heaven, the sub crew immediately noticed how an immaculate and well-organized submarine was being transformed into filth and chaos. Lieutenant Commander Olsen's after-action report paints the picture well:

> The entire ship's company [crew] was berthed in the after battery compartment except for torpedo watch-standers. Concerning the passengers: Men and boys lived in after torpedo rooms, women and children in the forward torpedo room. CPO [chief petty officers] quarters were inhabited by one woman with a two months old baby, one pregnant woman (8-months), one seriously ill girl (worms—temperature 104) and two elderly women. Ship was immediately infested with cockroaches, body lice, and hair lice. A large percentage of the passengers had tropical ulcers plus an odor that was unique in its intensity.

> All passengers showed signs of prolonged undernourishment. All were suffering from lacerated feet due to the long march to the embarkation point without footgear. One male passenger was temporarily insane, requiring a twenty-four hour watch. Two meals a day with soup at 2400 was put in effect at once, since it was apparent the ship did not have enough food aboard for a full three meals a day. Passengers ate ravenously from their arrival until they left the ship. Food was rationed until the night before our arrival at Darwin.

Habitability forward of the control room resembled the "black Hole" of Calcutta, a condition which resulted from children urinating and spitting on the deck, body odors and 47 persons sleeping forward of the control room. In spite of a constant watch at the head [toilet] it proved impossible to teach our passengers the proper use of this vehicle after two years in the hills. . . .

One for the book was the sight of a two-year old, half Filipino boy smoking (and inhaling) a cigar between gulps of his dinner which he was receiving at his mother's breast![20]

The biggest stressors on this twelve-day voyage to Darwin was thankfully not Japanese destroyers and depth charges but rather disease, clean air, claustrophobia, heat, and safe drinking water. The lone pharmacist's mate, "Doc" Needlinger, was constantly busy. When he saw Louise Spencer bulging at the seams in advanced pregnancy, he grew particularly worried. His shipmates needled him constantly about delivering her baby. However, despite the concern for Louise, Needlinger's time was primarily spent treating tropical diseases such as dysentery and tending to bruised and infected feet. He was also able to save one young girl from the brink of death caused by intestinal worms coupled with severe psychological shock due to war trauma. She became Doc Needlinger's favorite patient, and she improved greatly.

Clean air to breathe in a World War II submarine was rare. Submerged for long periods of time, the air grew stale and unhealthy. When the number of people on a submarine suddenly doubled, the problem became intense. Incredibly, at that time, people were even allowed to smoke inside a submarine, whenever the "smoking lamp" was lit, usually when the sub was surfaced.

Louise Spencer was particularly troubled by the lack of

oxygen. As her pregnancy advanced, she frequently felt short of breath. One day she passed out and had symptoms of a seizure. Fortunately, there was an oxygen tank on board, and periodic use of the oxygen brought her relief.[21]

When possible, the *Angler* would cruise on the surface at night. On these evenings, available external hatches were opened and fresh sea breezes would circulate belowdecks. The relief of the passengers was immediate. But when *Angler* was submerged for long hours, the carbon monoxide level could grow dangerous.

Toward the end of the voyage, the *Angler* encountered a serious and mysterious problem. Many of the crew and civilians became acutely nauseated. Much later it was discovered that the sub's drinking-water tanks had not been cleaned properly before departing on its mission, and the "safe" water had become tainted and toxic.[22] This did not prove fatal, and otherwise the cruise to Darwin remained quiet and uneventful.

Early on the morning of April 1, 1944, the *Angler* arrived in Darwin after a twelve-day voyage. Many refugee passengers rummaged through their small bags, trying to find clothing so they would look presentable when reentering civilization. Louise Spencer could find only a ripped and shredded green dress and a pair of tattered tennis shoes. Few of the refugees did better. Awkwardly they climbed up the ladders out of the depths of the submarine and stepped out onto the deck. Nearly blinded by the bright sun, they shielded their eyes and tried to get their bearings. What greeted them was the sight of the submarine crew standing in formation at rigid attention, saluting their weary passengers and paying tribute to their war effort and heroic survival. The refugees were stunned by this act of respect. Though efforts were made, no one could adequately express to the officers and crew their gratitude for their rescue. For the rest of their lives, fifty-eight desperate men, women, and children would remember the sight of the *Angler* bursting up out of the depths of the Sulu Sea and bringing to them the gift of life and a future. Captain Olsen would forever remain their hero and gruff guardian angel.[23]

The Panay evacuees were taken immediately to a quarantine center and then transferred to medical units and rehabilitation centers. Hot showers were a marvel, bedsheets luxurious, and a cafeteria line overwhelming. Slowly the reality settled in that there might be life after war. The next day they were all flown on three planes from Darwin to Brisbane, and General MacArthur sent a simple message to Colonel Peralta on Panay: "Evacuees and mail arrived."[24]

Epilogue

When the refugees from Panay began their temporary life in Australia, eighteen months of war in the Pacific theater still remained. How did the men and women who escaped adjust to their sudden rescue? Did they continue to contribute to the war effort? How did the war in the Pacific progress? And, with the war finally concluded, how did they live out the rest of their lives, as they scattered around the world?

General Douglas MacArthur and the Liberation of the Philippines

Even as the refugees from Panay set foot on Australian soil, it was far from clear whether General MacArthur and his armed forces would ever return in triumph to the Philippines. The problem was not so much the Japanese opposition. In fact, by the spring of 1943, Japanese forces in the Pacific were already in retreat and facing eventual defeat. Rather, what might delay liberation of the Philippines was a fierce difference of opinion among senior American military leaders. It boiled down to a conflict between the army and the navy.

By the time the Hopevale survivors arrived in Darwin on the *Angler*, MacArthur's New Guinea campaign was proving successful and gaining momentum. This campaign had a two-fold purpose. The primary purpose of conquering New Guinea was to defend Australia from attack and to secure the advances that American forces had already made in the southwest Pacific. The second purpose—which was gaining increasing importance each day—was to methodically advance northward and secure bases along the New Guinea coast from which to support an invasion of the Philippines.

In March 1944 the Joint Chiefs of Staff approved MacArthur's proposed landing at Hollandia, New Guinea, and also gave approval for Admiral Nimitz to unleash the navy and marines in an invasion of the Mariana Islands in June 1944. From soon-to-be constructed air bases on Saipan, Guam, and Tinian in the Marianas, the large, new B-29 bombers could soon commence bombing of Japan.

Anticipating success in New Guinea, MacArthur had his general headquarters staff draw up a proposed plan for the liberation of the Philippines, code-named "Musketeer." The plan projected a three-step invasion. First, American forces would land on southern Mindanao on November 15, 1944, and link up with Wendell Fertig's guerrilla forces. Then, leapfrogging to the central Visayan Islands, they would invade Leyte on December 20, 1944. Finally, the large northern island of Luzon, containing the vast majority of the Japanese troops, would be invaded through Lingayen Gulf, sometime in February 1945. By defeating roughly three hundred thousand Japanese soldiers and destroying their air and navy bases in the Philippines, a firm tactical platform for the future invasion of Japan would be secured, and—equally as important to MacArthur—the "Defender of the Philippines" would be able to avenge his honor and keep his great promise, "I Shall Return!!!"[1]

The navy and marines had other plans, however. Led by Admiral Ernest King, commander in chief, U.S. Fleet and chief of Naval Operations (COMINCH-CNO), the navy was beginning to advocate that the Philippines be bypassed and simply isolated and blockaded by naval forces. With good reason, the navy feared that the vast, sprawling Philippine archipelago could become a quagmire if invaded, causing multiple army divisions and supporting navy ships to become bogged down on far-flung islands losing much time in the approach to Japan. American casualties would predictably be high, and such loss of human life might be avoided if the Philippines were simply bypassed.

The navy's alternative plan was to attack the single island of Formosa—not a vast archipelago—several hundred miles north of the Philippines. From Formosa, the navy contended, they could police the southern shipping approach to Japan from the South China Sea and intercept Japanese tankers bringing oil from the Dutch East Indies—Japan's major source of petroleum. With no way to keep her industrial and military operations running without gas and oil, Japan could then be pounded into submission by constant bombing from bases on Tinian, Saipan, Guam, and other surrounding islands in American possession. All of this, they proposed, could be accomplished without liberating the Philippines, particularly the Japanese bastion of Luzon. The lives of thousands of American servicemen would be saved, and the timetable for attacking the Japanese homeland greatly advanced and expedited.[2]

Behind this plan, however, there was also political wrangling. The end result would be that Japan might be brought to her knees primarily by the might of the navy, marines, and the increasingly potent army air corps. The traditional army infantry would be left on the sidelines, and MacArthur with them. As MacArthur would later state in his memoirs, if Admiral King's plan had been accepted "all of my American forces, except a token group of two divisions and a few air squadrons, were to be transferred to the command of Admiral Nimitz, who was to continue to drive across the Central Pacific." This drew MacArthur's ire and underscored his belief that the navy's plan was fundamentally flawed and too simplistic.[3]

When MacArthur caught wind of the navy's plans and learned that even General George Marshall, chief of staff of the Army, was being influenced by Admiral King, he was livid. Not only did he fault King's approach as being strategically and tactically impaired, he considered it to be a personal affront to himself, American POWs in the Philippines, and the Filipino people. MacArthur later wrote that to bypass the Philippines was immoral and

> would result in death to the thousands of prisoners, including American women, children, and men civilians, held in Philippine concentration camps. Practically all of the 17,000,000 Filipinos remained loyal to the United States, and were undergoing the greatest privations and sufferings because we had not been able to support or succor them. To by-pass isolated islands was one thing, but to leave in your rear such a large enemy concentration as the Philippines involved serious and unnecessary risks.[4]

Infuriated, MacArthur fired off a communiqué to his superior, General Marshall, requesting that "I be accorded the opportunity of personally proceeding to Washington to present fully my views."[5]

While Marshall did not provide MacArthur a ticket to come to Washington, President Roosevelt—who would soon be running for reelection to an unprecedented fourth term—decided to meet with MacArthur in Hawaii. Contrary to his normal procedure, Roosevelt would not be accompanied by the Joint Chiefs of Staff. This meant that Admiral King would not attend the meeting, but rather would be represented by Admiral Chester Nimitz, commander in chief, Pacific Ocean Areas.[6]

In sending his communiqué to MacArthur to fly to Hawaii and meet with President Roosevelt, General Marshall gave MacArthur a chilling warning: "It seems to me that you are allowing personal feelings and Philippine political considerations to override our great objective which is the early conclusion of the war with Japan. Also that you confuse the word 'bypass' with 'abandonment.' The two are in no way synonymous in my view." MacArthur now knew that convincing the president to support the invasion of the Philippines was solely on his shoulders, and that he was up against great odds.[7]

MacArthur flew from Australia on July 26, 1944, and hours later was greeted by Admiral Nimitz at Hickam Field in Honolulu. Roosevelt had boarded the new heavy cruiser, the U.S.S. *Baltimore*, the day after accepting the Democratic Party's presidential nomination for the fourth time and had docked in Hawaii only hours before MacArthur's plane landed.[8] After much fanfare and festivity, the three men finally met alone and got down to business. MacArthur was ready and loaded for bear. Chosen to make his presentation first, MacArthur began by arguing that the tourniquet on the flow of oil from the Dutch East Indies to Japan could be much better applied from the Philippines than from Formosa. He stated, "The blockade that I will put across the line of supply between Japan and the Dutch East Indies will so strangle the Japanese Empire that it will have to surrender."[9]

Next, MacArthur argued that unlike small islands that had been successfully bypassed in the approach to the Philippines, the massive island of Luzon could not be bypassed easily nor effectively blockaded by the navy. There were too many Japanese bombers and fighter planes based on Luzon to allow such restraining tactics. In addition, the United States would be leaving a military force in excess of three hundred thousand Japanese soldiers in its rear. And Japanese land-based planes on Luzon could easily bomb and strafe American troops who invaded Formosa. To bypass Luzon, argued MacArthur, was not only shortsighted but strategically and tactically unsound.

Finally, MacArthur confidently claimed that if allowed to invade the Philippines, he could complete his offensive with victory within six months. A somewhat incredulous President Roosevelt replied, "Douglas, to take Luzon would demand heavier losses than we can stand."[10]

MacArthur replied to the president by reminding him that unlike Formosa, the Philippine islands were filled with hundreds of guerrilla organizations and thousands of Filipino patriots who would join with the Americans in a united effort. They would make quick work of the encircled Japanese.[11]

Perhaps MacArthur's most impassioned argument, however, did not deal with strategy or tactics. He simply reminded the president that thousands of Filipinos, as well as the American defenders of Bataan and Corregidor, felt that they had been betrayed and abandoned by the United States. They must not, MacArthur intoned, be disappointed again, for "promises must be kept!"[12]

Nimitz then presented the navy's position. Nimitz was professional, well prepared, evenhanded, and thorough. He spoke for nearly two hours. However, Nimitz did not have the captivating oratory of MacArthur, nor his dramatic passion. And Admiral Nimitz often saw the wisdom of MacArthur's approach. Indeed, Nimitz—unlike Admiral King—saw many merits in invading and securing the Philippines.[13] As the meeting concluded, no decision had been made, nor did it appear that a conclusion would be drawn immediately. President Roosevelt was here to listen. A decision would probably come after he returned to Washington.[14]

MacArthur decided to strike one more blow and go for broke before returning to Australia. He asked Roosevelt if he could speak with him alone for a few minutes. The president's advisers shook their heads negatively, but a tired Roosevelt agreed. When only the two great men remained in the room, MacArthur politely swiped at Roosevelt's political jugular vein. He found the audacity to warn Roosevelt that if it became known near election time that the president of the United States was going to bypass the Philippines and leave hundreds of imprisoned Americans to languish longer in prison, then, declared MacArthur, "I daresay that the American people would be so aroused that they would register most complete resentment against you at the polls this fall."[15]

Exactly how President Roosevelt reacted to this political finger wagging by a professional military officer is unknown. But MacArthur was relentless. What is known is that late that night, while preparing for bed, Roosevelt turned to his nearby physician and said, "Give me an aspirin before I go to bed." Then, after a moment, he continued, "In fact, give me another aspirin to take in the morning. In all my life nobody has ever talked to me the way MacArthur did."[16]

President Roosevelt ultimately sided with MacArthur and the Philippines was invaded. The decision to invade Mindanao first was dropped, and the invasion commenced on the island of Leyte on October 20, 1944. For the next ten months the bloodiest and costliest land battle that transpired in the Pacific theater raged. In fact, the fighting in northern Luzon still continued when two atomic bombs were dropped on Hiroshima and Nagasaki in August 1945, resulting in Japan's unconditional surrender.

When the total of American soldiers, aviators, sailors, and marines killed in action in the liberation of the Philippines is tallied, 20,569 paid the supreme cost of freedom. When this is combined with the 15,386 killed in action in the defense of the Philippines during the initial months of the war, the grand total of American military lives lost in the Philippines during World War II is 35,955. To put this in perspective, the second highest campaign losses in the Pacific were on Okinawa, where there were 12,183 Americans killed in action. American military losses in the Philippines are staggering and have never been fully realized by the American people.[17]

At the conclusion of the war, General Douglas MacArthur was selected to step on the deck of the battleship U.S.S. *Missouri* in Tokyo harbor and officially receive and sign the instruments of surrender from the Japanese delegates. During these long war years MacArthur had experienced the complete range of emotions from defeat and humiliation on Bataan and Corregidor to victory and vindication in Tokyo. He had gone the distance and emerged a national military hero.

MacArthur's personal history after World War II is well-known. He was chosen to be the supreme commander of the Allied Powers in postwar Japan, and proved to be a benevolent and progressive leader in its political and economic reconstruction. He served as its interim political leader from 1945 through 1948.

Prior to the end of World War II—and in anticipation of the reformation of Japan—MacArthur made prescient remarks to Robert E. Sherwood, the playwright who also served as a speechwriter for President Roosevelt, that proved to shape his political governance:

> "[Victory over Japan] will make us the greatest influence on the future of Asia. If we exert that influence in an imperialistic manner, or for the sole purpose of commercial advantage, then we shall lose our golden opportunity; but if our influence and our strength are expressed in terms of

essential liberalism, we shall have the friendship and the
cooperation of the Asiatic peoples far into the future."[18]

During the three years in which MacArthur molded Japan's
future, he instituted a democratic form of government, helped
write a new constitution that renounced future warfare, and
while protecting and honoring the age-old role of the Japanese
emperor, reduced his influence to one of a national figurehead.
Under MacArthur's leadership, a sound foundation was laid for
Japan to rise from the ashes and regain economic strength and
international respect. Many scholars believe that MacArthur's
molding of postwar Japan is his greatest contribution to world
history.

MacArthur transferred full authority to the newly formed
Japanese government in 1949 and remained in Japan temporarily. On June 25, 1950, North Korean forces invaded South Korea, and America was once again embroiled in war in Asia. The
United Nations Security Council quickly authorized a military
force to support South Korea, and MacArthur was selected to be
its commander.

Under MacArthur's leadership, the UN forces quickly drove
the North Korean army out of South Korea and then proceeded
to advance into North Korea, soon approaching the northern
Yalu River and the border of China. China gave subtle but clear
diplomatic notice that if they advanced farther, China would
defend her borders and invade North Korea. MacArthur ignored
their threat and the Chinese army advanced, mauling UN forces
and driving them out of North Korea. As Chinese forces advanced into South Korea, United Nations forces were able to
stabilize and stop the communist advance. However, an embarrassed MacArthur called for more aggressive action, demanding
the authority to bomb Chinese military installations inside the
Chinese border. President Truman, fearing that such an action
would bring the Soviet Union into the war, and that a nuclear

response would be triggered, restrained MacArthur and insisted that United Nations offensive operations not advance inside China's borders.

MacArthur became increasingly and publicly critical of his commander in chief and displayed his characteristic disregard for superiors. When he delivered an ultimatum to Chinese forces that undermined Truman's attempts to establish a cease-fire, Truman had the backbone to declare MacArthur insubordinate and relieve him of command, on April 11, 1951.

Though Truman's decision was controversial, the majority of Americans ultimately saw its wisdom. MacArthur and his family returned to the United States for the first time in eleven years. Though no further punitive action was directed toward him, and he returned to a hero's welcome and lifelong acclaim, his long military career was over, and any hope of a political future quickly dimmed.

For a short time MacArthur was head of Remington Rand Corporation, and he spent the remainder of his life in New York City, ensconced in a penthouse in the Waldorf Towers. Even in old age, MacArthur never lost his hero status or narcissistic ways. In 1962 he was honored by West Point with the Sylvanus Thayer Award for outstanding service to the nation. Two years later, on April 5, 1964, at the age of eighty-four, MacArthur slipped into a coma following emergency surgery and passed away. He was buried in Norfolk, Virginia, at the MacArthur Memorial complex, a gift of the city to honor MacArthur and preserve his papers and memory in perpetuity.

Jean MacArthur, the general's "constant friend, sweetheart, and devoted support," lived for thirty-five years following her husband's death. Remaining in New York City, she was involved in nonprofit cultural organizations such as the Metropolitan Opera. She frequently gave speeches pertaining to her life and experiences with General MacArthur, and in 1988 was awarded the Medal of Freedom by President Ronald Reagan. In 1993 the

Philippine government bestowed on her the Legion of Merit. At the age of 101, in 2000, Jean MacArthur died and was entombed next to her husband at the MacArthur Memorial Building in Norfolk.

Arthur MacArthur IV, after leading a most unusual life as a child in war-torn Philippines, Australia, and Japan, returned with his parents to New York when he was thirteen. Deciding not to follow a military career, he attended Columbia University and graduated with a degree in music. Following his father's death, Arthur MacArthur began to live more of an independent life and sought anonymity. Though he never formally changed his name, he lives in New York under an assumed name. Now in his late sixties, he is an attractive single man, having never married. Many say that he physically resembles his father and, like the general, is a voracious reader and engaging conversationalist.

Claude and Laverne Fertig

Six months after the Fertigs' arrival in Australia, American forces landed on the island of Leyte, on October 20, 1944, beginning the liberation of the Philippines. On March 18, 1945—exactly one year after the rescue of the Fertigs by the *Angler*—the Fortieth Infantry Division splashed ashore on Panay and joined forces with Colonel Peralta's 22,500 guerrillas, and they quickly subdued Japanese forces.[19]

In preparation for the invasion of the Philippines, Major Claude Fertig was assigned to the Allied Geographic Section of the U.S. Army in Australia, to work on maps and detailed terrain handbooks for the liberation of the Philippines. His knowledge of islands such as Masbate and Panay was invaluable.[20] Later, working with the Army Corps of Engineers, he went with the invasion forces to the Philippines. During the final weeks of the war, Claude was at last reunited with his brother, Wendell. By the war's end, Claude was promoted to the rank of lieutenant colonel.

Prior to the conclusion of the war, Laverne Fertig sailed from Australia to the United States with her daughter, Susan. *Life* magazine learned of her intense and dramatic experiences in the Philippines and interviewed her for a feature story to be published in April 1945. Photographers took photographs of Laverne and Susan, and the article was in the advanced stages of production. However, in the week the article was to be printed, President Roosevelt died unexpectedly, and all feature stories were canceled to allow his death and funeral to receive full at-

Claude, Laverne, and Susan Fertig, about 1946.   *Susan Fertig-Dykes*

tention. Laverne Fertig's story was never rescheduled or published.[21]

After the conclusion of World War II, Claude and Laverne Fertig were reunited in Colorado. Following a period of rest and recuperation, the Fertigs returned to the Philippines, where Claude continued in his profession as a mining engineer and consultant, and they spent a total of thirty-two years in the Philippines. During these years they lived primarily near Baguio, in northern Luzon, and in Manila. Their daughters, Susan and Kathy, were raised in the Philippines, educated in Baguio at Brent School, and returned to the United States to attend college.[22]

In 1969, Claude and Laverne said an emotional farewell to the Philippines and returned to the United States. Claude was sixty-four years old and approaching retirement. However, he continued to work as a senior mining engineer with the International Mineral Engineers of Golden, Colorado, until 1975. Claude died on February 19, 1986, followed by Laverne, on January 18, 1992. Inseparable in life and death, they are interred in Fort Logan National Cemetery in Denver, Colorado.

Wendell Fertig

After American submarines successfully delivered equipment and supplies to Wendell Fertig's guerrillas on Mindanao, he was able to expand his guerrilla functions and effectiveness. MacArthur sent clear instructions that Fertig was to "lie low" and not wage offensive operations against the Japanese. Rather, he was to gather critical information and report it to MacArthur's headquarters via his new radios. Fertig successfully set up a chain of coast-watchers' stations that monitored Japanese naval movements along the Mindanao coastline. Soon more than 150 coast-watching stations had been created by various guerrilla commands across the vast expanse of the Philippine archipelago.

In June 1944, one of the coast-watcher stations observed a large fleet of Japanese ships sailing between Samar and southern Luzon through the San Bernardino Strait. This detailed information on the fleet enabled the Americans at headquarters to immediately realize that this fleet was en route to ambush the vulnerable American amphibious attacks in the Mariana Islands. Because of this valuable information, the fleet was not surprised, and critical adjustments and preparations were made. The result was a major Japanese naval defeat in the Battle of the Philippine Sea. This victory greatly accelerated the return of American forces to the Philippines.

Such effective radio reconnaissance came at a great price, however. Frequently, Fertig's radio stations were detected by the Japanese, and infantry units were sent out to destroy the stations. Fertig and his guerrilla bands spent much of their time on the run during the months preceding MacArthur's return to the Philippines. But finally, radio messages to the guerrillas began to change in tone and direction. As the American invasion drew near, MacArthur's "lie low" orders changed to aggressive attack orders. The guerrilla units were now directed to blow up bridges and supply dumps and to "unleash maximum violence against the enemy." They did so with great excitement and effectiveness and paved the way for the liberation of the islands.[23]

By the time MacArthur returned to the Philippines, Wendell Fertig was commanding a guerrilla force on Mindanao that totaled approximately thirty-eight thousand men, roughly the equivalent of an army corps. Lieutenant Colonel Fertig's forces were perhaps the largest, best-equipped, and most effective guerrilla fighting force in World War II. MacArthur promoted Fertig to the rank of colonel and awarded him the Distinguished Service Cross.

After the war, Wendell joined his wife, Mary, and their two daughters, Pat and Jeanne, in Colorado. He returned to his mining career for the next fifteen years, and was then employed in 1960 by his alma mater, the Colorado School of Mines, as the executive secretary of the alumni association. Fertig served in this capacity until his death in 1975 at the age of seventy-four.

Even in peacetime Wendell Fertig was not far removed

from military life. Retired American guerrilla leaders from the Philippines, such as Colonel Fertig and Lieutenant Colonel Russell Volckmann, were called upon by the U.S. Armed Forces to help formulate the doctrine of unconventional warfare that became the cornerstone of the emerging Special Forces. Wendell Fertig was especially proud that he helped to found the Army Special Warfare School at Fort Bragg, North Carolina, and is considered by some to be the father of the U.S. Army's Special Forces.[24]

Cyril "Spence" and Louise Spencer

When Spence and Louise set foot on Australian soil, their primary focus was the safe birth of their baby. On May 9, 1944, Louise gave birth to a baby boy in an army hospital, the Forty-second General Hospital. He was named Reid Spencer, honoring Louise's maiden name of Reid. Louise missed birthing her baby on the submarine by five weeks.[25]

Shortly after the birth of their son, the Spencers returned to the United States, prior to the end of the war. Louise immediately began work on a first-person narrative of her wartime experience. In 1945 her exceptional book, *Guerrilla Wife*, was published by Thomas Y. Crowell Company and became a featured selection of the People's Book Club. The book was published on Victory Over Japan Day.[26]

After the end of World War II, Spence continued working for mining companies in Nicaragua, Bolivia, Chile, Peru, Mexico, and Costa Rica. Spence and Louise retired in 1970 and lived during their retirement years in the Kansas City area. Throughout the decades, the Spencers and Fertigs stayed in touch with one another. Their special friendship, forged in the drama of World War II, could never be diluted by time or distance.

Spence and Louise were married for sixty-two years. Spence died at age ninety-four on December 28, 1999, and Louise died at age eighty-nine on January 9, 2002.[27]

Susan Fertig-Dykes and Louise Spencer, 1983.   *Susan Fertig-Dykes*

The Meyer Brothers: Frederick Jr., Milton, and Richard

Frederick "Buddy" Meyer Jr. was an undergraduate at Yale Univesity when World War II began. He spent most of the war years at the University of Rochester Medical School, graduating in 1945 with his M.D. degree. Frederick was a career naval medical officer, and died at the age of seventy-four in October 1995.

Milton Meyer served in the U.S. Army, primarily in the Office of Strategic Services, for nearly three years. His final posting was in China. In late 1945, he was granted permission to return to the United States for demobilization via the Philippines in order to tend to his family's affairs.

Milton spent five weeks in the Philippines. He visited Panay

and journeyed to Capiz and Hopevale. He was able to recon-
struct the story of his parents' last days, and to recover their few
possessions and documents. By that time his parents had been
deceased nearly two years, and their remains buried under the

Frederick, Milton, and Richard Meyer, 1946.   *Milton Meyer*

altar of the small Baptist church in Katipunan. However, Milton's grief was fresh and his lonely pilgrimage home to Panay
required great courage and devotion.

Milton returned to the United States, completed his B.A. at
Yale, a master's from Columbia, and a Ph.D. in history from
Stanford. For thirty-five years he was a professor of American
and Asian histories at California State University, Los Angeles. He authored thirteen books relating to Asian history and
culture. Today he is the only surviving child of Frederick and
Ruth Meyer, and continues to maintain close ties to Central
Philippine University in Iloilo and to lifelong Filipino friends
on Panay.[28]

Richard "Dick" Meyer was one of 3,790 Americans and people of other nationalities liberated from the Santo Tomas prison

camp in Manila on February 3, 1945, in a dramatic raid by the First Cavalry Division. MacArthur's intelligence department had reason to believe that the Japanese intended to execute prisoners of war as American forces battled their way from the invasion beaches of Lingayen Gulf south to Manila. The First Cavalry Division and the Thirty-seventh "Buckeye" Division were sent on an urgent mission to penetrate the Japanese lines and rescue all internees and prisoners of war in Manila. Only hours before the executions were expected to be carried out, American tanks crashed through the gates of the Santo Tomas and nearby Bilibid internment camps and successfully rescued their civilian internees.

Richard was fourteen when he was separated from his parents on Panay, and seventeen when liberated. He was one of the first civilian internees to be repatriated to the United States, where he completed high school and later graduated from Yale University. Richard served in the U.S. Army, stationed in Germany, from 1950 to 1952.

During his teenage years in Santo Tomas, Richard fell in love with Elizabeth "Bim" Thomas, an Australian girl interned with her parents. On the day he left Santo Tomas in an army caravan, he turned to this tearful teenage girl and whispered, "I'm going to see you again, honey, someday, remember that." Richard kept his word. Following his stint in the army, Richard sailed to Sydney, Australia, in 1953, and continued his courtship with Bim. They were married and, while living most of their years in Australia, raised two daughters and a son. Richard died in 1994. Milton Meyer inurned his brother's ashes in the National Memorial Cemetery of the Pacific in Honolulu, Hawaii.[29]

The Covell Children: Peggy, David, and Alice

As World War II began, all three of the Covells' children were in the United States, attending either college or high school. In the spring of 1943, nine months before his parents' death, eighteen-year-old David joined the Marines. His fluent Japanese assured his assignment to intelligence, and to the interrogation of Japanese prisoners. David was involved in four amphibious assaults on Kwajalein, Saipan, Tinian, and Iwo Jima with the Fourth Marine Division.

David learned of his parents' deaths following the Kwajalein invasion, while on a rest and relaxation deployment in Maui, Hawaii, in the spring of 1944. During the combat at Kwajalein, his mail had been held in Hawaii. One day he was given his stack of accumulated letters and eagerly sat down to read them. The first letter he opened was dirty and tattered. To his amazed delight he discovered that the letter was from his parents at Hopevale and had been smuggled out by submarine. Tearing into it, David read as Jimmy and Charma poured out their love to their son and reassured him that they were safe and in good spirits.

Relieved, he opened the second letter. It was from his uncle, who informed David that he had been notified unofficially that David's parents had been killed by Japanese soldiers in December 1943. Devastated, David wandered in a daze until his buddies found him and took him to see Reverend Edwin Dozier, a missionary on Maui who had known his parents. Reverend Dozier spent time with David and helped him through the initial days of his grief crisis. David deployed from Hawaii with the Fourth Marines for their invasion of Saipan on June 15, 1944.

David recalls Iwo Jima as his most difficult combat experience, "where I learned to say my prayers." He remembered that while on Iwo Jima he once walked away from a campfire only seconds before a mortar hit, killing all the marines with whom he had been talking. His most painful memory was walking by an open field filled with dead Japanese bodies. David refused to look at their faces for fear he would recognize someone from his childhood in Yokohama.

Corporal David Covell was twenty years old and a tested veteran when he was discharged from the Marines on Thanksgiving Day 1945. After returning to the United States, David graduated from William Jewell College. When the Korean War erupted, he was married and his wife was pregnant. He was recalled to the Marines and sent to Korea, again assigned to intelligence.

David is now retired from a career with the General Electric Corporation and lives in New York.[30]

David's older sister, Peggy, graduated in the midst of World War II after majoring in social work at Keuka College in Keuka Park, New York. During the latter years of the war, and during the months following the Japanese surrender, she chose to work in an American internment hospital for Japanese prisoners of war located on the border of Colorado and Utah.

In his book *God's Samurai*, noted military historian Gordon W. Prange, tells a remarkable story of how Peggy Covell profoundly influenced a group of Japanese naval pilots who were recovering from wounds. The pilots noted how kind and caring Peggy was to them. Because of her fluency in Japanese, she spoke easily with them and earned their trust. One day a pilot asked her why she was so kind. She responded by telling of the execution of her parents by a Japanese terrorist squad in the Philippines. The pilots were astounded and embarrassed. Then Peggy explained that though her grief was intense, her understanding of the love of God had enabled her to love and forgive all Japanese, too. It was this sense of God's love, she emphasized, that caused her to choose to serve Japanese prisoners.

One of these pilots returned to Japan and told her story to his close friend Mitsuo Fuchida, who was the lead Japanese pilot in the attack on Pearl Harbor. Fuchida was experiencing deep postwar despondency and depression. When he heard Peggy Covell's story, its poignancy and irony struck him forcefully, and ultimately led to his conversion to Christianity. Fuchida recovered from his emotional turmoil and became a powerful advocate for world peace and international accord.[31]

David's younger sister, Alice, graduated from Colgate University after World War II. Her love of the Orient drew her to Hawaii, where she spent her life as a children's librarian. Both Peggy and Alice are deceased.

Donal Rounds

Shortly before his release from the Santo Tomas internment camp, Donal Rounds and Dick Meyer were informed by other Baptist missionaries—Dr. Fred Chambers and Dr. Henry Waters—that their parents and Donal's younger brother, Douglas, had been executed by Japanese soldiers on Panay.[32] Devastated by this news, the handsome seventeen-year-old tried to pull himself together, and he received support from his adopted family of friends in Santo Tomas. However, his grieving period was soon interrupted and distracted by the vanguard of the American troops fighting their way into Manila.

On the day the troops reached Santo Tomas, Donal remembered, "Our liberation occurred suddenly, when the First Cavalry broke in through the main gates. We rushed out to see what the commotion was all about. When we saw the [American] helmets there was confusion, because we thought in the dusk of day that the Germans had invaded our camp. But when the cavalry started shooting the Japanese we realized it was our men, not the German army. . . . [I learned later that] just prior to our liberation an edict had been put forth [by the Japanese] that all men over 17 (including me!) were to be executed the next day. The liberation was truly THAT—I had been saved!"[33]

With deliberate speed, the U.S. Army transported Donal and Richard Meyer back to their relatives in the United States. Years later he recalled, "Because several of us did not have parents, we were the first to be sent by truck to the airfield. Next we flew to Leyte to board a transport ship headed for the States. It was an amazing sight, looking around the harbor in Leyte filled with our ships as far as the eye could see. At last we were in friendly territory headed home."[34]

Donal arrived in California and lived with his guardian, his aunt Mildred, in Pasadena, where he attended high school. By good fortune, his girlfriend at the Santo Tomas internment camp, Dodie Peters, was also repatriated to California, in San Francisco. Though not able to see each other frequently, they did stay in close contact.

Following high school graduation, Donal enrolled at the

Donal Rounds and Dodie Peters (right foreground), 1946.   *Dodie Borroughs*

University of Redlands, and Dodie attended the University of California at Berkeley. Though a "first love" affection would remain between them for the rest of their lives, each gradually went their own way, finding fulfilling marriages and raising children.

Donal graduated from the University of Redlands in 1950

and enrolled in the School of Architecture at the University of Oregon. There he met his wife, Ula Mae, and they were married for forty-three years, raising three children, Dylan, Moira, and Rhys.

Donal spent his adult years as an architect, practicing primarily in Washington and Oregon; Ashland, Oregon was considered home. He died in 2006, at the age of seventy-eight.

Fred and Dorothy Chambers

For the first fourteen months of their internment, the Chambers and Waters families were imprisoned in Iloilo. Then, all of the prisoners there were sent to the Santo Tomas internment camp in Manila. Dr. Dorothy Chambers continued to use her medical skills at the Santo Tomas dispensary.

Slowly, everyone in Santo Tomas was affected by a steadily declining food supply. Beginning in 1944, rations were gradually cut from fourteen hundred calories a day to under seven hundred calories. During the last five months of the war, the patients that Dr. Chambers was seeing—including herself—were clearly suffering from starvation. Yet Dr. Chambers continued to serve others as long as she could stand. Before the war she had weighed 140 pounds. When she left Santo Tomas, she weighed less than 100 pounds.

With the sudden liberation of the Philippines, Dorothy and her small, thin, children, Carol and Bob, returned by ship to the United States in May 1945. Fred remained there, and returned to Iloilo to help restore and reopen Central Philippine College. He joined his family in Boulder, Colorado, in August 1945.

Immediately following the war, Fred became director of placement at the University of Colorado and Dorothy focused on raising their children and helping them adjust to the United States. Then, in 1954, Fred became the pastor of the American

Baptist Church at Fort Collins, Colorado. In 1958 he returned to academia, becoming the professor of missions at Central Baptist Theological Seminary in Kansas City, Kansas, until he retired. Upon his retirement, Fred and Dorothy joined hundreds of young Americans by becoming Peace Corps volunteers, and they served in Pakistan for one year.

Fred Chambers died of Alzheimer's disease in 1985. During her final years, Dorothy moved into a retirement center. Even when she was confined to a wheelchair, she would often roll herself down the hall when there was a medical emergency, announcing, "I'm a physician. Can I help?" When Dorothy was one hundred years old, she quietly passed away.

Henry and Anna Waters

Upon arriving at the Santo Tomas internment camp, Dr. Henry Waters joined Dr. Dorothy Chambers and seven other doctors in serving the over four thousand internees who were chronically unhealthy. Anna Waters also served as a nurse, but she had her hands full with three little children: Billy, George, and Mary Alice. All five survived their years of imprisonment and returned to the United States at the end of the war.[35]

After the war the Waterses returned to Iloilo for several years. Upon completing fifteen total years of service in the Philippines, the Waterses returned to the United States, and Dr. Waters opened a private pratice in the Marshfield, Wisconsin, community. They remained in Marshfield until their deaths.[36]

Reverend Delfin Dianala, Katipunan, and Hopevale

Reverend Dianala led a long and amazing life. He was born in 1884 and was one of the very first Baptist ministers on Panay.

Reverend Dianala was fifty-eight years old when the Baptist missionaries came to Hopevale in 1942. Following World War II, he and his wife, Beatriz, continued to rear the last of their six children, who bore them twenty grandchildren. Reverend Dianala faithfully remained as pastor of his church in Katipunan until his retirement, when he was in his early nineties. He died in 1996, when he was 112 years old, setting records for both longevity and contribution to his community of Katipunan and the work of Baptists in Panay. Through his long years he never wavered in courage, faith, or pioneering spirit.[37]

Katipunan continues its life as a vital barrio today. Hopevale, though still remote and in disrepair, is considered a special and venerated spot by Baptists in Panay. In 2005, when Central Philippine University celebrated its centennial, the remains of the Hopevale missionaries were exhumed from their burial place in Katipunan and transferred to a beautiful memorial on the university campus. The story of their sacrifice is told to each generation of students and continues in its power and witness.[38]

Captain Watanabe

Very little is known about Captain Watanabe, the leader of the Japanese penetrations and terrorist tactics on Panay. Though efforts have been made by several researchers to discover more information about him, these attempts have been unsuccessful. The most common and best substantiated opinion is that he did not survive the war.

However, new evidence is emerging even as the writing of this book comes to conclusion. In 2009 a book was published in the Philippines by Toshimi Kumai titled *The Blood and Mud in the Philippines: Anti-Guerrilla Warfare on Panay Island*. This book includes an interview (conducted prior to 1977) with a Japanese soldier who was a member of Captain Watanabe's punitive force. This soldier states that in December of 1943 the punitive force captured a Mr. King who under "stern interrogation" revealed that there were Americans living "near Egue close to the town of Tapaz, 13 kilometers north of Calinog." The author, Toshimi Kumai, states that this is "likely a part of the village of Katipunan in Tapaz, Capiz." It is quite obviously Hopevale.

The Japanese soldier stated in the interview that "Watanabe immediately dispatched the whole company to Egue and found more than 10 Americans in the village, including a couple of around 50 years of age and their son of 12 or 13 [likely Erle, Louise, and Douglas Rounds]. From their interrogation, we learned that there were still more Americans further in the mountains [likely the Fertigs and Spencers], and my platoon was sent to capture them."

When this Japanese soldier returned without finding the Americans and rejoined the Watanabe company, he discovered that Watanabe had executed all of the Americans. He was horrified and later exclaimed, "I had thought that all the captured Americans would naturally be sent to the internment camp in Manila, so I felt furious about the cruel approach of Captain Watanabe. On hearing the story, my subordinates were all compassionate and outraged: 'How could he kill the family of three since they were obviously civilians.'"

This Japanese soldier went on to say later in the interview that "Neither the Battalion Commander Ryoichi Tozuka nor Captain Kengo Watanabe said anything to anybody about the execution of the Americans, probably because of pricks on their conscience. [However], later on, I learned that it was Captain Watanabe who reported the capture to officers at the garrison headquarters in Cebu City and that he did the executions following their order. There were rumors that the order was to bury the fact that—unknown to others, including Manila headquarters—they wanted to avoid the complexity of formal procedures in dealing with these persons and their transport to Manila. . . . [I was later informed] that this unpleasant incident was big news in the United States and led to the submarine rescue of the remaining Americans in Panay."[39]

This interview highlights interesting insights into Captain Watanabe and also shows that his actions often infuriated his own soldiers.

One other intriguing story did emerge in postwar Japan pertaining to Captain Watanabe and his punitive force. One day Jim Sugaya, a former general secretary of the Japan Baptist Union, was riding on a train and became engaged in conversation with a Japanese man seated next to him. Jim gave him his business card, and when the man saw that Jim was a Baptist minister, he asked, "Did you ever know an American Baptist missionary named James Covell?" Jim quickly replied, "Why, yes! James Covell was my professor in college. How do you know of him?"

The man grew silent and he looked far away. He then began to relate an experience he had had during World War II, while he was a young soldier in the Philippines. One day he was sent with a platoon to round up some American Baptist missionaries hiding in the central mountains of Panay. He thought they would bring them back to Iloilo to be placed in a prisoner-of-war camp. However, on their way to find the missionaries they were joined by another Japanese squad, led by a colonel [captain]. Being the most senior officer, this colonel took command of the operation. Later, when the missionaries were found and captured, the colonel insisted that they be executed. It was in this moment that this young Japanese private saw James Covell speak with the colonel and, in perfect Japanese, ask that the missionaries be spared and be placed in a prison camp. When the colonel refused, this young Japanese then witnessed the harrowing execution of the missionaries, and was profoundly affected both by their deaths and by the courage they displayed. After the war he, too, became a Christian. Telling the general secretary of the Japanese Baptist Union this story was a moment of deep meaning for both men.[40]

The Submarines and Their Crews

Final reflections would not be complete without remembrance of the submarine crews that supplied the guerrillas and rescued Americans and Filipinos during the war years.

In summation, nineteen submarines participated in a total of forty-one secret missions to the Philippines, beginning with the first successful landing of the USS *Gudgeon* (SS-211) in January 1943 on the island of Negros. Seven of the submarine missions were to Panay. The final mission to the Philippines was by the USS *Stingray* (SS-186) on January 1, 1945. Over the course of two hazardous years, the guerrilla submarines delivered 331 military personnel there, evacuated 472 people, and delivered approximately 1,325 tons of supplies. Their missions were by nature secretive, and the details remain largely unknown and unheralded today. However, their contribution to Allied victory in the Philippines is incalculable and was made with great sacrifice and courage.[41]

The submarine that transported the Hopevale survivors to Australia, *Angler* (SS-240), completed six war patrols and was awarded six battle stars prior to the end of World War II. After the Japanese surrender it continued its service in the U.S. Navy until it was decommissioned and its name struck from the Naval Vessel Register on December 15, 1971. On February 1, 1974, it was removed from naval custody and broken up for scrap.

Author's Note

An Author and a Story

I was six years old when my family sailed to the Philippines on the SS *President Wilson* to be Baptist missionaries. My mother and father, Al and Dorothy Walker, were professors at the Philippine Baptist Theological Seminary in the resort city of Baguio, high in the pine forests of the Cordillera mountains of northern Luzon. The year was 1957, and World War II had come to its bloody conclusion only twelve years before.

Though the war was over, the memory of its savagery was fresh and the evidence of its destruction all around. Next to our house stood a tall, two-story, burned-out chimney, the remnants of a colonial home used as Japanese officers' quarters and destroyed by American bombs. As a wide-eyed and adventurous child, I used this chimney as a climbing wall, its elevated fireplace my hideout. The soot in the chimney often stained my hands and clothes, and I tried to imagine the Japanese officers who had built fires in the hearth on cold nights not so long before.

Interspersed throughout our community were large caves dug into the mountain hillsides by Japanese soldiers. These desperate young men had retreated to these caves, where they stubbornly resisted surrender and died at the hands of advancing American infantry. My favorite pastime was to track through this mountainous terrain with my young buddies, explore these haunted caves, and find abandoned weapons and ammunition. My friends and I lugged home a rusted machine gun, dug up hand grenades and spent bullets, and even discovered an abandoned Japanese tank deep in a secluded valley. My parents lived in dread that one day we might detonate abandoned ordnance or trip an aging booby trap, and blow our young, inquisitive selves to kingdom come. We were constantly warned not to enter caves, not to touch bullets and artillery shells, and never to bring relics into our house. But we would not listen. The lure of adventure and discovery was too strong.

Most of the adult Filipinos I knew who had survived the war had been affected in some way by its terror. When we went to church on Sundays I often sat by a handsome, middle-aged man who was blind. He had been a member of the elite Philippine Scouts and decorated for bravery. While defending Bataan, he was firing a machine gun at an advancing line of Japanese soldiers when a grenade exploded near him, blowing his eyes out and knocking him unconscious. Somehow he survived his wounds and, later, the Bataan death march. Now, disabled, he wrestled with the haunting memories of war and the grim reality of trying to support his family. He often held a Bible in his hands but could not read the words.

Many of the Americans I knew—the parents of some of my friends—had endured harsh years of captivity in prisoner-of-war camps. They told stories of what they ate to survive and how they felt when they were finally liberated. Their health still betrayed the strain of these traumatic years. Their tales of endurance became living history for me.

Even the Episcopal boarding school that I attended, Brent School, had a storied wartime history. It had been established in 1909 by Bishop Charles Henry Brent, the first American bishop of the Missionary Diocese of the Philippine Islands. The purpose of this new boarding school was to provide an American-style education for American children living in the Philippines and other Asian countries. Such a school would allow American parents to remain in the Philippines and not have to send their children back to the United States for their education. As an example, when Lieutenant Colonel Dwight David Eisenhower received orders in 1935 to join the staff of General Douglas MacArthur in the Philippines, he soon made arrangements for his son, John, to attend Brent School. John loved the school and regretted leaving when his father was transferred back to the United States in late 1939, two years before the outbreak of World War II.[1]

However, when war with Japan did erupt, the first Japanese bombers that attacked the Philippines flew directly over Brent School and dropped their bombs several miles away on Camp John Hay. Most of the seventy-six students who attended Brent School were soon interned in Camp Holmes, a prisoner-of-war camp in Baguio. Some of these students were separated from their parents for the duration of the war.

As an elementary school student, I often sat in the Brent School library and gazed at a large mural painted on the wall depicting the life of the school during this imprisonment. I found my young imagination wondering what I would do if I were separated from my parents and had to endure such captivity. Indeed, I would occasionally have nightmares that the Japanese had again invaded the Philippines, and that I was being chased through the woods and jungles. World War II was more than history to me. It was a living, breathing saga endured, it seemed, within my lifetime.

When I was twelve years old my mother came home one

day after attending a women's book club during which Laverne Fertig had shared her wartime experiences by giving a report on a book titled *Guerrilla Wife*, which has been written by her close friend, Louise Spencer. The book told of the months that the Spencers and Fertigs had spent eluding the Japanese on the island of Panay and their dramatic escape to Australia. Mother bought a copy of the book and gave it to me. Because I was attending Brent School with the Fertigs' youngest daughter, Kathy, I began to read the book and could not put it down. I was caught up in the intensity of this story and the tragedy that befell the Baptist missionaries—missionaries like my parents—with whom the Fertigs and Spencers were hiding. I never forgot the story. And the story never forgot me.

As I grew older I became an avid reader and student of World War II, especially the events that had taken place in the Philippines. Years later—indeed, forty years after reading *Guerrilla Wife*—I was still fascinated by this story, a saga that I knew was fading from public memory and would soon be lost in time. Yet I was also intrigued by what I did not know about the story. I wanted to understand more about the missionaries who had lost their lives hiding in the jungles of Panay. What happened to their surviving children? What was done to honor their memory and preserve their story? And what about the Filipinos and the guerrillas who played such an important role in this drama? I wanted to learn more, and so I began intensive research.

Though I had not seen or heard from Kathy Fertig since our days at Brent School, I looked her up and we rekindled a friendship. By now her parents were dead. Kathy put me in touch with her older sister, Susan, who had been born in the mountains of Panay in 1944. Kathy and I spent much time exchanging e-mails, talking on the phone, and traveling to visit each other on several occasions so that I could interview her. She encouraged me to write a book that would approach this story much more broadly, with new research and insight. So I began to track down the surviving children and grandchildren of the executed missionaries. I sought first-person accounts by Filipinos who were both guerrillas and civilians on Panay during World War II. I connected the parallel adventures of two brothers, Claude and Wendell Fertig. And I placed this singular story within the broader context and campaigns of the Pacific theater. Gradually a much larger, complex, and comprehensive story emerged.

In the midst of my research Kathy Fertig developed a brain tumor and died within a short time. I was deeply grieved by her death and became even more determined to pursue writing this book, for her. Upon discovering Dr. Milton Meyer, the sole surviving son of Dr. and Mrs. Frederick Meyer, I traveled to Los Angeles twice and spent enjoyable times with him. As Milton shared with me his personal stories and written recollections of his parents' life experiences, I once again affirmed that this story must not fade from memory.

Now, after six years of research and writing, a much fuller and interwoven story has developed, and this book has evolved. As I conclude, I ask myself the crucial questions: What have I learned? What have I gleaned through this story that can be distilled and written within the scope of a few succinct pages? My thoughts can best be conveyed through four of the most powerful and universal words that are spoken in all languages: faith, hope, love, and war.

Faith and Hope

Within days of their executions, Filipinos on Panay began to refer to the missionaries as "the Hopevale Martyrs." This phrase is still heard today, sixty-seven years later. The choice of the word martyr is an interesting one. It conjures up visions of bloody Roman arenas, snarling lions, torture chambers, and the great suffering of persecuted Christians. However, the root word for martyr is not primarily "one who suffers." Rather, it is "one who bears witness." What do the missionaries depicted in this book bear witness to? What are the themes that are painted on the canvas of their lives?

First, what drew these Hopevale martyrs together on the small island of Panay was a common commitment to make the world a better place. Whether the medium of improvement was education, medicine, agriculture, social work, or spiritual healing, the overriding purpose of their lives was to live so that "God's will is done on earth as it is in heaven." These men and women collectively spent decades attempting to do good, though they were limited by circumstances and their own human nature. They bore witness that life has an overarching purpose of seeking to love others and to meet human need. They had faith in the power and purpose of doing good. And their hope was that by living a life of faith, goodness would ultimately prevail.

Second, they bore vivid witness that those who seek to do good are not protected from the dangers, the terrors, and the tragedies of life. Indeed, to seek to do good is to thrust oneself into inevitable conflict and danger, to become more vulnerable to personal harm. Their testimony is that God does not place a protective barrier around those who live loving and charitable lives. Rather, these martyrs came to know in the most intense way what Jesus meant when he said, "But I say to you, love your enemies, and pray for those who persecute you in order that you may be sons of your Father who is in heaven; for He causes His sun to rise on the evil and the good, and sends rain on the righteous and the unrighteous." There is no promise of reward, special treatment, or safety when you seek to do good. You are not shielded from sun or storm. Goodness is done for no other sake than goodness. It takes faith to believe in goodness in the midst of a tragic world. And such faith produces a seasoned, tempered, and mature existential hope.

Third, the Hopevale martyrs bore witness that the human

spirit combined with the strength of God can overcome the worst that life can offer. By all accounts, none of the missionaries wanted to die. None were without gripping fear and horror as they faced their deaths. None would have refused to escape if it were possible. Yet, when each of them was ordered to literally kneel and bear their neck, they found that they had the God-given strength to do so. They bore witness that the human spirit has the incredible ability to rise to the most daunting occasion and overcome. When your knees are weak and tremble, it requires the strong hand of faith to grasp courage.

Fourth, the surviving children of the Hopevale martyrs have displayed an incredible sense of forgiveness toward those who executed their parents. Such forgiveness did not come easy. It took years for grief and forgiveness to come full term. But to a person, each of the surviving children that I have interviewed—now in their seventies, eighties, and nineties—have "embraced the enemy" and forgiven the unforgivable. Such forgiveness has brought tears to their eyes but peace to their souls. Forgiveness, too, is built on a faith in ultimate hope and goodness.

Finally, the most profound witness of the Hopevale martyrs is an unyielding belief in the existence and the goodness of God. Their story is not one that is filled with easy answers or simplistic theology. The God they served would appear to many to be a God who abandoned them in their time of deepest need, a distant God who did not answer their prayers or rescue them from evil. But their witness is the same gritty testimony of the biblical character of Job, who in the agony of the loss of his family, his health, and his home managed to utter one honest and angry sentence that sparked with profound faith: "Though God slay me, I will hope in Him. Nevertheless I will argue my ways to His face!"

Job never gave up on God. And Job never stopped asking the ultimate question: "Why do bad things happen to good people?" But there came a day when Job surrendered reason and ceased debate in order to embrace the ultimate mystery of God, and to say, "Though He slay me, I will hope in Him."

That same day came for the Hopevale martyrs. They walked to their executions singing a hymn of faith. They did not have answers. They could not penetrate the mystery of tragedy and suffering. With Job, they perhaps found the courage to argue and scream into the face of God. But to the end, they did not curse God. They clung to a faith that is beyond human understanding. For deepest faith is always shrouded in profound, disturbing, and sacred mystery. And mystery is the fount of hope.

The Hopevale martyrs did sing a hymn of faith. And the hymn they sang came not from a hymnal but from the witness of their lives and deaths.

Love

The gold miners were people of faith and hope as well. They came from different backgrounds than the missionaries. They were not pious. Their perspective was often different. They believed in hard labor and good business and making a profit. But they also believed in God in their own individual ways. And though they were "tough as boots" and rugged individualists, their love and concern for others was transparent and real.

There is no more moving moment in this story than when Louise Spencer determined that she would stick with the pregnant Laverne Fertig—come hell or divorce!—until Laverne gave birth to the baby. Despite the logical and emotional insistence of her husband that the two couples should split up for safety, Louise defied even her mate to stay with Laverne. This depth of love and friendship was spawned in the midst of the worst of times. It points to the nobility of the human character.

However, if there is one sterling hero within this story, it must be Reverend Dianala, who risked everything to protect and supply both the missionaries and gold miners who lived in Hopevale for eighteen months. The assistance and support that he and his fellow Filipinos in Katipunan rendered was not given out of compulsion, conscription, or guilty conscience. It was given freely and at high cost. That he and his family were not killed for their actions was against all odds.

Through this story I have come to agree with the Apostle Paul that the greatest of human gifts are faith, hope, and love. And that the greatest of these is love.[2]

War

As I conclude this book, above all else I want to express that it is not my conviction nor my desire to portray the Japanese people as being more violent or inhumane than any other nationality, society, or culture. War brings out the best—and certainly the absolute worst—in all peoples of all nations. This observation bears further explanation.

War has existed since the beginning of time, and it has never been good or laudable. Yet, the twentieth century represents the zenith of human destruction and depravity. In the preceding nineteenth century, it is estimated that 45 million people died due to wars, tyranny, slavery, genocide, and acts of inhumanity. A record number at that time. Yet for the twentieth century, a reasonable estimate projects that between 175 million and 200 million died from the same violent causes, roughly a fourfold increase in one short century. World War II alone resulted in approximately 72 million military and civilian deaths. And, as in all wars, the civilian deaths far exceeded military ones.

The wanton destruction of civilian populations is particularly disturbing in World War II as well as in the present time. In terms of American military history, the specific strategy and moral permission to wage open and unrestricted warfare on civilian populations began during the American Civil War. Several years ago I wrote a book about that war titled *Hell's Broke Loose in Georgia*. I discovered that it was on the battlefields of my own native state of Georgia that the assault upon a civilian population was most clearly planned, permitted, and accomplished. This singular action radically changed American military strategy.[3]

The year was 1864, and Americans—in both the North and South—were desperately weary of war. A generation of young Americans had been nearly bled to death. A presidential election loomed in November 1864. Abraham Lincoln knew that he had little chance of winning reelection if it could not be demonstrated that the Civil War was moving rapidly toward an unconditional surrender of the Confederacy and an imminent Union victory. Yet to accomplish this required a level and a scope of Union military success not yet obtained.

One of Lincoln's most eccentric but able generals understood this perfectly well, William Tecumseh Sherman. He knew that a Union victory must not only be achieved, it must be clearly gained prior to the presidential election, or a peace candidate would be elected and the preservation of the union of the United States would disappear. As Sherman invaded northern Georgia, he determined that come hell or high water he would conquer Atlanta and roughly subdue the civilian population of Georgia. He would create a spectacle of unleashed and destructive power. Only by slashing civilian support for the Confederacy through terror and intimidation would the South be quickly brought to its knees. Sherman decreed that he would "make Georgia howl!" Writing to the mayor of Atlanta, Sherman succinctly defined the emergence of modern warfare: "You cannot qualify war in harsher terms than I will. War is cruelty, and you cannot refine it."[4]

True to his word, Sherman rode roughshod over the citizens of a significant portion of Georgia as he marched from Atlanta to Savannah, demonstrating that the Union army could now move unimpeded in the South. Southern morale crumbled, and the Northern population realized that the collapse of the South was impending. As a result, Lincoln won reelection, and his goal of the unconditional surrender of the South and preservation of the Union was achieved.

So it was in World War II, eighty years later. The Japanese in the Philippines realized that they could not subdue the Philippines or win their Asian war in a timely fashion unless civilian populations were traumatized and terrorized into submission. They honed the art of individual cruelty and torture. The Japanese could not fight forever, and they needed to bring their war to a rapid conclusion before their resources were depleted and America had time to rebound and gain offensive momentum.

And so it was with the Americans. Roosevelt was running for an unprecedented fourth term as president. The American population was war weary. Some felt it was time to bring a cruel war to a close and secure a negotiated peace. Months before in Europe the decision to bomb civilian populations had been accepted by Allied military leadership.[5] Now an aerial conflagration was being unleashed not only over German cities, but over Japanese cities as well. Toward the end of the war nightly American air raids targeted major Japanese cities with incendiary bombs, intentionally wiping out civilian populations. On some nights over one hundred thousand Japanese civilians were burned and cremated by the American firebombing of densely populated areas—more deaths than resulted from the later dropping of two atomic bombs. Again the premise was expounded by the Americans: Break the hearts of the people and the war will end.[6]

In modern warfare, wars are not confined to battlefields and soldiers. They are won when civilian populations are subdued and traumatized. Firebombing cities and burning alive a hundred thousand men, women, and children each night is no more humane than bayoneting hog-tied young men in a public square or beheading helpless civilian prisoners. Bombing seems cleaner, more distant and sanitized. A bomber crew seldom sees its victims. A bayonet and a samurai sword appear more personal, brutal, and primitive. However, whether by sword or bomb, both forms of killing civilians are done for the same purpose—to expedite the winning of a war.

So what is the lesson learned? General Sherman put it succinctly. "War is hell!" And unless one wants to create hell and live in its uncontrollable fury, wars must be fought only when all other options have been denied and exhausted. Cultures that glorify war and raise it to the level of a competitive international game or a political power weapon are cultures that will reap the winds of destruction. I firmly believe that those who died at Hopevale would want their deaths to be a violent symbol—*a witness*—to the perverse lunacy of warfare, and a prophetic warning for the days in which we now live.

And so the conclusion comes. What can we learn from this story? Perhaps we can better understand the truth of the age-old proposition that faith, hope, and love are the only forces that conquer all. And despite all of the logical and political reasons to subscribe to the most current "just war" theory, it is a fact that whenever wars are waged, everyone loses. Simplistic? Yes. Ultimately true? I think so. These are lessons that can only be learned when you have seen and experienced the edge of terror.

Notes

Prologue

1. Gamaliel L. Manikan, *Guerilla Warfare on Panay Island in the Philippines: Historical Account of the Organization and Operations of the Wartime Sixth Military District, Philippine Army, Otherwise Known as the "Free Panay Guerilla Forces," During World War II in the Philippines*, 406–7.
2. Ibid., 408.

Chapter 1

1. Stanley Karnow, *In Our Image: America's Empire in the Philippines*, 104–5.
2. Karnow, *In Our Image*, 125; Gordon L. Rottman, *World War II Pacific Island Guide*, 270.

3. Harry A. Gailey, *The War in the Pacific: From Pearl Harbor to Tokyo Bay*, 9–10; Karnow, *In Our Image*, 10–12.

4. Karnow, *In Our Image*, 72–77.

5. Ibid., 112–17.

6. Ibid., 110.

7. Roland G. Simbulan, http://www.yonip.com/main/articles/apology.html.

8. Brian McAllister Linn, *The Philippine War, 1899–1902*, 311–14.

9. Rottman, *Pacific Island Guide*, 270.

10. Karnow, *In Our Image*, 170.

Chapter 2

1. Milton Walter Meyer, *Letters Home: A Personal History of Emmanuel Hospital, Capiz, and the Meyers, 1919–1943*, 67–68.

2. Interview with Milton Meyer, September 26, 2007.

3. "The Student Volunteer Mission: Evangelizing the World in Their Generation," *Christian History Institute*, no. 81, http://chi.gospelcom.net/GLIMPSEF/Glimpses/glmpses081.shtml; Meyer, *Letters Home*, 69–71.

4. Wilfred Grenfell, *A Labrador Doctor: The Autobiography of Sir Wilfred Thomason Grenfell*, 1–2; http://collections.ic.gc.ca/heirloom_volume5/300-303.htm.

5. Meyer, *Letters Home*, 68, 71; interview with Milton Meyer, September 26, 2007.

6. Meyer, *Letters Home*, 74.

7. Ibid., 81–82.

8. Ibid., 83.

9. Ibid., 89.

10. Gordon L. Rottman, *World War II Pacific Island Guide*, 268. Indonesia is the largest archipelago.

11. Meyer, *Letters Home*, 92; Allied Geographical Section, Southwest Pacific Area, Terrain Handbook 51: *Panay Island*, 92.
12. Terrain Handbook 51: *Panay Island*, 1–2.
13. On May 12, 1951, the municipality of Capiz was renamed Roxas City in honor of its son, President Manuel Roxas.
14. Meyer, *Letters Home*, 27.
15. Ibid., 3–52.

Chapter 3

1. Interview with Kathy Fertig, 2003; interviews with Susan Fertig, 2007, 2008; Claude Fertig, correspondence, http://www.mcguiresplace.net/They%20Fought%20Alone.
2. Jean Edward Smith, *FDR*, 319–22.
3. Interview with Kathy Fertig, 2003.
4. Colorado State Teachers College is now the University of Northern Colorado.
5. Interview with Kathy Fertig, 2003.
6. "Background Note: Philippines," U.S. Department of State, Bureau of East Asian and Pacific Affairs, September 2005, http://www.state.gov/r/pa/ei/bgn/2794.htm.
7. "Philippine Civilization and Technology," Asia Pacific University, http://www.geocities.com/Tokyo/Temple/9845/tech.htm?20068.
8. Rafal Swiecki, "Alluvial Exploration & Mining," http://www.minelinks.com/alluvial/gold1.html.
9. "History of FHL," Filipinas Heritage Library, http://www.filipinaslibrary.org.ph/history/default.asp.
10. Susan Drumheller, "Fertig: A Soldier's Story," *The Spokesman-Review*, February 26, 1996, 1B.
11. Interview with Kathy Fertig, 2003.

Chapter 4

1. Milton Walter Meyer, *Letters Home: A Personal History of Emmanuel Hospital, Capiz, and the Meyers, 1919–1943*, 95.
2. Ibid., 913–14.
3. Ibid., 110–11.
4. Ibid., 282, 533–34, 789–92, 905–7.
5. Ibid., 106–7.
6. Ibid., 565, 567, 842.
7. Ibid., 92.
8. Ibid., 167–68.
9. Ibid., 567.
10. Interview with Milton Meyer, September 26, 2007.
11. Meyer, *Letters Home*, 861.
12. Ibid., 862.
13. Ibid., 864.
14. Ibid., 867.
15. Ibid., 869.
16. Interview with Kathy Fertig, 2003.
17. Louise Reid Spencer, *Guerrilla Wife*, 155; interview with Kathy Fertig, 2003.
18. Spencer, *Guerrilla Wife*, 6; interview with Kathy Fertig, 2003.
19. Spencer, *Guerrilla Wife*, 3, 9.
20. Ibid., 3, 9, 27.
21. John Keats, *They Fought Alone*, 12.
22. Meyer, *Letters Home*, 849–50.
23. Arthur Zich, *The Rising Sun*, 87.
24. Stanley Karnow, *In Our Image: America's Empire in the Philippines*, 284; William H. Bartsch, *December 8, 1941: MacArthur's Pearl Harbor*, 192.

Chapter 5

1. "Life on the Newsfronts of the World: U.S. Cheerfully Faces War with Japan," *Life* 11, no. 23 (December 8, 1941): 38.

2. Harry A. Gailey, *The War in the Pacific: From Pearl Harbor to Tokyo Bay*, 117–19.

3. William H. Bartsch, *December 8, 1941: MacArthur's Pearl Harbor*, 192–93; Stanley Karnow, *In Our Image: America's Empire in the Philippines*, 288; William Manchester, *American Caesar: Douglas MacArthur, 1880–1964*, 200–1; 205–7; Geoffrey Perret, *Old Soldiers Never Die: The Life of Douglas MacArthur*, 243, 245–46.

4. Manchester, *American Caesar*, 208; Bartsch, *December 8, 1941*, 26–71.

5. Manchester, *American Caesar*, 205–6.

6. Bartsch, *December 8, 1941*, 276–77, 280–82.

7. Ibid., 287.

8. Ibid.

9. Ibid., 296.

10. Bartsch, *December 8, 1941*, 409; Sam McGowan, "Caught on the Ground," 1, no. 10, *WWII History: Pearl Harbor Attack*, 64–65,

11. Louis Morton, *The Fall of the Philippines*, 68–71; Arthur Zich, *The Rising Sun*, 91–92.

12. Louise Reid Spencer, *Guerrilla Wife*, 1–2.

13. Ibid., 4.

14. Ibid., 40.

15. Jesse Rodman Wilson, ed., *Through Shining Archway*, 39–43.

16. Ibid.

17. Louise Rounds, "Diary," December 8, 1941.

18. Ibid., December 9, 1941.

19. Ibid., December 17–18, 1941.

20. Ibid., December 17–18, 1941.
21. Milton Walter Meyer, *Letters Home: A Personal History of Emmanuel Hospital, Capiz, and the Meyers, 1919–1943*, 871.
22. Ibid., 872.

Chapter 6

1. Louise Rounds, "Diary," December 31, 1941.
2. Milton Walter Meyer, *Letters Home: A Personal History of Emmanuel Hospital, Capiz, and the Meyers, 1919–1943*, 872; Louise Reid Spencer, *Guerrilla Wife*, 42–43.
3. Meyer, *Letters Home*, 872.
4. Spencer, *Guerrilla Wife*, 13–14.
5. Ibid., 15–16.
6. Ibid., 20.
7. Ibid., 21.
8. Gamaliel L. Manikan, *Guerilla Warfare on Panay Island in the Philippines: Historical Account of the Organization and Operations of the Wartime Sixth Military District, Philippine Army . . .* , 43–44.
9. Spencer, *Guerrilla Wife*, 21; Laverne Fertig, "Memoir," 23.
10. Ibid., 30.
11. Stanley Karnow, *In Our Image: America's Empire in the Philippines*, 282.
12. Harry A. Gailey, *The War in the Pacific: From Pearl Harbor to Tokyo Bay*, 111.
13. Karnow, *In Our Image*, 282–283; Gailey, *War in the Pacific*, 50.
14. Gailey, *War in the Pacific*, 50–51; Karnow, *In Our Image*. 284.
15. R. M. Connaughton, *MacArthur and Defeat in the Philippines*, 160–61; Karnow, *In Our Image*, 292.
16. Gailey, *War in the Pacific*, 116–17.

17. Gailey, *War in the Pacific*, 117–18; Karnow, *In Our Image*, 284, 294, 299; James F. Dunnigan and Albert A. Nofi, *The Pacific War Encyclopedia*, vol. 2, 499; William Manchester, *American Caesar: Douglas MacArthur, 1880–1964*, 215.
18. Louis Morton, *The Fall of the Philippines*, 245.
19. John G. Doll, *The Battling Bastards of Bataan*, 41.
20. Karnow, *In Our Image*, 284, 292.
21. Ibid., 295.
22. Connaughton, *MacArthur and Defeat in the Philippines*, 100; Karnow, *In Our Image*, 281, 302.
23. John M. Fitzgerald, *Family in Crisis: The United States, the Philippines, and the Second World War*, 196.
24. John Keats, *They Fought Alone*, 104–5.

Chapter 7

1. William Manchester, *American Caesar: Douglas MacArthur, 1880–1964*, 250–53.
2. Ibid.
3. Louis Morton, *The Fall of the Philippines*, 360–66; Bradford Grethen Chynoweth, *Bellamy Park: Memoirs*, 235; Ed Cray, *General of the Army: George C. Marshall, Soldier and Statesman*, 302; Jonathan M. Wainwright, *General Wainwright's Story*, 68–70.
4. Duane Schultz, *Hero of Bataan: The Story of General Jonathan M. Wainwright*, 13–16.
5. Geoffrey Perret, *Old Soldiers Never Die: The Life of Douglas MacArthur*, 287–88.
6. Manchester, *American Caesar*, 256.
7. Manchester, *American Caesar*, 256; Douglas MacArthur, *Reminiscences*, 142; Wainwright, *General Wainwright's Story*, 5.

8. Schultz, *Hero of Bataan*, 199, 200; Cray, *General of the Army*, 301.

9. William L. White, *They Were Expendable*, 119.

10. "Tokyo Rose" was the nickname that American G.I.s used for any of the English-speaking women who broadcast Japanese propaganda over short-wave radio. See James Campbell, *The Ghost Mountain Boys: Their Epic March and the Terrifying Battle for New Guinea—The Forgotten War of the South Pacific*, 10.

11. Michael Green, *MacArthur in the Pacific: From the Philippines to the Fall of Japan*.

12. Schultz, *Hero of Bataan*, 201–4.

13. White, *They Were Expendable*.

14. Cray, *General of the Army*, 302.

15. Green, *MacArthur in the Pacific*, 35; Perret, *Old Soldiers Never Die*, 274.

16. Arthur Zich, *The Rising Sun*, 96.

17. Russell Volckmann, *We Remained*, 43.

18. Stanley Falk, *The March of Death*, 95.

19. Ibid., 84–85.

20. John M. Fitzgerald, *Family in Crisis: The United States, the Philippines, and the Second World War*, 37; Gailey, *War in the Pacific*, 122.

21. Zich, *The Rising Sun*, 97; Stanley Karnow, *In Our Image: America's Empire in the Philippines*, 301.

22. John Keats, *They Fought Alone*, 104–5.

23. Meyer, *Letters Home*, 873.

24. Louise Reid Spencer, *Guerrilla Wife*, 31.

25. Ibid., 32–33.

26. Ibid.

27. There is a discrepancy in the available primary sources as to the date of this meeting of twenty-four missionaries. In his memoirs, Fred Chambers places the date on Sunday, April 12. Milton Meyer (*Letters Home*, 874) seems to place

the event on Easter Sunday, April 5, as does Louise Rounds ("Diary," April 5, 1942, 18). However, Milton Meyer also states that on Sunday, April 12, "the army ordered the hospital [at Dumalag] closed and the staff to leave; nurses to be sent home" (*Letters Home*, 874). Thus, it seems the likely date is Easter Sunday, April 5. For the agreement that each family would make its own decision, see Fred Chambers, "Memoirs," 6.

28. Louise Rounds, "Diary," April 5, 18.
29. Dorothy Kinney Chambers, letter to Carol Chambers Park, March 10, 1983, 4.
30. Chynoweth, *Bellamy Park*, 259.
31. Meyer, *Letters Home*, 874–75.
32. John G. Doll, *The Battling Bastards of Bataan*, 55.
33. Meyer, *Letters Home*, 875.
34. Jesse Rodman Wilson, ed., *Through Shining Archway*, 4.
35. Interview with Elmo D. Familiaran, October 8, 2008; Elmo D. Familiaran, "No Greater Love," *The Centralian Link*, 15.
36. Katipunan is 2.48 miles from national highway 2.
37. Meyer, *Letters Home*, 875–76; Spencer, *Guerrilla Wife*, 41.
38. Spencer, *Guerrilla Wife*, 34–35.
39. Wilson, *Through Shining Archway*, 34.
40. Spencer, *Guerrilla Wife*, 35.
41. Wilson, ed., *Through Shining Archway*, 36–37.
42. Dorothy Kinney Chambers, letter to Carol Chambers Park, March 10, 1983, 4; Fred Chambers, "Memoirs," 1.
43. Ibid., 6–15.
44. Ibid.
45. Ted Lawson, edited by Robert Considine, *Thirty Seconds Over Tokyo*, 54–79; Zich, *The Rising Sun*, 108.
46. Meyer, *Letters Home*, 876–77; Spencer, *Guerrilla Wife*, 44–47, 50.
47. Spencer, *Guerrilla Wife*, 42, 52.
48. Terrance C. McGovern and Mark A. Berhow, *American*

Defenses of Corregidor and Manila Bay, 1898–1945, 4–11, 29.

49. Ibid., 29, 33.

50. McGovern and Berhow, *American Defenses of Corregidor*, 18–19.

51. Juanita Redmond, *I Served on Bataan*, 138–40.

52. Ibid., 144–47.

53. PBYs were flying boats/patrol bombers, often used in night attacks and search and rescue operations during World War II. Schultz, *Hero of Bataan*, 268–69.

54. Jonathan Mayhew Wainwright, *General Wainwright's Story*, 101–2; Elizabeth M. Norman, *We Band of Angels: The Untold Story of American Nurses Trapped on Bataan by the Japanese*, 104–7.

55. Keats, *They Fought Alone*, 105.

56. Ben D. Waldron and Emily Burneson, *Corregidor: "From Paradise to Hell," True Narrative by Ben Waldron, Prisoner-of-War*, 75–77.

57. Ibid., 77.

58. Richard Connaughton, *MacArthur and Defeat in the Philippines*, 299; Michael Miller, *From Shanghai to Corregidor: Marines in the Defense of the Philippines*, 29.

59. McGovern and Berhow, *American Defenses of Corregior*, 34; Miller, *From Shanghai to Corregidor*, 29–30.

60. Waldron and Burneson, *Corregidor*, 77.

61. John W. Whitman, "Hell Broke Loose This Morning" in *Command* 43 (May 1997), 29.

62. Ibid.

63. Ibid.

64. Connaughton, *MacArthur and Defeat in the Philippines*, 299.

65. Wainwright, *General Wainwright's Story*, 121. In addition to military personnel, the population of Corregidor

included Filipino civilians who were working for the American forces and their children.

66. Miller, *From Shanghai to Corregidor*, 41.
67. Schultz, *Hero of Bataan*, 290–91.
68. Wainwright, *General Wainwright's Story*, 124.
69. Ibid., 124–27.
70. Ibid., 129–30.
71. Ibid., 130–32.
72. John G. Doll, *The Battling Bastards of Bataan*, 63.
73. Ibid., 64.
74. John M. Fitzgerald, *Family in Crisis: The United States, the Philippines, and the Second World War*, 126–28; Doll, *Battling Bastards of Bataan*, 65.
75. Admiral Ernest J. King, *U.S. Navy at War 1941–1945*, 46.
76. Ibid., 47.
77. Zich, *The Rising Sun*, 142.

Chapter 8

1. Louise Reid Spencer, *Guerrilla Wife*, 56–57.
2. Jennie Clare Adams, *The Hills Did Not Imprison Her*, 5.
3. Spencer, *Guerrilla Wife*, 39, 43, 53, 60–66.
4. Milton Walter Meyer, *Letters Home: A Personal History of Emmanuel Hospital, Capiz, and the Meyers, 1919–1943*, 877.
5. Spencer, *Guerrilla Wife*, 68.
6. Louise Rounds, "Diary," July 6, 31.
7. Spencer, *Guerrilla Wife*, 71.
8. Louise Rounds, "Diary," June 27, 29.
9. Spencer, *Guerrilla Wife*, 69–70.
10. Meyer, *Letters Home*, 883.
11. Adams, *The Hills Did Not Imprison Her*, 40; Spencer, *Guerrilla Wife*, 72–75.

12. Adams, *The Hills Did Not Imprison Her*, 15–16.
13. Spencer, *Guerrilla Wife*, 29.
14. Ibid., 70.
15. Meyer, *Letters Home*, 877–88.
16. Fred Chambers, "Memoirs," 15.
17. Spencer, *Guerrilla Wife*, 70.
18. Ibid.
19. Jesse Rodman Wilson, ed., *Through Shining Archway*, 3–4; *American Baptists in Missions*, Summer 2000; interview with David Covell; Spencer, *Guerrilla Wife*, 70; Donald W. Lambert, *Dr. Dorothy Kinney Chambers*, 2.
20. Founded in 1884 as the Baptist Theological Seminary of Yokohoma, the school received its Japanese name of Kanto Gakuin University in 1919; it is also known by its English name, Mabie Memorial College. Wilson, ed., *Through Shining Archway*, 17–19; *American Baptists in Missions*, Summer 2000; interview with David Covell.
21. Louise Rounds, "Diary," February 14, 1942, and March 5, 1942.
22. Donal Rounds, "Memories of Santo Tomas, Philippines, 1942–1944," 1.
23. Ibid., 1.
24. Ibid., 1.
25. Donal Rounds, "Memories of Santo Tomas," 1. There is evidence from Donal Rounds's mother's diary that Donal and Richard Meyer were temporarily released from Santo Tomas, likely due to their young ages and missing parents. However, if this happened, they were soon returned to the prison camp for the rest of the war. See Louise Rounds, "Diary," February 28, 1942, and Tressa R. Cates, *Infamous Santo Tomas*, 41.
26. Frances B. Cogan, *Captured: The Japanese Internment of American Civilians in the Philippines, 1941–1945*, 208–9. It is estimated that there were 7,800 civilian internees in the

Philippines. This number comprised approximately 4,200 men, 2,300 women, and 1,300 children. Of this group, nearly 6,000 were American citizens. The next largest group were from the British Commonwealth. The Santo Tomas civilian internment camp was by far the largest. Smaller camps were scattered throughout the Philippines in cities such as Baguio, Bacolod, Cebu, Davao, and Los Banos in southern Luzon. By the final months of the war, most civilian internees had been transferred and centralized in Santo Tomas, swelling the population to over 7,000 internees.

27. A. V. H. Hartendorp, *The Japanese Occupation of the Philippines*, 1:11.
28. Ibid., 12.
29. Georgiana "Dodie" Peters Borroughs, "Interned in the Philippines: A Memoir of Survival and Perseverance," 9; Hartendorp, *Japanese Occupation*, 1:11.
30. Donal Rounds, "Memories of Santo Tomas," 1; Borroughs, "Interned in the Philippines," 20.
31. Donal Rounds, "Memories of Santo Tomas," 1.
32. Ibid., 2.
33. Ibid.
34. Ibid.
35. Borroughs, "Interned in the Philippines," 11.
36. Donal Rounds, "Memories of Santo Tomas," 2.
37. Ibid., 3.
38. Ibid.
39. Meyer, *Letters Home*, 880–82; Milton Walter Meyer, "This Is the Place Where They Died," *Missions* 37, no. 4 (April 1946), 211.
40. Roscoe Creed, *PBY: The Catalina Flying Boat*, 95–98; John Keats, *They Fought Alone*, 105.
41. Rafael Steinberg and the editors of Time-Life Books. *Return to the Philippines*, 22–24.
42. Ibid., 24.

43. Prepared by his General Staff, editor in chief, Charles
    A. Willoughby, *Reports of General MacArthur: The Campaigns
    of MacArthur in the Pacific*, 308.

Chapter 9

1. Prepared by his General Staff, editor in chief, Charles
   A. Willoughby, *Reports of General MacArthur: The Campaigns
   of MacArthur in the Pacific*, 1:315–16; Eliseo D. Rio, *Rays of
   a Setting Sun: Recollections of World War II*, 161.
2. Gamaliel L. Manikan, *Guerilla Warfare on Panay Island in
   the Philippines: Historical Account of the Organization and
   Operations of the Wartime Sixth Military District, Philippine
   Army . . .* , 121.
3. Ibid., 128–29.
4. Ibid., 131–32.
5. Ibid.
6. Ibid., 133.
7. Ibid., 134.
8. Ibid., 154.
9. *Reports of General MacArthur*, 1:300; Manikan, *Guerilla
   Warfare*, 121, 157.
10. Manikan, *Guerilla Warfare*, 203, 243; Louise Reid Spencer,
    Guerrilla Wife, 97.
11. Manikan, *Guerilla Warfare*, 473.
12. Ibid., 208.
13. Milton Walter Meyer, *Letters Home: A Personal History of
    Emmanuel Hospital, Capiz, and the Meyers, 1919–1943*,
    882, 885, 887; Spencer, *Guerrilla Wife*, 78–82.
14. Meyer, *Letters Home*, 886–87.
15. Ibid.
16. Ibid., 887–88.

17. Ibid., 889.

18. Spencer, *Guerrilla Wife*, 96–97.

19. Ibid.

20. Ibid., 76.

21. Manikan, *Guerilla Warfare*, 138–39.

22. Ibid., 174.

23. Ibid., 173.

24. Ibid., 181.

25. Fertig, "Memoir," 129.

26. Spencer, *Guerrilla Wife*, 95–97.

27. Manikan, *Guerilla Warfare*, 203–5.

28. Meyer, *Letters Home*, 884.

29. Manikan, *Guerilla Warfare*, 182.

30. Ibid., 185.

31. Ibid., 207.

32. Spencer, *Guerrilla Wife*, 97.

33. Jennie Clare Adams, "Planes," *The Hills Did Not Imprison Her*, 23.

34. Meyer, *Letters Home*, 884–85.

35. Spencer, *Guerrilla Wife*, 98.

36. Ibid., 98–99.

Chapter 10

1. Peralta, *Guerrilla Warfare*, 155–6.

2. Peralta, *Guerrilla Warfare*, 132, 219; *Terrain Handbook 51: Panay Island*, 92. In 1939, there were 201 American residents on Panay, of whom 176 lived in Iloilo province, 22 in Capiz province, and 3 in Antique province. Most Americans lived in Iloilo City.

3. Ibid., 211, 224–25.

4. Ibid., 224–25.

5. Aklan became a separate province from Capiz province on November 8, 1956.

6. Ibid., 205.

7. Louise Reid Spencer, *Guerrilla Wife*, 102.

8. Milton Walter Meyer, *Letters Home: A Personal History of Emmanuel Hospital, Capiz, and the Meyers, 1919–1943*, 885.

9. Meyer, *Letters Home*, 886; Spencer, *Guerrilla Wife*, 103.

10. Ibid., 171.

11. Meyer, *Letters Home*, 886.

12. Jennie Clare Adams, "Weary of War," *The Hills Did Not Imprison Her*, 25.

13. Meyer, *Letters Home*, 886.

14. Spencer, *Guerrilla Wife*, 104–5, 124–28.

15. Ibid., 127.

16. Ibid., 132–33.

17. Meyer, *G.I. Joe: 1943–1945*, 1.

18. Ibid., 2.

19. Interview with David Covell, March 15, 2006.

20. Roberta Stephens and Ann Borquist, "From Suffering and Sacrifice Comes Joy: The Story of the Covell Family," *American Baptists in Mission*, Summer 2000, http://www.abc-usa.org/inmissn/summ00/6summ00.htm.; Gordon William Prange, Donald M. Goldstein, and Katherine V. Dillon, *God's Samurai: Lead Pilot at Pearl Harbor*, 202–3, 217.

21. Meyer, *Letters Home*, 887.

22. Meyer, *Letters Home*, 887; Gamaliel L. Manikan, *Guerilla Warfare on Panay Island in the Philippines: Historical Account of the Organization and Operations of the Wartime Sixth Military District, Philippine Army . . .* , 243.

23. Spencer, *Guerrilla Wife*, 150; Meyer, *Letters Home*, 887.

24. Meyer, *Letters Home*, 888–89.

25. Ibid., 889–90.

26. Ibid., 890.

27. Manikan, *Guerilla Warfare*, 249–50; 297–300; Spencer, *Guerrilla Wife*, 135.

28. Spencer, *Guerrilla Wife*, 135–36.

29. Edward Dissette and Hans C. Adamson, *Guerrilla Submarines*, 58.

30. David Hinkle, editor, *United States Submarines*, 13, 133; Clay Blair, *Silent Victory: The U.S. Submarine War Against Japan*, 100–1, 107–12; USS *Gudgeon* (SS-211), http://en .wikipedia.org/wiki/USS_Gudgeon_(SS-211).

31. Dissette and Adamson, *Guerrilla Submarines*, 60–63; Manikan, *Guerilla War*, 298–300; Blair, *Silent Victor*, 392–94.

32. Spencer, *Guerrilla Wife*, 140–42. A year after landing supplies on Panay, on April 7, 1944, the USS *Gudgeon* disappeared without trace while on its twelfth war patrol near Johnston Island. The mystery of its disappearance has not been solved. Prior to its disappearance, Commander Bill Post, who landed supplies on Panay, had been transferred to another submarine. Commander Post survived the war.

33. Spencer, *Guerrilla Wife*, 142.

34. Interview with Kathy Fertig.

35. Spencer, *Guerrilla Wife*, 144.

36. Ibid., 147–48.

Chapter 11

1. Gamaliel L. Manikan, *Guerilla Warfare on Panay Island in the Philippines: Historical Account of the Organization and Operations of the Wartime Sixth Military District, Philippine Army . . .* , 317.

2. Ibid., 318.

3. Ibid., 321.

4. Ibid., 324.

5. Ibid., 324–25.

6. Ibid., 330.

7. Ibid., 331.

8. Ibid., 358.

9. Milton Walter Meyer, *Letters Home: A Personal History of Emmanuel Hospital, Capiz, and the Meyers, 1919–1943*, 890–94.

10. Ibid., 894.

11. Louise Reid Spencer, *Guerrilla Wife*, 149–50.

12. Theodore Roscoe, *United States Submarine Operations*, 512–13; Meyer, *Letters Home*, 888. Milton Meyer notes that the last letters received from Hopevale—one written by Dr. Meyer and the other by Mr. Rose to the American Baptist Mission Board—likely found their way on board an American submarine.

13. Manikan, *Guerilla War*, 338; Clay Blair, *Silent Victory: The U.S. Submarine War Against Japan,* 397; Roscoe, *United States Submarine Operations*, 273.

14. Donald L. Miller, *Masters of the Air: America's Bomber Boys Who Fought the Air War Against Nazi Germany*, 471.

15. Spencer, *Guerrilla Wife*, 150.

16. Meyer, *Letters Home*, 894.

17. Spencer, *Guerrilla Wife,* 150–51.

18. Meyer, *Letters Home*, 894.

19. Spencer, *Guerrilla Wife,* 170.

20. Ibid., 169.

21. Ibid., 168.

22. Ibid., 155, 171–81.

23. Ibid., 155–56.

24. Ibid., 173.

25. Delfin Dianala, *The Hopevale Martyrs*, 107.

26. Meyer, *Letters Home*, 895.

27. Ibid., 895.

28. Spencer, *Guerrilla Wife*, 174–79.

29. Dianala, *The Hopevale Martyrs*, 107.

30. Ibid., 179.

31. Jesse R. Wilson, ed., *Through Shining Archways*, 27.

32. Ibid., 21–28; Dianala, *The Hopevale Martyrs*, 107; Spencer, *Guerrilla Wife*, 180.

33. Spencer, *Guerrilla Wife*, 181–86.

34. Dianala, *The Hopevale Martyrs*, 107.

35. Roberta Stephens and Ann Borquist, "From Suffering to Sacrifice Comes Joy: The Story of the Covell Family," *American Baptists in Mission*, Summer 2000, http://www.abc-usa.org/inmissn/summ00/6summ00.htm.; Meyer, *Letters Home*, 899; Spencer, *Guerrilla Wife*, 194–96.

36. Meyer, *Letters Home*, 899.

37. Laverne Fertig, "Memoir," 214; Spencer, *Guerrilla Wife*, 193–94, 206.

38. Dianala, *The Hopevale Martyrs*, 107.

39. Ibid., 107.

40. Ibid., 111.

41. Ibid.

Chapter 12

1. Louise Reid Spencer, *Guerrilla Wife*, 188–208.

2. Travis Ingham, *Rendezvous by Submarine: The Story of Charles Parsons and the Guerilla-Soldiers in the Philippines*, 182.

3. Gamaliel L. Manikan, *Guerilla Warfare on Panay Island in the Philippines: Historical Account of the Organization and Operations of the Wartime Sixth Military District, Philippine Army . . .* , 335, 471. On August 4, 1943, Lieutenant Colonel

Peralta was promoted to colonel. At age thirty, he became the highest-ranking officer in the Philippine Army not in captivity. Spencer, *Guerrilla Wife*, 213.

4. Manikan, *Guerilla War*, 471–72.

5. Spencer, *Guerrilla Wife*, 213–28.

6. Clay Blair, *Silent Victory: The U.S. Submarine War Against Japan*, 580.

7. Blair, *Silent Victory*, 580; Edward Dissette and Hans C. Adamson, *Guerrilla Submarines*, 113–14; Theodore Roscoe, *United States Submarine Operations*, 527.

8. Ibid., 580–81.

9. Roscoe, *Submarine Operations*, 514–15.

10. Manikan, *Guerilla Warfare*, 472.

11. Dissette and Adamson, *Guerrilla Submarines*, 114.

12. Spencer, *Guerrilla Wife*, 236–37.

13. Dissette and Adamson, *Guerrilla Submarines*, 114.

14. Spencer, *Guerrilla Wife*, 235–39.

15. Dissette and Adamson, *Guerrilla Submarines*, 114.

16. Ibid., 239.

17. Spencer, *Guerrilla Wife*, 239.

18. Ibid., 240.

19. Dissette and Adamson, *Guerrilla Submarines*, 116.

20. Roscoe, *Submarine Operations*, 370.

21. Spencer, *Guerrilla Wife*, 241–42.

22. Blair, *Silent Victory*, 581.

23. Spencer, *Guerrilla Wife*, 242.

24. Manikan, *Guerilla Warfare*, 473.

Epilogue

1. Geoffrey Perret, *Old Soldiers Never Die: The Life of Douglas MacArthur*, 401.

2. Ibid., 400.

3. Perret, *Old Soldiers Never Die*, 380; Douglas MacArthur, *Reminiscences*, 197.

4. MacArthur, *Reminiscences*, 198; Perret, *Old Soldiers Never Die*, 383; Jean Edward Smith, *FDR*, 621.

5. Perret, *Old Soldiers Never Die*, 401.

6. E. B. Potter, *Nimitz*, 376–77.

7. Courtney Whitney, *MacArthur: His Rendezvous with History*, 123; Perret, *Old Soldiers Never Die*, 401.

8. Smith, *FDR*, 620.

9. Whitney, *MacArthur*, 123; Perret, *Old Soldiers Never Die*, 405.

10. Perret, *Old Soldiers Never Die*, 406.

11. William Manchester, *American Caesar: Douglas MacArthur, 1880–1964*, 368–69.

12. Ibid., 368.

13. Potter, *Nimitz*, 382–85.

14. Smith, *FDR*, 621; Manchester, *American Caesar*, 368.

15. Manchester, *American Caesar*, 369; Perrot, *Old Soldiers Never Die*, 406.

16. Manchester, *American Caesar*, 369.

17. Richard K. Kolb and the editors of *VFW* magazine, eds., *Faces of Victory: Pacific*, 226–27.

18. Ibid., 426.

19. Gordon L. Rottman, *World War II Pacific Island Guide*, 308–9.

20. *Filipino Times*, "Widow of American WWII Guerrilla Dies," February 1992, 7; Allied Geographical Section, Southwest Pacific Area, Terrain Handbook 51, *Panay Island*, December 10, 1944.

21. Interview with Kathy Fertig, 2003.

22. Résumé of Claude E. Fertig, 2.

23. Rafael Steinberg and the editors of Time-Life Books, *Return to the Philippines*, 22–33.

24. http://stackingswivel.blogspot.com/2005/05/wendell-fertig-american-hero.html.

25. Spencer, *Guerrilla Wife*, 243.

26. Obituary of Beatrice Louise Spencer, *Kansas City Star*, January 11, 2002.

27. Obituary of Beatrice Louise Spencer, *Kansas City Star*, January 11, 2002; obituary of Cyril L. Spencer, *Kansas City Star*, December 30, 1999; Sherry Armel, "Jungle Was Refuge for Couple on Run During War Years," *Kansas City Star*, July 1, 1993.

28. Milton Walter Meyer, *Letters Home: A Personal History of Emmanuel Hospital, Capiz, and the Meyers, 1919–1943*, 895–900; Milton Walter Meyer, *G.I. Joe 1943–1945*, 179–200.

29. Interview with Milton Meyer, September 26, 2007; Elizabeth Meyer, *Teenage Diary*, 262.

30. Interview with David Covell, March 15, 2006.

31. Gordon William Prange, Donald M. Goldstein, and Katherine V. Dillon, *God's Samurai: Lead Pilot at Pearl Harbor*, 202–4, 206–9, 217.

32. Interview with Carol Chambers Park concerning her memory of her father, Dr. Fred Chambers, sharing with Dick Meyer and Donal Rounds the news of their parents' deaths, October 7, 2008.

33. Donal Rounds, "Memories of Santo Tomas, Philippines, 1941–1944," 4.

34. Ibid., 5.

35. A. V. H. Hartendorp, *The Japanese Occupation of the Philippines*, 2.155–56.

36. Obituary of Anna Waters, March 5, 2008. http://www.blindliving.com/jhistory.htm.

37. Inteview with Elmo D. Familiaran, grandson of Reverend Delfin Dianala, October 8, 2008.

38. Familiaran, "No Greater Love," *The Centralian Link*, January–February 2008, 15.

39. Toshimi Kumai, *The Blood and Mud in the Philippines: Anti-Guerrilla Warfare on Panay Island* (Iloilo City, Philippines: Malones Printing Press and Publishing House, 2009), 72–73.

40. Taylor, Familiaran, and Qualls, "No Greater Love," 79–80.

41. Thomas Holian, *Saviors and Suppliers: World War II Submarine Special Operations in the Philippines*, http://www.navy.mil/navydata/cno/n87/usw/issue_23/saviors.htm.

Author's Note

1. James J. Halsema, *Bishop Brent's Baguio School: The First Seventy-five Years*, 29, 152.

2. I Corinthians 13:13.

3. Scott Walker, *Hell's Broke Loose in Georgia*, 188–89.

4. Letter to James M. Calhoun, mayor of Atlanta, September 12, 1864.

5. Michael Miller, *Masters of the Air*, 35–37, 52–55, 109.

6. Ibid., 454–55, 484; Gordon Thomas and Max Morgan Witts, *Enola Gay*, 98; Geoffrey Perret, *Winged Victory: The Army Air Forces in World War II*, 454–59.

Bibliography

Primary Sources

Unpublished Manuscripts, Diaries, Journals, Letters, Memoirs

Borroughs, Georgiana "Dodie" Peters. "Interned in the Philippines: A Memoir of Survival and Perseverance." Edited by Kacey Morgan. Unpublished memoir. Private collection.

Chambers, Dorothy Kinney. Collected Letters. Private collection.

Chambers, Fred. Autobiography and memoirs. Private collection.

Fertig, Laverne. Memoir. Private collection.

Lambert, Donald W. "Dr. Dorothy Kinney Chambers: A Woman Ahead of Her Time," Funeral Eulogy for Dr. Chambers, December 4, 2001.

Rounds, Donal. "Memories of Santo Tomas, Philippines, 1941–1944." Unpublished memoir. Private collection.

Rounds, Louise. Diary. Private collection.

Books and Pamphlets

Adams, Jennie Clark. *The Hills Did Not Imprison Her*. New York: Woman's American Baptist Foreign Mission Society, 1947.

Cates, Tressa R. *Infamous Santo Tomas*. San Marcos, Calif.: Pacific Press, 1957, 1981.

Chynoweth, Bradford Grethen. *Bellamy Park: Memoirs*. Hicksville, N.Y.: Exposition Press, 1975.

Coleman, John S. *Bataan and Beyond: Memoirs of an American POW*. College Station: Texas A&M University Press, 1978.

Foley, Betty Halsema. *Keepsake: An Autobiography*. Scottsdale, Ariz.: Paper & Ink, 2001.

Gause, Damon. *The War Journal of Major Damon "Rocky" Gause*. New York: Hyperion, 1999.

Hartendorp, A. V. H. *The Japanese Occupation of the Philippines*. 2 vols. Manila: Bookmark Publishers, 1967.

Hind, R. Renton. *Spirits Unbroken*. San Francisco: John Howell, Publisher, 1946.

Hubbard, Preston John. *Apocalypse Now: My Survival of Japanese Imprisonment During World War II*. Nashville, Tenn.: Vanderbilt University Press, 1990.

Hunt, Ray C., and Bernard Norling. *Behind Japanese Lines: An American Guerrilla in the Philippines*. Lexington: University of Kentucky Press, 1986.

King, Ernest J., and Walter Muir Whitehill. *Fleet Admiral King: A Naval Record*. New York: W. W. Norton, 1952.

Lapham, Robert L., and Bernard Norling. *Lapham's Raiders: Guerrillas in the Philippines, 1942–1945*. Lexington, Ky.: University Press of Kentucky, 1996.

Lawson, Ted W. *Thirty Seconds over Tokyo*. Edited by Robert Considine. New York: Random House, 1943.

Lawton, Manny. *Some Survived: An Epic Account of Japanese Captivity During World War II*. Chapel Hill, N.C.: Algonquin Books of Chapel Hill, 1984.

Lee, Clark. *They Call It Pacific: An Eye-Witness Story of Our War Against Japan from Bataan to the Solomons.* New York: Viking Press, 1943.

MacArthur, Douglas. *Reminiscences.* New York: McGraw-Hill, 1964.

Manikan, Gamaliel L. *Guerilla Warfare on Panay Island in the Philippines: Historical Account of the Organization and Operations of the Wartime Sixth Military District, Philippine Army, Otherwise Known as the "Free Panay Guerilla Forces," During World War II in the Philippines.* Quezon City, Philippines: Bustamante Press, 1977.

Mansell, Donald E., with Vesta W. Mansell. *Under the Shadow of the Rising Sun.* Namp, Idaho: Pacific Press Publishing Association, 2003.

Meyer, Elizabeth "Bim." *Teenage Diary: Santo Tomas Internment Camp,* ed. Milton Walter Meyer. Philippine Monographs, no. 1. Claremont, Calif.: Paige Press, 2005.

Meyer, Milton Walter. *G.I. Joe: 1943–1945.* Claremont, Calif.: Paige Press, 2003.

———. *Letters Home: A Personal History of Emmanuel Hospital, Capiz, and the Meyers: 1919–1943.* Claremont, Calif.: Paige Press, 2003.

Miles, Fern Harrington. *Captive Community: Life in a Japanese Internment Camp, 1941–1945.* Jefferson City, Tenn.: Mossy Creek Press, 1987.

Miller, E. B. *Bataan Uncensored.* Long Prairie, Minn.: Hart Publications, 1949.

Morrill, John, and Peter Martin. *South from Corregidor.* New York: Simon and Schuster, 1943.

Petillo, Carol M. *The Ordeal of Elizabeth Vaughan: A Wartime Diary of the Philippines.* Athens: University of Georgia Press, 1985.

Ramsey, Edwin Price, and Stephen J. Rivele. *Lieutenant Ramsey's War.* New York: Knightsbridge, 1990.

Redmond, Juanita. *I Served on Bataan.* New York: J. B. Lippincott, 1943.

Rio, Eliseo D. *Rays of a Setting Sun: Recollections of World War II.* Manila: De La Salle University Press, 1999.

Salvador, Maximo G. *Panay Guerrilla Memoirs.* Self-published, 1973.

Sams, Margaret. *Forbidden Family: A Wartime Memoir of the Philippines, 1941–1945.* Madison, Wis.: University of Wisconsin Press, 1989.

Spencer, Louise Reid. *Guerrilla Wife.* New York: Thomas Y. Crowell, 1945.

Thompson, Dorothy Davis. *The Road Back: A Pacific POW's Liberation Story.* Lubbock, Tex.: Texas Tech University Press, 1996.

Volckmann, Russell W. *We Remained: Three Years Behind Enemy Lines in the Philippines.* New York: W. W. Norton, 1954.

Wainwright, Jonathan. *General Wainwright's Story.* Edited by Robert Considine. Garden City, N.Y.: Doubleday, 1949.

Waldron, Ben D., and Emily Burneson. *Corregidor: "From Paradise to Hell"; True Narrative of Ben Waldron, Prisoner-of-War.* Freeman, S. Dak.: Pine Hill Press, 1988.

Whitehead, Arthur Kendal. *Odyssey of a Philippine Scout: Fighting, Escaping, and Evading the Japanese, 1941–1944.* Bedford: Penn.: Aberjona Press, 2006.

Whitfield, Evelyn. *Three Year Picnic: An American Woman's Life Inside Japanese Prison Camps in the Philippines During WWII.* Corvallis, Ore.: Premiere Editions International, 1999.

Wills, Donald H., with Rayburn W. Myers. *The Sea Was My Last Chance: Memoir of an American Captured on Bataan in 1942 Who Escaped in 1944 and Led the Liberation of Western Mindanao.* Jefferson, N.C.: McFarland, 1992.

Articles and Parts of Books

Adams, Jennie C. "The Frail Baby That Cried in the Night." *Missions,* 33, no. 8 (October 1942), 498.

Dianala, Delfin. "The Hopevale Martyrs." *Book of Remembrance: Convention of Philippine Baptist Churches Golden Jubilee, 1900–1950*, 107–108, 111.

Meyer, Frederick W. "Many Were Restored to Health and Others Died." *Missions*, 32, no. 6 (June 1941), 341–342.

Meyer, Milton Walter. "This Is the Place Where They Died." *Missions*, 37, no. 4 (April 1946), 206–211.

Waters, Henry S. "Here They Died and Their Remains Rest Here." *Missions*, 146, no. 4 (April 1948), 208–210.

Secondary Sources

Books

Alip, Eufronio M. *Philippine History: Political, Social, Economic.* Manila: Alip and Sons, 1954.

Astor, Gerald. *Crisis in the Pacific: The Battles for the Philippine Islands by the Men Who Fought Them; An Oral History.* New York: Donald I. Fine, 1996.

Bain, David Haward. *Sitting in Darkness: Americans in the Philippines.* Boston: Houghton Mifflin, 1984.

Bantug, Asuncion Lopez-Rizal. *Indio Bravo: The Story of José Rizal.* Makati, Philippines: Tahanan Books, 1997.

Bartsch, William H. *December 8, 1941: MacArthur's Pearl Harbor.* College Station: Texas A&M University Press, 2003.

———. *Doomed at the Start: American Pursuit Pilots in the Philippines, 1941–1942.* College Station: Texas A&M University Press, 1992.

Beck, John Jacob. *MacArthur and Wainwright: Sacrifice of the Philippines*. Albuquerque: University of New Mexico Press, 1974.

Blair, Clay, Jr. *Silent Victory: The U.S. Submarine War Against Japan*. New York: Bantam Books, 1975.

Breuer, William B. *MacArthur's Undercover War: Spies, Saboteurs, Guerrillas, and Secret Missions*. New York: John Wiley, 1995.

Campbell, James, *The Ghost Mountain Boys: Their Epic March and the Terrifying Battle for New Guinea; The Forgotten War of the South Pacific*. New York: Crown, 2007.

Cannon, Hamlin M. *Leyte: The Return to the Philippines*, vol. 5 of *United States Army in World War II: War in the Pacific*, Kent Roberts Greenfield, gen. ed. Washington, D.C.: Government Printing Office, 1954.

Caraccilo, Dominic J. *Surviving Bataan and Beyond: Colonel Irvin Alexander's Odyssey as a Japanese Prisoner of War*. Mechanicsburg, Penn.: Stackpole Books, 1999.

Cates, Tressa R. *Infamous Santo Tomas*. San Marcos, Calif.: Pacific Press, 1981.

Cogan, Frances B. *Captured: The Japanese Internment of American Civilians in the Philippines, 1941–1945*. Athens: University of Georgia Press, 2000.

Connaughton, Richard. *MacArthur and Defeat in the Philippines*. New York: Overlook Press, 2001.

Cray. Ed. *General of the Army: George C. Marshall, Soldier and Statesman*. New York: W. W. Norton, 1990.

Creed, Roscoe. *PBY: The Catalina Flying Boat*. Annapolis, Md.: Naval Institute Press, 1985.

Davis, Kenneth S. *FDR: The War President, 1940–1943*. New York: Random House, 2000.

Daws, Gavan. *Prisoners of the Japanese: POWs of World War II in the Pacific* New York: William Morrow, 1994.

De Morga, Antonio. *History of the Philippine Islands*, 2 vols. BiblioBazaar, 2006.

D'Este, Carlo. *Eisenhower: A Soldier's Life*. New York: Henry Holt, 2002.

Dioguardi, Ralph. *Roll Out the Barrel . . . The Tanks Are Coming: The Liberation of the Santo Tomas Internment Camp*. Bennington, Vt.: Merriam Press, 2003.

Dissette, Edward, and H. C. Anderson. *Guerrilla Submarines*. New York: Ballantine Books, 1972.

Doll, John D. *The Battling Bastards of Bataan: A Chronology of the First Days of World War II in the Philippines*. Bennington, Vt.: Merriam Press, 2002.

Driskell, Frank A., and Dede W. Casad. *Chester W. Nimitz: Admiral of the Hills*. Austin Tex.: Eakin Press, 1983.

Elson, Robert T. *Prelude to War*. World War II. Alexandria, Va.: Time-Life Books, 1977.

Falk, Stanley L. *The March of Death*. London: Robert Hale, 1962.

Fellowes-Gordon, Ian. *The World's Greatest Escapes*. London: Odhams Books, 1966.

Fitzgerald, John M. *Family in Crisis: The United States, the Philippines, and the Second World War*. Bloomington, Ind.: 1st Books Library, 2002.

Fleming, Thomas. *The New Dealers' War: F.D.R. and the War Within World War II*. New York: Basic Books, 2001.

Fluckey, Eugene B. *Thunder Below! The USS Barb Revolutionizes Submarine Warfare in World War II*. Champaign: University of Illinois Press, 1992.

40th Infantry Division: The Years of World War II, 7 December 1941–7 April 1946. Baton Rouge, La.: Army and Navy Publishing Company, 1947.

Frankel, Stanley A. *The 37th Infantry Division in World War II*. Washington, D.C.: Infantry Journal Press, 1948.

Gailey, Harry A. *The War in the Pacific: From Pearl Harbor to Tokyo Bay*. Navato, Calif.: Presidio Press, 1995.

Glusman, John A. *Conduct Under Fire: Four American Doctors and*

Their Fight for Life as Prisoners of the Japanese, 1941–1945.
New York: Viking Press, 2005.

Go, Julian, ed. *The American Colonial State in the Philippines: Global Perspectives.* Durham, N.C.: Duke University Press, 2003.

Green, Michael. *MacArthur in the Pacific: From the Philippines to the Fall of Japan.* Osceola, Wis.: Motorbooks, 1996.

Griffith, Thomas E., Jr. *MacArthur's Airman: General George C. Kenny and the War in the Southwest Pacific.* Lawrence: University Press of Kansas, 1998.

Guerrero, Leon Maria. *The First Filipino: A Biography of José Rizal.* Manila: National Historical Commission, 1974.

Halsema, James. *Bishop Brent's Baguio School: The First 75 Years.* Baguio, Philippines: Brent School, 1987.

Harkins, Philip. *Blackburn's Headhunters.* New York: W. W. Norton, 1955.

Hersey, John. *Men on Bataan.* New York: Alfred A. Knopf, 1943.

Hopkins, William B. *The Pacific War: The Strategy, Politics, and Players That Won the War.* Minneapolis: Zenith Press, 2008.

Hoyt, Edwin P. *Japan's War: The Great Pacific Conflict.* New York: Cooper Square Press, 1986, 2001.

Ingham, Travis. *Rendezvous by Submarine: The Story of Charles Parsons and the Guerilla-Soldiers in the Philippines.* Doubleday, Doran, 1945.

Ishida, Jintaro. *The Remains of War: Apology and Forgiveness; Testimonies of the Japanese Imperial Army and Its Filipino Victims.* Guilford, Conn.: Lyons Press, 2001.

Jocano, F. Landa. *Growing Up in a Philippine Barrio: Case Studies in Education and Culture.* New York: Holt, Rinehart and Winston, 1969.

Karnow, Stanley. *In Our Image: America's Empire in the Philippines.* New York: Random House, 1989.

Keats, John. *They Fought Alone: A True Story of a Modern American Hero.* New York: J. P. Lippincott, 1963.

Kerr, E. Bartlett. *Surrender and Survival: The Experience of American POW's in the Pacific 1941–1945*. New York: William Morrow, 1985.

King, Ernest J. *U.S. Navy at War: 1941–1945. Official Report to the Secretary of the Navy by Fleet Admiral Ernest J. King, U.S. Navy*. Washington, D.C.: Government Printing Office, 1946.

Kolb, Richard K., editor. *Faces of Victory, Pacific: The Fall of the Rising Sun*. Kansas City, Mo.: Addax Publishing Group, 1995.

Krieger, Herbert W. *Peoples of the Philippines*. Smithsonian Institution War Background Studies, no. 4. Washington, D.C.: Smithsonian Institution, 1942.

Kumai, Toshimi. *The Blood and Mud in the Philippines: Anti-Guerrilla Warfare on Panay Island*. Iloilo City, Philippines: Malones Printing Press and Publishing House, 2009.

Lee, Clark, and Richard Henschel. *Douglas MacArthur*. New York: Henry Holt, 1952.

Linn, Brian McAllister. *The Philippine War, 1899–1902*. Lawrence: University Press of Kansas, 2000.

Manchester, William. *American Caesar: Douglas MacArthur, 1880–1964*. Boston: Little, Brown, 1978.

McCoy, Alfred W., ed. *Southeast Asia Under Japanese Occupation*. Yale University Southeast Asia Studies, no. 22, 1985.

McGovern, Terrance C., and Mark A. Berhow. *American Defenses of Corregidor and Manila Bay, 1898–1945*. Botley, Oxfordshire, U.K.: Osprey Publishing, 2003.

Mellnik, Stephen M. *Philippine War Diary: 1939–1945*. New York: Van Nostrand Reinhold, 1981.

Miller, Donald L. *Masters of the Air*. New York: Simon and Schuster, 2006.

Miller, Edward S. *War Plan Orange: The U.S. Strategy to Defeat Japan: 1897–1945*. Annapolis, Md.: Naval Institute Press, 1991.

Miller, J. Michael. *From Shanghai to Corregidor: Marines in the Defense of the Philippines*. Marines in World War II Commemorative Series. Washington, D.C: Marine Corps Historical Center, 1997.

Miller, Stuart Creighton. *Benevolent Assimilation: The American Conquest of the Philippines, 1899–1903*. New Haven, Conn.: Yale University Press, 1984.

Morton, Louis. *The Fall of the Philippines*, vol. 4 of *United States Army in World War II: War in the Pacific*, Kent Roberts Greenfield, gen. ed. Washington, D.C.: Government Printing Office, 1953.

Moseley, Leonard. *Marshall: Hero for Our Times*. New York: Hearst Books, 1982.

Musicant, Ivan. *Empire by Default: The Spanish-American War and the Dawn of the American Century*. New York: Henry Holt, 1998.

Nadeau, Kathleen. *The History of the Philippines*. Westport, Conn.: Greenwood Press, 2008.

Norling, Bernard. *The Intrepid Guerrillas of North Luzon*. Lexington: University Press of Kentucky, 1999.

Norman, Elizabeth M. *We Band of Angels: The Untold Story of American Nurses Trapped on Bataan by the Japanese*. New York: Random House, 1999.

Panay Island: Philippine Series. Terrain Handbook 51, Allied Geographical Section, Southwest Pacific Area, December 10, 1944. New York: Random House, 1999.

Perret, Geoffery. *Old Soldiers Never Die: The Life of Douglas MacArthur*. New York: Random House, 1996.

———. *Winged Victory: The Army Air Forces in World War II*. New York: Random House, 1993.

Petillo, Carol Morris. *Douglas MacArthur: The Philippine Years*. Bloomington: Indiana University Press, 1981.

Potter, E. B. *Nimitz*. Annapolis, Md.: Naval Institute Press, 1976.

Prange, Gordon W. *God's Samurai: Lead Pilot at Pearl Harbor*. Washington, D.C.: Brassey's, 2004.

Ratti, Oscar, and Adele Westbrook. *Secrets of the Samurai: The Martial Arts of Feudal Japan*. Edison, N.J.: Castle Books, 1973, 1999.

Reports of General Douglas MacArthur: The Campaigns of MacArthur in the Pacific, vol. 1. Prepared by his General Staff. Washington, D.C.: Government Printing Office, 1966.

Roscoe, Theodore. *United States Submarine Operations in World War II*. Annapolis, Md.: United States Naval Institute, 1949

Rottman, Gordon L. *World War II Pacific Island Guide: A Geo-Military Study*. Westport Conn.: Greenwood Press, 2002.

Russell of Liverpool, Edward, Lord. *The Knights of Bushido: A Short History of Japanese War Crimes*. London: Greenhill Books; Mechanicsburg, Penn.: Stackpole Books, 2002.

Schaller, Michael. *Douglas MacArthur: The Far Eastern General*. New York: Oxford University Press, 1989.

Schultz, Duane. *Hero of Bataan: The Story of General Jonathan M. Wainwright*. New York: St. Martin's Press, 1981.

Sibley, David J. *A War of Frontier and Empire: The Philippine-American War, 1899–1902*. New York: Hill and Wang, 2008.

Smith, Jean Edward. *FDR*. New York: Random House, 2007.

Smith, Robert Ross. *The Approach to the Philippines*, vol. 3 of *United States Army in World War II: The War in the Pacific*, gen. ed., Kent Roberts Greenfield. Washington, D.C.: Government Printing Office, 1953.

———. *Triumph in the Philippines*, vol. 10 of *The United States Army in World War II: War in the Pacific*, gen. ed., Stetson Conn. Washington, D.C.: Government Printing Office, 1963.

Smith, Steven Trent. *The Rescue: A True Story of Courage and Survival in World War II*. New York: John Wiley, 2001.

Spector, Ronald H. *Eagle Against the Sun: The American War with Japan*. New York: Free Press, 1985.

Steinberg, David Joel. *Philippine Collaboration in World War II*. Ann Arbor: University of Michigan Press, 1967.

Steinberg, Rafael. *Return to the Philippines.* World War II. Alexandria, Va.: Time-Life Books, 1979.

Taylor, Wilma Rugh, and Elmo Familiaran, eds. *No Greater Love: Triumph and Sacrifice of American Baptist Missionaries During WWII Philippines and the Martyrdom in Hopevale.* Greenlake, Wis.: World Wide Gifts of Green Lake Conference Center, 2007.

Thomas, Gordon, and Max Morgan Witts. *Enola Gay.* New York: Stein and Day, 1977.

Toland, John. *But Not in Shame: The Six Months After Pearl Harbor.* New York: Random House, 1961.

United States Coast Pilot Philippine Islands: Luzon, Mindoro, and Visayas, part 1. 3rd edition. Washington, D.C.: Government Printing Office, 1940.

Wise, William. *Secret Mission to the Philippines: The Story of "Spyron" and the American-Filipino Guerrillas of World War II.* Dutton, 1968.

White, William L. *They Were Expendable.* New York: Harcourt, Brace, 1942.

Whitman, John W. *Bataan: Our Last Ditch.* New York: Hippocrene Books, 1990.

Whitney, Courtney. *MacArthur: His Rendezvous with History.* New York: Alfred A. Knopf, 1956.

———. *Queens Die Proudly.* New York: Harcourt, Brace, 1943.

Wilson, Jesse Rodman, ed. *Through Shining Archway.* New York: American Baptist Foreign Mission Society and Woman's American Baptist Foreign Mission Society, 1945.

Wright, B. C. *The First Cavalry Division in World War II.* Tokyo: Toppan Printing, 1947.

Zaide, Gregorio F. *José Rizal: Life, Works, and Writings.* Manila: Villanueva Bookstore, 1957.

Zich, Arthur. *The Rising Sun.* World War II. Alexandria, Va.: Time-Life Books, 1977.

Articles, Parts of Books, and Pamphlets

Beightler, Robert S. *Report on the Activities of the 37th Infantry Division, 1940–1945.*

Childress, Clyde. "Wendell Fertig's Fictional 'Autobiography'; Critical Review of 'They Fought Alone.'" *Bulletin of the American Historical Collection Foundation: The American Era in the Philippines*, 1, no. 2 (2003).

Clayton, Edward H. "The Sacred Legacy of Hopevale." *Missions*, 37, no. 3 (March 1946), 154–156.

Drumheller, Susan. "Fertig: A Soldier's Story." *The Spokesman-Review*, February 26, 1996, 1B.

Facts and Figures About the Philippines. War Department Pamphlet No. 31–3. Washington, D.C.: November 1944.

"Liberation of the Philippine Islands Brings News of Death and Destruction." *Missions*, 36, no. 6 (September 1945), 298–299.

"Life on the Newsfronts of the World: U.S. Cheerfully Faces War with Japan." *Life* 11, no. 23 (December 9, 1941), 38.

McGowan, Sam. "Caught on the Ground: U.S. Forces in the Philippines . . ." *WWII History: Pearl Harbor Attack*, 1, no. 10 (Winter 2007), 58–65.

"Missionary Martyrs in the Philippine Islands." *Missions*, 36, no. 7 (September 1945), 383–386.

Parsons, Peter. "Special Mission Subs in the Philippines: The Chick Parsons Connection." *Bulletin of the American Historical Collection*, vol. 9, no. 1 (January–March 2003), Manila, Philippines.

"Religion: In the Hills of Panay." *Time* magazine, June 11, 1945.

Simbulan, Roland G. "U.S. Government Must Officially Apologize for Atrocities in Philippine-American War." http://www.yonip.com/main/articles/apology.html.

Skoglund, John E. "Wild Orchids Now Bloom Where the Missionaries Died." *Missions*, 38, no. 6 (June 1947), 336–339.

Stephens, Roberta, and Ann Borquist. "From Suffering and

Sacrifice Comes Joy: The Story of the Covell Family." *American Baptists in Mission* (Summer 2000). http://www.abc-usa.org/inmissn/summ00/6summ00.htm.

Steward, Harold D. *The First Was First: The Story of the First Cavalry Division*. Manila: Santo Tomas University Press, March 1945.

"The Student Volunteer Mission: Evangelizing the World in Their Generation." *Glimpses of Christian History,* no. 81, http://www.christianhistorytimeline.com/GLIMPSEF/Glimpses/glmps081.shtml.

Whitman, John W. "Delaying Action in the Philippines." *WWII,* 11, no. 4 (November 1998), 42–48.

———. "Hell Broke Loose This Morning: The First Philippine Campaign, 1941–42." *Command,* 43, (May 1997), 18–29.

Index